C0-AWW-630

PROBLEM SOLVING, REASONING, AND COMMUNICATING, K–8
Helping Children Think Mathematically

Arthur J. Baroody
University of Illinois at Urbana-Champaign

with Ronald T. Coslick, Niskayuna (New York) Middle School

Merrill, an imprint of
Macmillan Publishing Company
New York

Maxwell Macmillan Canada
Toronto

Maxwell Macmillan International
New York Oxford Singapore Sydney

Editor: Linda James Scharp
Developmental Editor: Linda Kauffman Peterson
Production Editor: JoEllen Gohr
Art Coordinator: Peter A. Robison
Cover Designer: Russ Maselli
Production Buyer: Corinne Folino

This book was printed and bound by Semline, Inc., a Quebecor America Book Group Company. The cover was printed by Phoenix Color Corp.

Copyright © 1993 by Macmillan Publishing Company, a division of Macmillan, Inc. Merrill is an imprint of Macmillan Publishing Company.

Printed in the United States of America

All rights reserved. Instructors of classes using Arthur J. Baroody's *Problem Solving, Reasoning, and Communicating, K–8: Helping Children to Think Mathematically*, may reproduce material from the textbook for classroom use. Otherwise, no part of this book may be reproduced or transmitted in any form or by any means, electronic or mechanical, including photocopy, recording or any information storage and retrieval system, without permission in writing from the Publisher.

Macmillan Publishing Company
113 Sylvan Avenue, Englewood Cliffs, NJ 07632

Library of Congress Cataloging-in-Publication Data

Baroody, Arthur J.
    Problem solving, reasoning, and communicating, K–8 : helping
children think mathematically / Arthur J. Baroody.
        p.   cm.
    ISBN 0-02-306488-9
    1. Mathematics—Study and teaching (Elementary)   I. Title.
QA135.5.B2849   1993
372.7—dc20   92-27749
                                                                          CIP

Printing: 2 3 4 5 6 7 8 9 Year: 5 6 7

CONTENTS

PREFACE

As we began thinking about writing this book for you, we had to grapple with our conviction that memorizing basic arithmetic skills does not foster a meaningful understanding of mathematics. Instruction today needs to focus on the development of mathematical thinking, and this entails helping children construct their own understanding of mathematics as well as the cultivation of critical thinking, reasoning, and problem-solving skills. We have tried to translate this conviction into a text that will enable you to learn to teach beyond the level of memorization of facts and skills.

This minibook on problem solving is an attempt to fashion an elementary mathematics methods course that enables prospective teachers to implement the daring reforms recommended by the National Council of Teachers of Mathematics (1989) in the *Curriculum and Evaluation Standards for School Mathematics* (NCTM *Curriculum Standards*). These efforts have led us to find, adapt, or develop course materials which actively involve you in mathematical activities that allow you to construct mathematical meaning for yourself.

To accomplish this goal, we have implemented a unique format that requires more interaction with the text material than is required in traditional textbooks. As much as possible, we want to give preservice teachers an opportunity to reflect on and use the content to solve both mathematical and pedagogical problems. To accomplish these ends, we not only discuss reasoning and mathematical problem-solving skills, but invite you to use these skills by presenting genuine problems to solve. In effect, we will model for you how to teach these skills in your classrooms. Our hope is that you will become a more capable mathematical and pedagogical problem solver than you might be if you simply read a traditional textbook.

To help you, we have devised **probes,** which ask you to investigate genuine situations or issues associated with problem solving, **activities** that stretch your mathematical knowledge and ask you to apply it to new situations, **notes** that ask you to reflect on the content, **dialogues** between students and teachers, and **case studies** and real-world situations involving principles of problem solving. In addition, many of the activities and probes are perfect for collaborating with your peers in groups as you investigate new avenues in understanding mathematics.

We have fashioned learning experiences that also model, at least to some degree, the kinds of learning experiences recommended by the NCTM (1989) *Curriculum Standards*. As you learn and apply the standards as you interact with this book, so, too, will your students learn from you when you become the orchestrator of their learning in your classroom. After all, this is our ultimate goal—to make you better teachers and, as a result, your students will become more successful learners of mathematics.

Our comprehensive mathematics methods textbook (of which this minibook is one chapter) is still very much a work in progress. Your reaction to this minibook version will be an important indication as to whether or not our experimental format is successful. Your comments and suggestions will be helpful in making the final version of our forthcoming methods textbook a valuable and usable resource, so please take time to send us your comments and reactions on the form provided at the end of the text.

ACKNOWLEDGMENTS

This book builds on the research and writing of numerous mathematics educators and psychologists, only some of whom are cited in the text. We are particularly grateful to the following colleagues for their invaluable comments and suggestions on an earlier draft of this book: N. Bezuk (San Diego State University), R. Charles (San Jose State), C. Dockweiler (Texas A & M), D. Peck (University of Utah), and L. Zech (University of Nevada, Las Vegas). Thanks are also due to Sharon C. Baroody, Linda Peterson (Developmental Editor for Macmillan), Joan Campagnolo, Ellen Satrom, and Barbara Rudell for carefully reading the text and their many suggestions. Special thanks are due to June Chambliss and Selena Douglass of the Word Processing Unit in the UIUC College of Education, who diligently prepared the typed text and graphics. We also want to recognize the invaluable contributions of another member of the Unit, Donna Auble, who tragically died in a car accident. We are grateful to the many classroom teachers who contributed their ideas, particularly Mylinda Ostergren and Patti Stoffel of the Urbana, Illinois, School District. We are indebted to Jo Lynn Baldwin, Diane Dutton, and Linda Moore of the Mahomet, Illinois, School District for sharing their classroom with us so that we could try out instructional ideas described in this text. Last but not least, we want to express our appreciation to the many elementary and college-level students whose questions and strategies were a constant source of amazement and edification. We are particularly grateful for the opportunity to learn from Alison, Alexi, and Arianne.

CREDITS

Page 1-1: PEANUTS reprinted by permission of UFS, Inc.

Pages 2-2 through 2-3: Reprinted by permission from *Curriculum and Evaluation Standards for School Mathematics*, copyright © 1989 by the National Council of Teachers of Mathematics, Reston, VA.

Figure 2.2 (page 2-4): THE FAR SIDE copyright 1987 Universal Press Syndicate.

Table 2.1 (page 2-13): Reprinted by permission of the publisher from Arthur J. Baroody, *CHILDREN'S MATHEMATICAL THINKING: A Developmental Framework for Preschool, Primary, and Special Education Teachers*, Table 14.2 (New York: Teachers College Press, © 1987 by Teachers College, Columbia University. All rights reserved.)

Figure 2.4 (page 2-14): FOX TROT copyright 1990 Universal Press Syndicate.

Figure 2.5 (page 2-15): PEANUTS reprinted by permission of UFS, Inc.

Page 2-15: Revised version of a vignette (The Case of Sherry) In Herb Ginsburg and Arthur J. Baroody, "The Constructivist Views on the Teaching and Learning of Mathematics" (JRME Monograph #4), edited by R. B. Davis, C. A. Mahr, and N. Noddings, copyright © 1980 by the National Council of Teachers of Mathematics, Reston, VA.

Pages 2-22 and 2-122: The Cow-Fence problem and the House problem from *The Pattern Factory: Elementary Problem Solving Through Patterning* by Ann Roper and Linda Harvey, copyright © 1980 by Creative Publications, Sunnyvale, CA. Reprinted by permission.

Box 2.7 (page 2-32): From *Addison-Wesley Mathematics, Grade 3* by Robert Eicholz et al. (Menlo Park, CA: Addison-Wesley Publishing Company, 1991), p. 38. Reprinted by permission.

Page 2-39: From R. I. Charles and F. K. Lester, *Teaching Problem Solving: What, Why and How*, pp. 42–43 (Menlo Park, CA: Dale Seymour Publications, 1982). Reprinted by permission.

Figure 2.9 (page 2-58): PEANUTS reprinted by permission of UFS, Inc.

Page 2-64: Adapted from *Mathematics: A Human Endeavor* by H. R. Jacobs (San Francisco: W. H. Freeman), p. 44. Used with permission.

Page 2-71: From Arthur J. Baroody and Margaret Hank, *Elementary Mathematics Activities: A Teacher's Guidebook.* Copyright © 1990 by Allyn and Bacon. Reprinted with permission.

Figure 2.10 (page 2-99): PEANUTS reprinted by permission of UPS, Inc.

Page 2-120: The problem "Palindromes" and the activity "Cross-Out Singles" from *About Teaching Mathematics*, copyright © 1992 by Math Solutions Publications, 150 Gate 5 Road, Suite 101, Sausalito, CA 94965. Reprinted by permission.

Page 2-121: From Maria Morolda, *Activities with Attributes: Experiences in Logical Problem Solving* (Menlo Park, CA: Dale Seymour Publications, 1993). Reprinted by permission.

Page 2-121: The activity "The Chain Letter" reprinted by permission from COMAP, Inc., Lexington, MA, publisher of *The Elementary Mathematician*.

Pages 2-121 through 2-122: From *Make It Simpler* by Carol Meyer and Tom Sallee (Menlo Park, CA: Addison-Wesley Publishing Company, 1983), p. 224. Reprinted by permission.

Pages 2-122 through 2-123: From *The Problem Solver 3: Activities for Learning Problem Solving Strategies*, page T-89, by Shirley Hoogeboom and Judy Goodnow, copyright © 1987 by Creative Publications, Sunnyvale, CA. Reprinted by permission.

Page 2-124: From *The I Hate Mathematics! Book* by Marilyn Burns. Copyright © 1978 by the Yolla Bolly Press. By permission of Little, Brown and Company.

Page 2-125: Reprinted by permission from Chapter 12, "Problem Solving Using the Calculator," by J. Duea et al. in the 1980 NCTM Yearbook (Problem Solving in School Mathematics, edited by S. Krulik and R. E. Reys), copyright © 1980 by the National Council of Teachers of Mathematics, Reston, VA.

Page 2-125: From *The Problem Solver with Calculators*, p. 3, by T. G. Coburn, Shirley Hoogeboom, and Judy Goodnow, copyright © 1989 by Creative Publications, Sunnyvale, CA. From *Cooperative Problem Solving with Calculators*, p. 26, by Ann Roper, Shirley Hoogeboom, and Judy Goodnow, copyright © 1991 by Creative Publications, Sunnyvale, CA. Reprinted by permission.

Pages 2-125 through 2-126: From *Using the Math Explorer Calculator* by Gary Bitter and Jerald Mikesell (Menlo Park, CA: Addison-Wesley Publishing Company, 1990), p. 133. Reprinted by permission.

1 PROLOGUE

Figure 1.1: Problems with Math Problems

PEANUTS reprinted by permission of UFS, Inc.

THIS CHAPTER

*M*any students—like Peppermint Patty in the Figure 1.1 above—react to mathematical problems with helpless anxiety. Many teachers react in the same way when confronted with the prospect of teaching mathematical problem solving. Yet, the elementary classrooms of tomorrow will need to put much more emphasis on problem solving (Lindquist, 1989; National Council of Teachers of Mathematics or NCTM, 1989). This book is an effort to help prospective and in-service teachers meet this challenge, so that you and your students will actually welcome opportunities for mathematical inquiry.

This chapter first outlines the aims of the book, a rationale for those aims, and some of the arguments for and against focusing on problem solving. It then describes the features of the book, particularly the more novel features for a book on elementary mathematics teaching methods. The last section of the Prologue provides some suggestions about how the book might be used. The main text (Chapter 2) has three units: Problem Solving, Reasoning, and Communicating. Each unit discusses why it is important for instruction to focus on the topic; the developmental task confronting children, including common difficulties; and specific instructional guidelines and activities for promoting mathematical thinking.

AIMS

This book focuses on how to foster a mathematical way of thinking among elementary-level children. In other words, it examines how K-8 instruction can nurture the *processes* essential to mathematical inquiry: problem solving, reasoning, and communicating. More specifically, this book has four interrelated aims:

(1) promote a better understanding of the nature of mathematics and mathematical inquiry;

(2) foster an understanding of how children's mathematical thinking develops;

(3) nurture understanding and reflection about methods for cultivating problem solving, reasoning, and communicating skills; and

(4) further the reader's own mathematical thinking.

RATIONALE FOR THE AIMS

Why are the four aims of this book important to you as a classroom teacher? We all have beliefs about what knowledge is, how it is learned, and the best ways of helping children learn mathematics. Whether conscious or not, these beliefs are the cornerstones on which we base our teaching practices—how we approach the task of teaching. Moreover, our own willingness and ability to engage in mathematical thinking can have a profound impact on the development of our students' mathematical thinking.

The Nature of Mathematics

What role should problem solving, reasoning, and communicating play in your mathematics curriculum? How this question is answered depends on your beliefs about the nature of mathematics (Schoenfeld, 1992).

Traditional View. Most people think of mathematics merely as a body of information. Many equate it with arithmetic: a collection of number facts, arithmetic rules, formulas, and computational procedures. Mathematicians are popularly viewed as gifted individuals who have managed to master this body of knowledge and who can, for example, perform calculations with exceptional proficiency. They are also commonly viewed as loners who pursue their work in solitude. In this view, problem solving, reasoning, and communicating are, at best, secondary aspects of mathematics.

Reflective View. In fact, mathematics is much more than so much subject matter. It is essentially a method of inquiry: a way of thinking about the world, organizing our experience, and solving problems. Mathematics is, at heart, an effort to find patterns. Indeed, it has been described as the science and language of patterns (Steen, 1990a, p. iii). "Seeing and revealing patterns are what mathematicians do best," (Steen, 1990b, p. 1). Like any science, doing mathematics requires reasoning and communicating. The latter is important because mathematics is, in fact, a social enterprise: mathematicians build on each other's work and frequently work in teams to solve a problem. In brief, problem solving, reasoning, and communicating are the basic tools for mathematical inquiry—the science and language of patterns.

The Development of Children's Mathematical Thinking

How should instruction promote problem-solving, reasoning, and communicating skills? How this question is answered depends on your beliefs about the learning process (Schoenfeld, 1992).

Traditional View. Most people, including many teachers, believe that learning is essentially a receptive or passive process. Children are viewed as uninformed, and learning is viewed as a process of absorbing needed information. The role of children is to "stay on task"—listen carefully and practice diligently what has been taught—so that they can memorize what they need to know. In a traditional view, how to solve problems, reason, and communicate—if taught at all—are treated as information that children need to memorize.

Reflective View. Recent cognitive research suggests that meaningful and usable knowledge is not merely absorbed but must be actively constructed. In this view, an understanding of mathematics and a mathematical way of thinking cannot be imposed on children from without but must be actively built from within by the children themselves. Recent research also indicates that children are not utterly uninformed or blank slates when they begin school. Typically, even young children have considerable informal mathematical knowledge and thinking skills: mathematical competencies developed through everyday life. The implications for instruction are that children need to be *actively* engaged in problem solving, reasoning, and communicating and, if encouraged to use their informal knowledge, are capable of a surprising amount of self-regulated learning and thinking.

The Nature of Instruction

Why do so many students—like Peppermint Patty in Figure 1.1—react to mathematical problems with helpless anxiety and fail miserably in their efforts to solve them? Is there anything a teacher can do to help children like Peppermint Patty? The answer to the first question can be found in how elementary mathematics has traditionally been taught. The answer to the second depends largely on whether or not you can resist traditional beliefs about learning and teaching and *act on* those stemming from a reflective view.

Traditional View. Traditionally, elementary instruction has focused on the mastery of basic skills: the facts, rules, formulas, and computational procedures needed to study higher mathematics or to become a productive member of society. In the traditional classroom, the teacher is the authoritative source of this knowledge and children passively memorize what is dictated. Memorization is accomplished largely by doing numerous written worksheets—frequently without reflection or understanding. In brief, how mathematics has traditionally been taught has encouraged children to be dependent rule-followers, rather than independent thinkers. When they encounter a mathematical problem requiring thought, is it any wonder that children feel ill prepared, helpless, or even anxious?

Reflective View. There is wide consensus that schools should shift their focus from memorizing basic skills to promoting understanding and problem solving (NCTM, 1989). Table 1.1 compares a conceptual approach and a problem-solving approach with the traditional skills approach to teaching mathematics. It should be noted that the conceptual (a meaningful-content) approach is not inconsistent with the problem-solving (process) approach. Indeed, as we note in Chapter 2, the two can be integrated.

To develop mathematical thinking and the autonomy to solve challenging mathematical problems, children need to *do* mathematics (National Research Council, 1989, 1990). Doing mathematics here does not mean doing rows and rows of computational "problems." It entails:

- solving challenging problems;
- exploring patterns;
- formulating educated guesses (conjectures) and checking them out;
- drawing conclusions (reasoning); and
- communicating ideas, patterns, conjectures, conclusions, and reasons.

Table 1.1: Three Approaches to Teaching

Skills Approach	Conceptual Approach	Problem-Solving Approach
Aim: To foster the mastery of basic skills—memorization of arithmetic and geometric facts, rules, formulas, and procedures	**Aim:** To foster meaningful learning—understanding of facts, rules, formulas, and procedures	**Aim:** To foster the development of mathematical thinking
Focus: Procedural content (e.g., *how* to divide with fractions)	**Focus:** Meaningful content (e.g., *why* you invert and multiply when dividing fractions)	*Focus: Processes* of mathematical inquiry: problem solving, reasoning, and communicating
Roles: Teacher-directed; student passive	**Roles:** Teacher-directed; student active	**Roles:** Teacher-guided; student active
Organizing principle: Sequential instruction based on a hierarchy of skills—build from simplest to most complex skill	**Organizing principle:** Sequential instruction based on the readiness of students to construct understanding	**Organizing principle:** Posing problems that are neither too simple nor too difficult, whether or not students have received formal instruction on the content involved
Methods: • Direct instruction; primarily teacher talk • Practice, with an emphasis on written worksheets	**Methods:** • Teacher-directed use of manipulatives, (e.g., linking concrete models to symbolic mathematics • Discovery-learning activities	**Methods:** • Student discussion of problems, solution strategies, and answers • Content instruction done incidentally as needed

Reflective Teaching

What role should teachers play in elementary mathematics instruction? What status should teaching have? The answer to these questions again depends on your beliefs about learning and teaching.

The Role of Teachers. In a traditional view, a teacher's primary role is to communicate knowledge: Tell and show children what they need to know. A teacher also serves as task master and judge: Ensure sufficient practice and serve as the final authority over what is correct.

In a reflective view, a teacher serves as a guide. This is *not* a passive role. The teacher must select appropriately challenging problems, know when to intervene, know how and how much to help, and so forth. Teachers must, for example, introduce problems (or content material) that are neither so unfamiliar that children cannot make sense of it or so familiar as to be unchallenging. In other words, they need to present problems and content material in a manner consistent with Piaget's moderate novelty principle: Only information that is moderately novel can both be understood and pique interest. After all, children—like anyone—have little interest engaging in something so novel they cannot understand it, or something so obvious they take it for granted. The implication of the moderate novelty principle is that a teacher must continually gauge the progress of his or her students and pose material and problems just beyond their reach.

Teachers as Technicians or Professionals. Traditionally, teachers have served as technicians: merely implementing a prescribed course of mathematical instruction. Typically, they simply followed the instructions and syllabi in their teacher's edition of their textbooks.

However, there are no simple, universal recipes for good mathematics instruction, particularly that which focuses on problem solving. Although a textbook can prescribe general instructional guidelines and outline specific instructional activities, each class—each child—is different and brings new challenges. There is simply no way of preparing prospective or in-service teachers for every situation they will encounter. Particularly in a program that emphasizes problem solving, they will need to make innumerable pedagogical decisions themselves. To do so effectively, teachers need to have considerable insight into the three cornerstones of instruction: the subject matter, the learner, and instructional methods. Moreover they need to be comfortable with the role of decision maker and have proficiency in solving pedagogical problems. In brief, it is essential that teachers be prepared as *reflective* practitioners—as *professionals* who autonomously can make informed decisions.

Teachers as Mathematical Thinkers

Teachers need to develop a mathematical way of thinking so that they can serve as role models for their students. They need to practice mathematical problem solving for several reasons. It is important to develop your own problem-solving skill so that you are better able to guide the development of your students' problem-solving skill. Moreover, actual experience solving problems can give you a better appreciation for the value of problem-solving strategies outlined in the text and the difficulties children may have in their problem-solving efforts.

ARGUMENTS FOR AND AGAINST A PROBLEM-SOLVING APPROACH

Is a problem-solving approach really practical? Won't focusing on problem solving take too much time away from teaching the basic skills? Won't performance on achievement tests suffer? What can I tell parents and other teachers who expect children to master the basic skills? Isn't problem solving just too difficult for most children? Can teachers with weak mathematical training themselves implement such an approach?

Some teachers feel that focusing on problem solving is impractical and simply continue in their traditional manner. A growing number are convinced that such a focus is essential and are trying to implement this approach in their classrooms. Yet, others feel uncertain about a problem-solving approach: They agree, in principle, that students should do more problem solving but are unsure, for example, how much time should be spent on it or if they are capable of implementing such an approach. Consider the arguments for and against focusing on problem solving offered by the three teachers in Box 1.1: Mrs. Battleaxe, a crusty and mentally encrusted traditionalist; Ms. Wise, an experienced and progressive teacher; and Miss Brill, an open-minded but uncertain new teacher.

Box 1.1: Some Pros and Cons of a Problem-Solving Approach

Miss Brill had been raised to believe that ladies did not argue; she was ill-prepared for her initial grade-level meeting.

Ms. Wise, who long had emphasized problem solving in her class, began, "I believe the District has taken a significant step forward in advocating we focus on problem solving. I'd be happy to share the materials I've collected over the years and to hear your ideas."

Mrs. Battleaxe, who believed that mathematics had to be stuffed into children's heads, grumped, "I've been teaching for over 40 years and I've seen many educational fads come and go. This problem-solving stuff is just the latest flash in the pan. What really matters—what has always mattered—is whether students have mastered the basic computational skills. Focusing mainly on problem solving is unrealistic. There is barely enough time to get through the book now. If we focus on problem solving, there won't be enough time to teach and practice basic arithmetic skills."

"I don't care what those bloated bureaucrats down at the District Puzzle Palace *say* about focusing on problem solving," continued Mrs. Battleaxe building up a full head of steam, "Their bottom line is how well the kids do on the standardized test and the standardized test basically tests computational skills, not problem solving." Suddenly directing her comments to a now wide-eyed Miss Brill, Mrs. Battleaxe threatened, "Look Missy, you don't have tenure. What the principal and the school board will look at is whether or not your students do well on those standardized tests. You can focus on problem solving if you want, but you will be held accountable." (The A-word sent a shudder of fear down Miss Brill's back.)

"What are you going to tell parents who think their children should be doing worksheets to practice facts and procedures?" exclaimed Mrs. Battleaxe, now red with anger. "Are you going to tell successful doctors, lawyers, and business people that what was good enough for them isn't good enough for their children? Ha! What are you going to tell the sixth-grade teachers and principal when you pass on students who haven't mastered fifth-grade arithmetic skills? Do you want Dent, Gomez,

and Finklestein, the terrible trio of gossip, telling the whole school you didn't prepare your students for the sixth grade? Do you want the principal to think you are one of those loose-at-the-ends kind of teacher—the kind that isn't in control?"

"Besides, problem solving is difficult for children, particularly those having problems mastering the basic arithmetic skills," added Mrs. Battleaxe beginning to calm down a bit. "For those having problems, especially, it makes sense to spend our time practicing computational skills."

Miss Brill thought of another reason, "I'm not very good in math myself; I always had to struggle with word problems. I still have nightmares where I am standing on a railroad track with two trains approaching me from opposite directions and I can't move until I've calculated where they are going to meet. I never could do those train problems. How am I supposed to teach problem solving to children?"

Ms. Wise could see that Miss Brill had been thoroughly shaken by Mrs. Battleaxe's arguments. "There are several reasons," she noted, "why it is essential that teachers take the time to help children develop problem-solving competence. One is that mastering basic computational skills is no longer enough to prepare children for today's economy. Another is that focusing on solving problems is *not* incompatible with learning computational skills. In fact, research indicates that when teachers focus on problem solving, their students do better than traditionally taught students on tests of basic computational skills, as well as on tests of problem solving." In response to the incredulous stares of her cohorts, Miss Wise added, "It makes sense; solving problems provides a purposeful and meaningful context for learning and practicing computational skills. Children, or adults, for that matter, are more likely to learn something if it makes sense to them and there is a real reason for learning it."

"The issue of testing needs to be put into perspective," continued Ms. Wise. "First of all, I have real problems accepting that a standard test should dictate what and how we should teach. After all, tests are supposed to be tools for evaluating whether or not we have achieved our educational goals, not

Box 1.1 continued

for dictating what our goals should be. Second, if we teach to the test, we do our students a great disservice. The use of traditional standardized tests basically ensures that children achieve a *minimal* level of mathematical competency. That's not what I want for my students! Indeed, good performance on a standardized test does not mean that a child really *understands* or *can apply* mathematics. Third," concluded Ms. Wise, "standardized tests are beginning to change—to better reflect the importance of understanding and problem solving. Note that our state achievement test puts less emphasis on computation and more on thinking."

Changing gears, Ms. Wise next observed, "I believe it is part of my professional responsibility to help other teachers and parents see the importance of focusing on problem solving. Our job is a lot easier than some, because our new principal, Mrs. Dew-Wright, actively supports reforming the math curricula."

"Solving genuine problems," continued Ms. Wise," can be challenging, if not downright difficult. But how are children going to learn how to tackle challenging and difficult problems in the real world if we don't help now? Besides, children can be surprising; they enjoy a good challenge, or

can learn to enjoy one. Also they can often do much more than we adults give them credit for. I've been astounded over the years by the problems my students have posed and solved. As for children with learning difficulties, many don't try to learn because they see no point to it or don't understand what is being taught. Solving problems is particularly useful for such children, because it can help them learn mathematics in a purposeful and meaningful fashion."

"Finally," concluded Ms. Wise, "you do not need to be an expert problem solver yourself to use a problem-solving approach. In a traditional classroom where the teacher is the source of all wisdom, expertise is essential. In a problem-solving classroom where the teacher is a guide and a participant, you don't have to know everything. Don't get me wrong, the more you know about mathematics and problem solving, the better a guide you will be. However, a lack of expertise is not a reason for not focusing on problem solving. In some ways it's an advantage: It forces you to be more of a participant and less of a traditional authority figure. I know that's scary, but think how much you can learn along with your kids."

Miss Brill still had doubts but was ready to give problem solving a try.

FEATURES OF THE BOOK

Chapter Introduction

Chapter 2 is introduced with a bulletin-board display and segments titled THIS CHAPTER and WHAT THE NCTM CURRICULUM STANDARDS SAY.

Bulletin-Board Display. This graphic illustrates a bulletin board you can use to promote a spirit of inquiry in your own class.

This Chapter. This segment provides a brief rationale for the chapter and an overview of it.

What the NCTM *Curriculum Standards* **Say.** This segment summarizes the recommendations made by NCTM (1989) *Curriculum Standards* regarding problem solving, reasoning, and communicating. The general aims for grades K - 4 and 5 - 8 are listed separately.

Text

Chapter 2 consists of a text and Action Tasks. The former involves the kinds of things usually found in a textbook such as explanations, examples, tables, and figures. The following symbols are used to call attention to other key features:

✐ The pencil indicates a **teaching point**: an instructional recommendation.

🍎 The apple indicate **Activity Files** or **instructional activities**—classroom-tested activities for actively involving a whole class, a small group, and/or an individual.

■ The black box indicates a **problem**—all of which can be used or adapted for use in the elementary grades.

✚ The aid symbol, a cross, indicates a general **problem-solving aid** or helper.

✦ The four-pointed star indicates an extension of a problem.

🔑 A key next to a problem or question indicates that a hint or the answer can be found in the ANSWERS TO SELECTED QUESTIONS section in the back of the text.

The text also includes boxes ,which present the following additional features:

• case studies illustrating children's often-surprising mathematical strengths and their learning difficulties;

• student-teacher or teacher-teacher dialogues that raise issues, prompt questions about instructional practices, or illustrate common teaching difficulties or effective teaching techniques;

• extensions of material discussed in the text; or

• good and bad examples of instructional material.

Samples from *The Math Book From Hell* illustrate ineffective materials.* Throughout the chapter, you will encounter installments about the adventures of various teachers, particularly Miss Brill, a first-year teacher. Although the characters are fictional, the

---

* Samples from this fictional textbook are not intended as a general condemnation of all textbooks. They serve to underscore—we hope humorously—the need for teachers to be reflective. Although textbook publishers are making earnest efforts to meet the spirit of the NCTM (1989) *Curriculum Standards*, the extent to which textbook series embody the NCTM's recommendations varies considerably. Moreover, many schools do not have the latest edition of a textbook series. The textbook used by my (AB) children's school was published in 1988 and, unfortunately, shares many of the characteristics of *The Math Book From Hell*. Also, as teachers move further toward a problem-solving approach, they will undoubtedly rely less on standard textbooks. Even so, textbooks can play a role (e.g., a resource for exploring ideas generalized from problem-solving efforts).

situations described are often based on real classroom events and dialogues. Moreover, the problems Miss Brill encounters, the feelings she expresses, and the questions she asks might be those of any teacher.

Key terms and questions are italicized. Many of the questions were asked by children, in-service teachers, or pre-service teachers we have known. Perhaps some are questions you have. Ideally, they will pique your interest and entice you to read the text.

Action Tasks

The textbook attempts to involve readers actively with Action Tasks. As you read through the text, you will be directed to Action Tasks by a pointing-finger symbol: ☞ . These tasks can be used to prompt small-group or whole-class discussions. We believe that most people would benefit substantially by tackling the Action Tasks in a small group and discussing the tasks with others—whether in a small group, with the whole class, or both. The three types of Action Tasks you will encounter are: challenges, probes, and activities.

Challenges. These Action Tasks ask the reader to solve a mathematical problem found in the text or to answer pedagogical questions related to the text. Challenges are dispersed throughout the text.

Probes. These Action Tasks involve analyzing curriculum materials, solving mathematical problems, trying out teaching techniques, and answering challenging questions about pedagogy. Probes appear at the end of a subunit in the order mentioned by the didactic texts. They are printed on colored paper and are marked with an arrow symbol ↗ .

Sometimes you will be asked to tackle a probe before you read the relevant text. Ideally, this will raise questions and provide an incentive to read the text. We recommend you give a probe an earnest effort, read the text, retry the probe if necessary, and only then check ANSWERS TO SELECTED QUESTIONS located at the end of Chapter 2. This will take more time and effort on your part, but we believe you will learn more this way than by looking up the answers immediately or skipping the probe altogether. Other times you will be instructed to try some probes after reading a segment of text. These probes require you to apply the text material in some way (e.g., solving a pedagogical or mathematical problem). This should help you consolidate your understanding, identify remaining gaps or inaccuracies in your concepts, and—with any luck—raise further questions for discussion.

Activities. These Action Tasks introduce material by means of guided discovery learning and double as a lesson plan you can follow with your own class. Like Probes, they appear at the end of a subunit on colored paper but are marked with an open apple: 🍎 .

For Further Exploration

This section of Chapter 2 includes a description of some instructional resources, a sample of children's literature, tips on using technology, questions to consider, suggested activities, questions to check understanding, and problems.

Some Instructional Resources. This section provides a small sample of commercially available resources. Such resources can be invaluable whether you are just starting out in teaching or have been teaching for many years. In most cases, we try to pique your interest about a resource by describing or illustrating an activity, game, or problem from the resource. To prompt reflection about these materials, we also include some questions about each.

A Sample of Children's Literature. This section describes a small sample of children's books that can help make K-8 mathematics instruction more interesting. It includes books written specifically to discuss mathematical ideas with children. As with the instructional resources, we describe a sample of the book so that you have some sense of how the resource can be used, and we include some questions to prompt reflection.

Tips on Using Technology. This section describes several resources on using calculators and computers to help foster problem solving and reasoning.

Questions to Consider. These questions typically explore the issues raised in a chapter in more depth and, thus, serve to extend the discussion in the text. An instructor might wish to use these questions to foster discussion or as a way of challenging a group of students who complete in-class problems or assignments before other groups.

Suggested Activities. This section includes things you can do to prepare for classroom instruction and things you can do in your classroom.

Questions to Check Understanding. These questions are based directly on the chapter text and serve to check your comprehension of the text material. Some questions involve realistic pedagogical problems. Many of the questions could be used by classroom teachers to evaluate children.

Problems. The problems at the end of Chapter 2 give you the opportunity to practice problem-solving skills. Nearly all of the problems could be used with upper elementary children. Some would be appropriate for primary-level children. Yet others could be adapted for use with younger children.

Answers to Selected Questions.

This last section of Chapter 2 provides an answer key for selected problems and questions appearing in the text, the Action Tasks, and some parts of the FOR FURTHER EXPLORATION section. It does not include answers for QUESTIONS TO CHECK UNDERSTANDING or PROBLEMS. Some instructors may wish to use these sections to select material for homework assignments, classroom discussions, or tests.

USES OF THE BOOK

This text can be used in various ways:

1. Some or all of the Action Tasks could be done in class to prompt class discussions and to provide a student-centered, problem-solving approach to instruction. Additional questions, activities, and problems for class use could be drawn from the material in the text and from FOR FURTHER EXPLORATION.

2. Some or all of the Action Tasks could be done outside of class in small, cooperative-learning groups. Study groups could also be assigned questions and problems from FOR FURTHER EXPLORATIONS.

3. Some or all of the Action Tasks and selected questions and problems from FOR FURTHER EXPLORATIONS could be assigned to individuals as homework.

4. Some combination of group and individual work in and out of class could be fashioned.

An advantage of Approach 1 is that it models the kind of instruction recommended by the text and the NCTM (1989) *Curriculum Standards*. An advantage of Approaches 1, 2 and 4 is that working in cooperative-learning groups gives students firsthand experience with this important teaching technique. It gives them a real opportunity to discover the technique's strengths and weaknesses and can provide a basis for discussing issues regarding this technique.

There is no one right way to carry out small group work. Some groups may prefer to tackle tasks together from beginning to end. Other groups may prefer to work on tasks individually first and then meet as a group to compare and discuss their efforts and to settle on answers. Some groups may wish to meet together to ensure everyone understands the task and is headed off in the right direction. After working on the task individually, they may then reconvene to discuss their individual progress.

An issue you will need to decide for group work is how the group will make its decisions: Will the group adopt as its answer the one with the largest number of votes, that which has at least half of the votes (a simple majority), that which receives all the votes (a unanimous decision)?

☞ Consider the following question: *What are the advantages and disadvantages of each decision method above?*

It is important to keep in mind that learning how to become a better teacher of mathematics is an ongoing process—indeed, a career-long process. There is probably more in this text than can be covered in a single methods course or that can be comprehended in a single reading. One hope is that the book helps you get started in the challenging and exciting task of fostering children's mathematical thinking. Ideally, you will revisit the text again and again throughout your teaching career as the need arises.

It is also important to keep in mind that the tone of a classroom is set by its teacher. Your attitude toward teaching mathematics can have a profound impact on that of your students. We hope, then, that the book piques your interest in fostering problem solving, reasoning, and communicating and helps you feel more comfortable with a process approach to mathematical instruction. Furthermore, we hope that you will enjoy using the text and will look forward to learning more about mathematics, mathematics learning, and mathematics teaching.

2 PROBLEM SOLVING, REASONING, AND COMMUNICATING

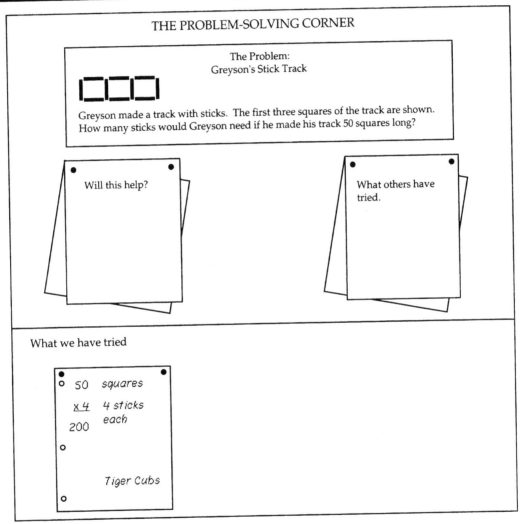

THE PROBLEM-SOLVING CORNER

The Problem:
Greyson's Stick Track

Greyson made a track with sticks. The first three squares of the track are shown. How many sticks would Greyson need if he made his track 50 squares long?

Will this help?

What others have tried.

What we have tried

50   squares
x 4   4 sticks
200   each

Tiger Cubs

A problem-solving bulletin board can consist of (a) a statement of the problem (The Problem); (b) some tips on understanding the problem and/or developing a solution, such as "Look for a pattern" (Will this help?); (c) a sample of possible solution methods (What others have tried); and (d) a place for individuals or groups to display their solution attempts (What we have tried) (Jacobson, Lester, & Stengel, 1980). To encourage autonomy and creativ-ity, you may wish to post "What others have tried" after students have displayed their solutions.

☞ What is the solution to the problem above? Evaluate the Tiger Cubs' solution posted on the bulletin board above. Consider how you, as a teacher, would respond to their solution. Reconsider this question after reading the chapter.

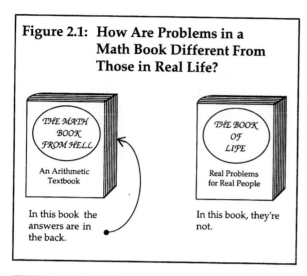

Figure 2.1: How Are Problems in a Math Book Different From Those in Real Life?

THE MATH BOOK FROM HELL

An Arithmetic Textbook

In this book the answers are in the back.

THE BOOK OF LIFE

Real Problems for Real People

In this book, they're not.

THIS CHAPTER

*I*n the words of Bob Dylan, "the times they are changin'." During the industrial age, mathematical literacy simply entailed mastery of basic skills. A key aim of school was to prepare workers who were literate about numbers, computational procedures, and shapes. To ensure the memorization of basic facts, rules, formulas, and procedures, schools typically spoon-fed students, encouraging them to depend on authorities like their teachers and textbooks. If students did not know an answer, they simply asked the teacher or looked it up in the textbook.

In our post-industrial, information-based, and technological-oriented age, mathematical literacy requires more than mastery of basic mathematical skills. In our increasingly complex and rapidly changing world, the memorization of facts, rules, and procedures is not enough. Business, industry, and government increasingly need workers capable of using the power of mathematics to solve new problems (Lappan & Schram, 1989). Computation is typically done by computers. What is needed are people who can tell the computers what to do and check whether the results are sensible. What is needed are people who can analyze and think logically about new situations, devise unspecified solution procedures, and communicate their solution clearly and convincingly to others.

Because change is occurring so rapidly, no education can prepare children in advance to solve all the problems they will encounter. Thus, schools today need to arm students with general problem-solving skills. Moreover, it is essential that schools

foster autonomy: an ability to think about and answer questions for oneself. After all—as Figure 2.1 implies—in the real world, the answers to many, often the more important, problems cannot be looked up in an answer key or obtained from some authority.

Chapter 1 discussed a problem-solving approach to mathematics and equated it with a process approach to instruction. The three units of this chapter focus on the basic processes of mathematical inquiry: problem solving, reasoning, and communicating. These are the basic tools of a mathematician or any user of mathematics. The chapter illustrates how problem solving, reasoning, and communicating can be integral aspects of content instruction.

WHAT THE NCTM CURRICULUM STANDARDS SAY

Mathematics as Problem Solving

Standard 1 for both grades K to 4 and grades 5 to 8 is *Mathematics as Problem Solving*.

Grades K-4. "The study of mathematics should emphasize problem solving so that students can:

- ◆ use problem-solving approaches to investigate and understand mathematical content;
- ◆ formulate problems from everyday and mathematical situations;
- ◆ develop and apply strategies to solve a wide variety of problems;
- ◆ verify and interpret results with respect to the original problem;
- ◆ acquire confidence in using mathematics meaningfully" (p. 23).

Grades 5-8. "The mathematics curriculum should include numerous and varied experiences with problem solving as a method of inquiry and application so that students can:

- ◆ use problem-solving approaches to investigate and understand mathematical content;
- ◆ formulate problems from situations within and outside mathematics;
- ◆ develop and apply a variety of strategies to solve problems, with emphasis on multi-

step and nonroutine problems;

◆ verify and interpret results with respect to the original problem situation;

◆ generalize solutions and strategies to new problem situations;

◆ acquire confidence in using mathematics meaningfully" (p. 75).

Mathematics as Reasoning

Standard 3 for both grades K to 4 and grades 5 to 8 is *Mathematics as Reasoning*.

Grades K-4. "The study of mathematics should emphasize reasoning so that students can:

◆ draw logical conclusions about mathematics;

◆ use models, known facts, properties, and relationships to explain their thinking;

◆ justify their answers and solution processes;

◆ use patterns and relationships to analyze mathematical situations;

◆ believe that mathematics makes sense" (p. 29).

Grades 5-8. "Reasoning shall permeate the mathematics curriculum so that students can:

◆ recognize and apply deductive and inductive reasoning;

◆ understand and apply reasoning processes, with special attention to spatial reasoning and reasoning with proportions and graphs;

◆ make and evaluate mathematical conjectures and arguments;

◆ validate their own thinking;

◆ appreciate the pervasive use and power of reasoning as a part of mathematics" (p. 81).

Mathematics as Communication

Standard 2 for both grades K to 4 and grades 5 to 8 is *Mathematics as Communication*.

Grades K-4. "The study of mathematics should include numerous opportunities for communication so that students can:

◆ relate physical materials, pictures, and diagrams to mathematical ideas;

◆ reflect on and clarify their thinking about mathematical ideas and situations;

◆ relate their everyday language to mathematical language and symbols;

◆ realize that representing, discussing, reading, writing, and listening to mathematics are a vital part of learning and using mathematics" (p. 26).

Grades 5-8. "The study of mathematics should include opportunities to communicate so that students can:

◆ model situations using oral, written, concrete, pictorial, graphical, and algebraic methods;

◆ reflect on and clarify their own thinking about mathematical ideas and situations;

◆ develop common understandings of mathematical ideas, including the role of definitions;

◆ use the skills of reading, listening, and viewing to interpret and evaluate mathematical ideas;

◆ discuss mathematical ideas and make conjectures and convincing arguments;

◆ appreciate the value of mathematical notation and its role in the development of mathematical ideas" (p. 78).[†]

[†]The standards above are reprinted with permission of the National Council of Teachers of Mathematics, Reston, VA.

MATHEMATICS AS PROBLEM SOLVING

Figure 2.2 A Common Reaction to Story Problems

THE FAR SIDE reprinted by permission of UPS.

Hell's library

Many students and teachers equate problem solving with story or word problems. As Figure 2.2 suggests, many people view word problems as dense, difficult, discouraging, deflating, disturbing, debilitating, disgusting, deadening, demonic and/or damnable—to mention a few of the more polite adjectives. Asked how she was doing in mathematics, one first-grade girl summarized her dislike for word problems by saying, "I'm doing well, except I don't like those *problem words!*"[1]

This unit begins by examining the nature of problem solving by defining problem solving and outlining what it takes to be a successful problem solver. It explores why traditional instructional practices, such as using the word problems historically found in textbooks, have failed miserably to interest students in problem solving or develop their considerable and surprising potential for problem solving. To help you improve your own problem-solving skills and put you in a position to help students develop theirs, the unit explores general problem-solving strategies. The unit ends with tips

on how to make word problems and problem solving challenging and interesting to students. With any luck, the unit will help you see that teaching problem solving is not, as many teachers think, an overwhelmingly difficult task—that, indeed, it can be enlightening and exciting for a teacher as well as students.

THE CASE OF THE LOOSELY USED TERM

This subunit addresses the question: *What is problem solving?* It distinguishes among exercises, problems, and enigmas and discusses why this distinction is difficult to make in practice.

A Distinction Among Exercises, Problems, and Enigmas

What's the difference among exercises, problems, and enigmas? Miss Brill examined the newly revised *District Curriculum Guide for Mathematics.* A team of teachers and administrators had worked on it for over a year in an effort to update the district's guidelines in light of the NCTM (1989) *Curriculum Standards.* The district's guide noted that mathematics educators have long advised putting more emphasis on problem solving and that the NCTM (1989) *Curriculum Standards* recommended making problem solving a focus of mathematics instruction.

Although emphasizing problem solving seemed like a good idea, Miss Brill had only a hazy notion of what this entailed. An examination of her textbook did not clarify the matter. Her teacher's edition stated: "Consistent with the NCTM *Curriculum Standards,* the third edition of the *The Math Book From Hell* focuses on problem solving. Students are regularly asked to solve problems, including story problems." However, Miss Brill found many things in the textbook called *problems,* including: "5 + 3 = ☐. What goes in the box?" She also found many things labeled *problem solving,* including drill exercises for practicing basic computational facts and procedures. "Is finding the answers to symbolic expressions—rows and rows of symbolic expressions—really problem solving?" she wondered.

Miss Brill went next door to get some advice. Ms. Wise nodded sympathetically and noted, "There is a great deal of confusion about what constitutes problem solving. To define problem solving requires specifying what a problem is, and there's the hitch. Different people have rather different ideas about what a problem is. Even my Webster's (New Twentieth Century Unabridged) Dictionary (2nd ed.) suggests two different definitions for *problem*. Here on page 1434 it says:

(1) 'In mathematics, a problem is anything required to be done....'

(2) 'A problem is a question...that is perplexing or difficult.'"

Exercises. "The dictionary's first definition," noted Ms. Wise, "equates a problem with an assignment. Teachers commonly introduce a procedure or a formula and then, to provide practice, assign numerous computational 'problems': 'For your seatwork, do *Problems* 1 to 1,300 on page 8 of your workbook.' However, when a person already has a strategy for finding the solution to a task, many mathematics educators prefer to call the task an *exercise*. Because a way of determining the answer is known, an exercise can be done rather automatically and, even thoughtlessly."

Problems. "Actually, the dictionary's second meaning more closely captures the view of a problem held by mathematicians," continued Ms. Wise. "Although the term problem can, in everyday use, refer to either a required task or a puzzling situation, many mathematics educators reserve the term problem for a puzzling task for which a person does not have a readily available solution strategy."

A problem can further be defined as a puzzling situation for which a person wants or needs to find a solution. A person may find many things puzzling. However, the person may have no interest in making sense of some of these perplexing situations and, thus, make no effort to resolve them. Because it is useful to distinguish between puzzles that do and do not motivate interest and action, let's agree that *a problem entails (a) a desire to know something, (b) the lack of an obvious way to find a solution, and (c) an effort to find the solution* (Charles & Lester, 1982). Because a way of determining the answer is not known and an answer is desired, problems require a thoughtful analysis and, perhaps, an extended effort.

Enigmas. Let's call a task a person simply ignores or accepts as unsolvable an enigma. Because a person has no interest in finding an answer or is convinced it cannot be found, enigmas typically are not given a second thought and are quickly dismissed.

Distinguishing Among Exercises, Problems, and Enigmas

☞ Consider Probe 2.1 (page 2-7) before going on.

The Task Confronting a Teacher. In theory, it is relatively easy to distinguish among exercises, problems, and enigmas. In practice, determining whether a task is an exercise, a problem, or an enigma can be a genuine pedagogical problem for a teacher. A teacher must decide if a child already knows how to solve a task and, if not, whether it is within the child's grasp to understand and solve. The teacher must also decide whether the task is sufficiently interesting that the child will want to tackle it. In brief, whether a task constitutes a genuine problem depends on (a) a child's readiness and (b) the attractiveness of the task to the child (Charles & Lester, 1982).

Note that a problem for one child may simply be an exercise for another and an enigma for a third (Charles & Lester, 1982; Schoenfeld, 1985). Moreover, what may constitute an enigma for a child at one time, may—with experience—become a problem and, eventually, simply an exercise. (Indeed, one aim of mathematics is to reduce problems to the realm of exercises.) To ensure that tasks are genuine problems—challenging but not overwhelming—teachers must constantly evaluate their students' thinking and interests.

Clearly, then, simply labeling an activity "problem solving" does not make it a genuine problem. Consider, for example, the activities in Probe 2.1. For most kindergartners and first graders, pages 18 and 27 would be exercises, not problem-solving activities. Indeed, for page 18, the teacher *tells* the children what to do. The children then merely use (practice) color identification, coloring, and counting skills. Page 27 would probably be a genuine problem for extremely few first graders. It simply provides practice counting two collections to determine the total amount. Although this builds on children's informal approach to arithmetic, it does not really involve puzzling situations for which the children do not have a readily available strategy. It is also unclear why children would be interested in finding the solutions to these "problems"—other than to collect rewards or avoid punishment. On the other hand, for children with insufficient informal mathematical knowledge or those who failed to see a connection with their informal knowledge, workbook page 27 might constitute an enigma.

A Word on Word Problems. *Can word problems be considered genuine problems?* Miss Brill commented that their textbook had numerous word problems, which should provide students ample problem-solving experience. She was surprised by Ms. Wise's reaction, "Working on a word problem may *or* may *not* involve problem solving."

As with any task, whether or not a word problem is an enigma, a genuine problem, or an exercise, depends on the developmental level of a child and the nature of the word problem. Word problems for which a child is not developmentally ready would be enigmas. Word problems that require a thoughtful analysis to devise a *new* strategy or to use existing strategies in *new* ways would constitute a genuine problem. Those that require a thoughtful analysis to decide among existing strategies (e.g., whether to add or subtract) might also be considered genuine problems in the sense that they lack an obvious solution procedure. Word problems in which a child can readily identify and apply a solution strategy are more like routine practice exercises. Unfortunately, this is how word problems have historically been used in instruction (see Box 2.1).

Box 2.1: The Traditional Use of Problems in Instruction—Problems as Routine Practice Exercises

"Problems have occupied a central place in the school mathematics curriculum since antiquity, but problem solving has not" (Stanic & Kilpatrick, 1989, p. 1). Traditionally, "problems" have been used as a means for teaching content. More specifically, problems have most often been used as a vehicle to practice facts, rules, formulas, or procedures. Typically, students are *shown* a specific technique for solving a particular type of problem. Then, to practice and master the technique, they are asked to "solve" sets of similar "problems."

The ancient Egyptians, Chinese, and Greeks apparently used problems as routine practice exercises as early as 1650 B.C. Textbooks in the 19th and most of the 20th century followed suit. A classic example is a "train problem," such as:

■ The *City of New Orleans* leaves Chicago and a freight train leaves Champaign at the same time and head toward each other on the same track. If the trains begin 120 miles apart, the *City of New Orleans* travels at an average speed of 40 miles per hour, and the freight train travels at 20 miles per hour, how far outside Chicago would they crash?

Many students (and their parents) are terrified by the mere mention of a train problem. Frequently, they have been shown a prescribed method for solving this class of problems—a prescription they do not understand. Because they cannot remember the senseless prescription and have not learned general problem-solving skills for attacking novel problems, they feel utterly helpless when confronted with such problems.

Questions for Reflection

1. For people described in the paragraph above, is the train problem an exercise, a problem, or an enigma?

2. Is the train problem above an exercise, a problem, or an enigma for students who have *not* been taught a specific technique for solving it but who nonetheless welcome the challenge of solving it intuitively?

3. Can you recall the technique for solving the train problem above? Whether you can or not, try solving it using an intuitive approach.

4. Kilpatrick (1985b) described Polya's classification of pedagogical problems:

   • **One rule under your nose**: mechanically apply a rule just presented.

   • **Application with some choice**: decide which of two or more previously presented rules applies.

   • **Choice of a combination**: requires using two or more rules as shown previously in class.

   • **Novel combination**: entails deciding how to combine two or more rules in a previously untaught manner.

   a. Rank the four types of problems in terms of their degree of difficulty, their value in provoking students to think.
   b. Rank the four types of problems in terms of their frequency in a textbook, a class you are observing, or your own elementary experience. Compare this ranking with the ranking done above for the previous question. What are the implications of this comparison?
   c. Some worksheets provide mixed practice (e.g., a child has to decide whether to add or subtract). How would such problems be classified according to Polya's scheme?

→ Probe 2.1: Analyzing Problem-Solving Activities in Textbooks I

Aware that problem solving had become a hot buzz word in mathematics education, the Boring Books Publishing Company made sure that their latest elementary textbook series incorporated plenty of "problem solving." Analyze the following problem-solving activities from page 18 of their kindergarten workbook and page 27 of their first-grade workbook. What is the aim of these activities? Given our agreed upon definition of problem solving, do these activities deserve to be so labeled? Why or why not?

THE MATH BOOK FROM HELL: Kindergarten
Boring Books Publishing Co., Inc.

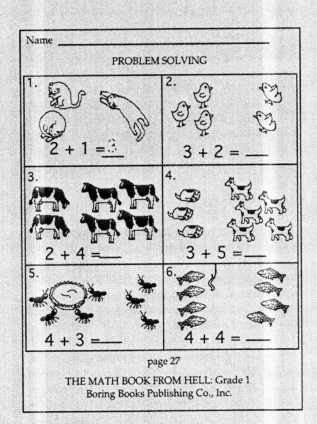

THE MATH BOOK FROM HELL: Grade 1
Boring Books Publishing Co., Inc.

THE TASK CONFRONTING CHILDREN

This subunit addresses the question: *What are the requirements for effective problem solving?* The chances of solving genuine problems are affected by three sets of factors: (a) cognitive, (b) affective, and (c) metacognitive factors (cf. Charles & Lester, 1982). Cognitive factors include conceptual knowledge (*understanding*) and strategies for applying existing knowledge to new situations (*general problem-solving strategies*). Affective factors influence children's *disposition* to solve problems. Metacognition includes *self-regulation*: the ability to think through problems on your own. Besides having sufficient understanding, adequate problem-solving strategies, a positive disposition toward mathematical problem solving, and a capacity for self-regulation, effective problem solvers typically have another characteristic: *flexibility*.

Understanding

In general, the broader and better organized a person's mathematical knowledge base, the more problems he or she can solve. As their content knowledge of mathematics grows and becomes more interconnected, then, students increase their ability to understand and to find solutions for more and more difficult problems.

Solving a genuine problem begins with understanding the problem, which entails constructing an appropriate mental representation of the problem (Riley, Greeno, & Heller, 1983). Clearly, the greater a child's conceptual understanding, the more likely he or she will be able to construct an appropriate mental representation. Box 2.2 illustrates the importance of constructing an accurate mental representation. It also underscores the key point that informal—as well as formal—experiences can play a significant role in the development of the knowledge base needed to understand and solve problems.

A well-connected body of knowledge also increases the number of solution strategies a person can bring to bear on a problem and, thus, the probability of finding an efficient procedure, or any solution procedure for that matter. Primary children might understand Problem 2.1 below, for instance, but they probably would not have sufficient knowledge to construct a solution strategy. Older children who were familiar with making scale drawings could solve the problem (see Figure 2.3 on page 2-9), but

---

> ## Box 2.2: Solving a New Kind of Problem
>
> At $7\frac{1}{2}$, Arianne had finished first grade but had not yet been introduced to word problems like the one below:
>
> ■ Austin has 8 marbles, and Michael has 5 marbles. How many more marbles does Austin have than Michael?
>
> After the problem was read to her, Arianne asked how much each boy had and counted out a collection of eight pennies and another of five. She paused to think for awhile and then responded, "That's [eight] more than that [five]." Apparently, Arianne did not appear to understand that the word problem was asking for the difference of the two sets, not simply which was larger.
>
> The interviewer prompted: "How much more?"
>
> After reconsidering the situation for a moment, Arianne counted five of the pennies in the collection of eight, pushed them aside, and noted: "Three." Thus, when the feedback made it clear her conception of the problem was incorrect, the girl had sufficient informal understanding of comparative situations to comprehend the meaning of the interviewer's prompt and to construct an informal solution strategy.

this would be a relatively inefficient approach. Students who recognized that the formula for the circumference of a circle (c = πd) was applicable and who recalled that π was about 22/7 could solve the problem quickly: $c = \frac{22}{7} \cdot 21$ feet ≈ 66 feet).*

■ **Problem 2.1: A Pool Barrier.** Mr. Wilson bought a circular above-ground pool. The widest distance across the pool was 21 feet. Because the wall of the pool was only four feet high, he was afraid his young children might be able to climb over it. He decided to put a wire mesh around the rim of the pool to discourage any unsupervised jaunts into the pool. The wire mesh was sold by the length. What length does Mr. Wilson need?

---

* The symbol ≈ means about.

Figure 2.3: A Concrete Solution to a Pool-Barrier Problem

Step 1: Draw a circle to scale.

Scale: ⊔ ($\frac{1}{8}$ inch) = 3 feet

Step 2: Place a string around the rim of the circle, and mark how far around the string must be wrapped.

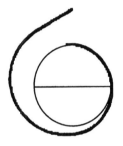

Step 3: Straighten out the string and use the scale to determine the distance around the circle's rim.

22 3-foot lengths ➜ 66 feet

General Problem-Solving Strategies

Recalling existing knowledge, however, is not sufficient to solve novel tasks or genuine problems. Now we can attack such problems in a hit-or-miss (trial-and-error) fashion. However, a thoughtful analysis makes it more likely that we will understand a problem and find a solution to it. General strategies for helping us to do this include a systematic approach to solving problems and general problem-solving tips or aids called *heuristics*. The more heuristics we have at our disposal, the more likely we will be able to analyze a problem successfully and devise an effective solution procedure.

Disposition

Sometimes children and adults actually have sufficient knowledge to understand a problem and sufficient skill to solve it but don't try. Why? Quite simply, they lack drive—the desire or willingness (disposition) to grapple with the problem. The drive to struggle with genuine problems is affected by interest, self-confidence, perseverance, and beliefs (Lester, 1980; Silver & Thompson, 1984).

Interest. Children and adults alike will lavish effort on problems that intrigue them. For example, some spend hours figuring out the tricks to video games so that they can improve their play. Like most people, children will spend as little time as possible on problems that appear irrelevant or unimportant to them.

Self-Confidence. Like most things with significant payoffs such as making investments, playing a championship game, or falling in love, problem solving involves taking risks (House, 1980). There is the uncertainty of not knowing exactly what to do and of making choices. This raises the possibility of—aggh—being wrong and all the anxiety that can inspire. Let's face it, solving problems can be nerve-wracking. You need considerable confidence to confront uncertainty and the possibility of failure.

Perseverance. Like many worthwhile activities, solving genuine problems usually takes time. Indeed, because it is not clear how to solve such problems, there may be false starts and the need to begin again. People who are easily discouraged are not likely to solve genuine problems. Solving such problems usually requires perseverance.

Beliefs. Beliefs influence interest, self-confidence, and perseverance (e.g., Schoenfeld, 1985, 1992; McLeod, 1992). Thus, they are a critical factor in determining an individual's drive to solve problems. Effective problem solvers have a set of convictions about mathematics and themselves that energize problem-solving efforts. For example, they view problems as an interesting challenge rather than as a burden or a threat. Effective problem solvers tell themselves, "I might be able to solve this problem if I try," not "I doubt that I could solve it no matter how hard I try." Such people realistically recognize that genuine problems may require extended time and effort, rather than unrealistically believe that they can be solved quickly.

Self-Regulation

Understanding, general problem-solving strategies, and a positive disposition, though, are not sufficient for ensuring effective problem solving (Palincsar, 1986). There must be an awareness of what resources a problem requires and management of the resources used (Reeve & Brown, 1985). In other words, solving genuine problems entails a thoughtful analysis of the problem-solving *process* as well as of the problem. Knowledge about how our resources (mathematical knowledge, general problem-solving strategies, and other thinking processes) can be applied to a task, and the active monitoring and control of these resources, is called metacognition (Garofalo, 1987).

Metacognitive skills underlie self-regulated problem solving. Problem solvers with well-developed metacognitive skills might ask or tell themselves: "What do I know that applies to this problem?"; "What heuristics might be useful?"; "Watch your tendency to be impulsive"; "Am I still on track?"; "This is not working; I had better change that previous step"; "Does the answer make sense?".

Flexibility

Solving a problem often depends on using or viewing existing knowledge in a new way. Creativity or flexibility combines cognitive, affective, and metacognitive elements and can entail questioning or overcoming entrenched assumptions. Consider Problem 2.2, which dates from the 1700's (Pappas, 1989).

> ■ **Problem 2.2: The Farmer's Dilemma.** A farmer needed to take a wolf, goat, and cabbage to market but had to cross a river. He could only take one thing across the river at a time. If he took the cabbage first, the wolf would eat the goat. If he took the wolf first, the goat would eat the cabbage. How could the farmer get everything across the river safely?

Clearly, on the first trip across the river, the farmer needs to take the goat. At this point many people get stuck. What should the farmer take next? If he takes the cabbage, the goat will eat it before he returns. If he takes the wolf over next, the goat will be eaten before he returns. Accustomed to straight-forward algorithmic thinking, many people assume that once a subtask is done, it cannot be undone. This assumption prevents them from solving the Farmer's Dilemma.

A CASE OF STUNTED GROWTH

This subunit examines children's natural problem-solving ability, schoolchildren's performance on problem-solving tasks, and what effects schooling has on children's problem-solving ability.

Informal Skill

What problem-solving skill do children have before they receive formal instruction? Conventional wisdom holds that children are not capable of analyzing and solving before they have received arithmetic instruction. Indeed, it is commonly assumed that word problems are difficult for children and that they should be introduced *after* formal arithmetic instruction. The assumption is that children must first learn the skills and concepts needed to work problems before they are asked to tackle problems. Seems plausible, doesn't it?

In fact, research indicates that *before* formal arithmetic training begins, children can use their informal knowledge to analyze and solve simple arithmetic word problems (e.g., Carpenter, 1986). Indeed, word problems are often more meaningful to young children than symbolic arithmetic. Consider the case of Mark (Baroody, 1987). Shown the written addition problem 5 + 1 and asked how much five and one were altogether, the kindergartner appeared confused and did not respond. When asked: "How much are five candies and one more candy," Mark thought a moment and responded "Oh, six." He then responded correctly to five more symbolic problems involving the addition of 1.

How do young children solve simple addition and subtraction word problems? When first introduced to arithmetic word problems, children try to model the meaning of the problem, usually with objects. That is, they represent the quantities mentioned in the problem, use the representations to imitate the action implied by the problem, and count to determine the answer (Carpenter, 1986). To solve a simple addition problem such as Problem 2.3 on the next page, young children often model the problem concretely: (a) first counting out five blocks, fingers, or other objects to represent the amount Ruffus began with; (b) then counting out another three items to represent how much was added; and (c) lastly, counting all the items to determine the total. In brief, without training, children commonly use their everyday knowledge, concrete materials, and common sense to solve simple but novel arithmetic problems.

■ **Problem 2.3: Ruffus' Bones.** Ruffus the dog had five bones. He tipped Mr. Purdy's garbage can over and got three more bones. How many bones does Ruffus have altogether now?

The Problem-Solving Skill of U.S. Schoolchildren

How do U.S. schoolchildren measure up in terms of problem-solving ability?

Performance on Routine and Nonroutine Word Problems. One useful way to characterize word problems is to distinguish between routine and nonroutine word problems. A routine word problem entails a one-step solution process. The basic task posed by such a problem is deciding what operation is appropriate (LeBlanc, Proudfit, & Putt, 1980). For example, to determine the answer for Problem 2.4 below, a child simply has to identify subtraction as the appropriate operation and apply it to the two numbers.

■ **Problem 2.4: Ruffus and the Case of the Missing Doughnuts.** Mary set out 9 doughnuts for a party. Ruffus, her voluminous dog, consumed 7. How many doughnuts does Mary have left for the party?

Because routine word problems are a common feature of traditional textbooks and instruction, solving such problems may not be a good indication of problem-solving skill. For this reason, tests like the National Assessment of Educational Progress (NAEP) include nonroutine word problems. Such problems include some kind of twist. They may, for example, involve two or more steps (operations) or include extra and unneeded information. Because nonroutine word problems require more than the identification and application of a single arithmetic operation, they provide a greater challenge to children's thinking than do routine word problems. Additionally, children have far less, if any, exposure to nonroutine word problems. Thus, this type of word problem is more likely to constitute a genuine problem for children.

Results from the NAEP show that, generally, students at all ages successfully solve the routine, one-step word problems typically found in traditional textbooks (Carpenter, Matthews, Lindquist, & Silver, 1984). Most, however, have difficulty with nonroutine word problems that require some analysis or thinking (Carpenter, Corbitt, Kepner, Lindquist, & Reys, 1980; Carpenter et al., 1984; Kouba, Carpenter, & Swafford, 1989). For two-step word problems such as Problem 2.5 below, for example, less than a third of the third graders participating in the Fourth NAEP and less than four-fifths of the seventh graders correctly determined the answer was 6 cents. Although many children simply made a computing error and answered 16 cents, about one-sixth of the third graders simply completed the first step and answered 94 cents. In a similar vein, fewer than a tenth of the seventh graders were able to solve multistep problems involving the multiplication and subtraction of two-digit whole numbers (Silver & Carpenter, 1989).

■ **Problem 2.5: Chris' Change.** Chris buys a pencil for 35 cents and a soda for 59 cents. How much change does she get back from $1.00?

For Problem 2.6 below, which contains extra information, children commonly add all three numbers mentioned and answer "nine." Such children apparently made no effort to analyze the word problem and determine what information was needed and what was not needed.

■ **Problem 2.6: A Problem with Extra Information.** Jim bought a bag of marbles. There were 2 red marbles and 3 blue marbles in the bag. The bag of marbles cost 4¢. How many marbles did Jim buy altogether?

The Effects of a Skills Approach

Why do children who begin school with such promise become such poor problem solvers? Why doesn't a traditional skills approach promote problem solving? Certainly the problems posed to older children are more difficult than those that children just beginning school can solve. But with schooling, why don't children develop the skill to solve such problems? A key reason for poor problem-solving skills is how mathematics has traditionally been taught in the U.S. An optimist might rate our national efforts to promote problem-solving proficiency a D-: inadequate. A pessimist might rate our efforts an FFF: downright destructive.

Mathematical Understanding. Because of its focus on memorizing facts, rules, formulas, and procedures, a traditional skills approach frequently fails to cultivate an understanding of school mathematics. NAEP results, for example, have shown that schools are generally successful in fostering basic skills but far less successful in encouraging conceptual learning. Thus, a traditional skills approach often fails to cultivate an important basis for understanding nonroutine or genuine problems.

More specifically, when children memorize mathematical knowledge by rote, they usually cannot use this unconnected knowledge to model problems; they cannot create an accurate mental representation of a problem (Davis, 1992). Thus, even if children have memorized the appropriate calculational procedure, they frequently do not use it to solve problems. For example, Ling, a fifth grader, was given Problem 2.7 below:

■ **Problem 2.7: A Shared Candy Bar.** Jane had 1/3 of a candy bar. She gives 1/2 of what she has to Mike. How much of the candy bar does she give to Mike? (Maher & Alston, 1989 cited in Davis, 1992).

Apparently misrepresenting the problem, the girl divided 1/3 by 1/2 and got an answer of 2/3. Ling's difficulty was not that she did not know how to multiply fractions, but that she did not know it applied to this problem situation. (Interestingly, the girl was able to solve the problem informally with wooden Pattern Blocks.)

☞ Consider Probe 2.2 (page 2-16) before and after reading Problem-Solving Strategies.

Problem-Solving Strategies. A traditional skills approach does little to encourage thoughtful analyses of problems or to promote the development of general problem-solving strategies. For example, one important strategy is gauging whether or not there is sufficient information available to solve a problem. However, only 13% of the third graders and 38% of the seventh graders on the Fourth NAEP correctly indicated there was not enough information to solve Problem 2.8 below:

■ **Problem 2.8: A Tall Team.** Everyone on the team is tall. If Jane is tall, then [what can we conclude about Jane?]

In a skills approach, word problems are typically assigned after an operation is introduced and serve merely as exercises for practicing basic computational skills. Frequently, assignments consist exclusively of routine problems, which—unlike genuine problems—usually do not require a thoughtful analysis. Moreover, assignments often involve a single operation, which further minimizes the thought required. In brief, children in traditional programs have little or no experience in thoughtfully analyzing problems.

For many children, instruction on problem-solving strategies is basically limited to key-word training. Teachers and traditional textbooks often have children focus on *key words* in a word problem to help them decide what operation to choose. Children are instructed, for example, "whenever you see 'and' ('more,' 'altogether,' or 'in all'), add; whenever you see 'left' (or 'take away'), subtract" (see Probe 2.2). In some textbooks, the use of such a strategy will allow children to solve nearly all the word problems presented (Schoenfeld, 1982).

Although encouraging children to pay careful attention to the words used in word problems can be helpful, simply having them zero in on key words can be misleading. In Problem 2.9 below, the mindless application of the "and-means-add" rule would lead a child to add and to answer, "Seven." In Problem 2.10, the blind use of the "left-means-subtract" rule would lead a child to subtract and answer, "One" (Kilpatrick, 1985a).

■ **Problem 2.9: An Early Retirement Program for Mail Carriers.** Ruffus had forced 5 mailmen to retire, *and* Bruno the Beagle had forced 2 to retire. How many more mailmen had Ruffus forced to retire than Bruno?

■ **Problem 2.10: The Case of the Unwelcomed Deposits.** Ruffus *left* 3 messes in Mr. Purdy's yard and Bruno *left* 2. How many messes did the dogs leave in Mr. Purdy's yard?

Another problem with teaching children to look for specific words such as "in all" or "left" is that they are not the only terms to indicate addition or subtraction. A key-word strategy, then, may not be helpful in other contexts, such as on an achievement test that uses "What remained?" instead of "What was left?". Additionally, such a strategy will not be helpful when solving many nonroutine problems. In brief, mechanically learning superficial tricks like the key-word rules may encourage children not to analyze problems carefully and may actually interfere with problem-solving efforts (Carpenter, 1986).

Disposition. A traditional skills approach often undermines children's disposition to solve problems. For one thing, it can sabotage interest in problem solving. For example, when word problems are used exclusively or largely to practice basic skills, children may view them as just another monotonous and uninspiring burden. Under such circumstances, it is not surprising that many report disliking word problems.

Moreover, the use of word problems as routine practice exercise gives children an inaccurate notion of real problem solving (see Table 2.1), which fosters beliefs that undermine a disposition to engage in genuine problem solving (e.g., Schoenfeld, 1985, 1992). The hidden message of simple one-step word problems is that mathematics does not require hard thinking and creativity but attentiveness and dutiful memorization (Davis, 1992). Implicitly, or even explicitly, children learn that there is *one* correct (the school-taught) method for readily solving a mathematical task. The cumulative effect of such instruction is that children lose confidence in their intuitive or informal strategies. Effectively cut off from perhaps their best or only chance of solving problems, many—sooner or later—meet with failure, become discouraged, and resist risking further problem-solving attempts. Because a skills approach effectively teaches children that you either know the correct procedure for readily performing a task or you don't, many come to expect that if you cannot determine the solution to a problem in a few minutes, you might as well stop trying. Because aptitude is often equated with an ability to respond efficiently, many children interpret their inability to solve a problem as a lack of mathematical aptitude (see Figure 2.4 on the next page), which discourages them from further problem-solving efforts.

Self-Regulation. Traditional educational practice tends to ignore the metacognitive components of learning (Campione, Brown, & Connell, 1989). Students are seldom encouraged to reflect on their learning and problem-solving activities. Thus, other than understanding that practice is important

Table 2.1: Routine Word Problems Versus Real Problems†

Routine Word Problems Often Found in Traditional Textbooks	Problem-Solving Endeavors Common to Everyday Life and Mathematics
The unknown is specified or readily apparent.	The unknown may not be specified or obvious.
Only the specific information needed to calculate the answer is provided.	Too much or too little information is available.
One correct solution procedure is obvious.	Many solution procedures, which may or may not be apparent, apply.
There is one correct answer.	There may be a number of answers or even no answer.
The answer can be quickly computed.	Significant problems are often time consuming to solve.

†Based on Table 14.2 from *Children's Mathematical Thinking: A Developmental Framework for Preschool, Primary, and Special Education Teachers* by Arthur J. Baroody, © 1987. Reprinted by permission of Teachers College Press, Columbia University, New York. All rights reserved.

Figure 2.4: Many Students Believe That If They Can't Solve a Problem Quickly, They Lack the Ability To Solve It at All

FOX TROT reprinted by permission of U P S.

for memorizing information, they may understand little about these processes (see Box 2.3). When students are not given the underlying reasons for procedures, they are left with few means to monitor the use of procedures. Moreover, students are seldom coached on how to monitor their learning and problem-solving activities effectively.

Indeed, a traditional skills approach undermines the development of autonomy or self-regulation.

Box 2.3: Study Those Number Facts!

Tommy, age 8 and from an upper middle-class family, had just completed the fourth grade at the time he was interviewed. He was labeled learning disabled by his school and was behind in memorizing the basic arithmetic combinations. Asked how he might help a first grader learn all the basic addition combinations, Tommy replied: "Yeah, just by telling them the answers.... Make them study it."

Interestingly, Tommy recommended a method that had apparently failed him miserably. He equated learning with how he had learned mathematics: An authority tells you what to do, and then you practice it. Other ways of learning did not occur to him. For example, he did not consider that students might look for and use patterns.

Implicitly or explicitly, the expectation is created that students are not supposed to figure out methods by themselves (Schoenfeld, 1992). Such an approach, then, encourages passivity and reliance on external authorities such as a teacher or textbook. Children are seldom given practice solving problems on their own so that they can practice and develop self-regulatory skills. As a result, when confronted with a nonroutine word problem or other unfamiliar problems, many children feel utterly helpless (see Figure 2.5 on the next page).

This is often true even when the problem is only slightly different from what students have studied in school. Wertheimer (1945/1959) tells about a visit he took to a classroom that just learned how to determine the area of a parallelogram. The students had been taught to measure the length of the base and height of a parallelogram and multiply these two values (see Frame A of Figure 2.6). After watching children successfully complete several "problems," Wertheimer stepped to the board, drew a picture similar to the one in Frame B of Figure 2.6 and asked what its area was. The children could not determine the answer. He reported that some students were "obviously taken aback. One pupil [noted]: 'Teacher, we haven't had that yet' " (p. 15). Other students tried applying the procedure they had been taught but soon became bewildered. In brief, confronted with a somewhat novel task, most of the students did not see how their school-taught procedure applied and were at a loss.

Figure 2.5: Spoon-feeding Children Fosters Helplessness

PEANUTS reprinted by permission of UFS, Inc.

Figure 2.6: Determining the Area of a Rectangle

A. School-taught procedure

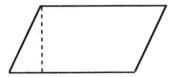

Measured height: 4 units
Measured base: 8 units

$A = b \times h = 8 \times 4 = 32$

B. Variation on the practiced task

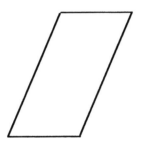

Flexibility. With its focus on rotely memorizing *the* correct (school-taught) procedure, the traditional skills approach discourages flexibility. There is real danger in routinely requiring children to memorize procedures that they do not understand and then asking them to use this knowledge to solve word problems. Consider the case of Sherry (Box 2.4). Believing she had to use the school-taught procedure, the girl struggled with a problem that could easily have been solved with common sense.

Box 2.4: The Case of Sherry[2]

Sherry, a junior high school student, noted she had been learning how to convert measurements from one unit to another. The problem below should have been relatively simple to solve.

■ A computer is programmed to read measurements in feet. Your first measurement, however, is 3 feet 6 inches. What are you going to feed into the computer?

Instead of reflecting on the problem and arriving at the common-sense conclusion that 6 inches is one-half a foot and that the answer must be 3.5 feet, Sherry immediately tried to apply her school-taught conversion algorithm: (a) Retrieve an equivalent measure (12 inches = 1 foot); (b) let X = the unknown; (c) set up a proportion (6 inches/12 inches = X/1 foot); (e) cross multiply and simplify the expression ($12 \cdot X = 6 \cdot 1$ foot; $X = 6/12$ feet = 0.5 feet); (f) add the converted amount to the whole number of feet (3 feet + 0.5 feet = 3.5 feet). Unfortunately, because she did not understand the underlying rationale for the algorithm, Sherry could not remember how to execute it correctly. She eventually came up with an answer of less than 3 feet. Recognizing her answer was not correct, Sherry became flustered. The interviewer tried to help by asking if there was any other way to solve the problem. "No," she responded sharply. "That's the way it *has* to be done." The interviewer then suggested examining the numbers involved to see if there might be an easier way to find the answer. Even more impatiently, Sherry retorted, "This is the way I learned in school, so it has to be *the* way."

➤ **Probe 2.2: Analyzing Problem-Solving Activities in Textbooks II**

❢ Evaluate the page of a first-grade workbook shown below. Your analysis should include whether the word problems constitute an enigma, a genuine problem, or an exercise; whether the problems are routine or nonroutine; and how word problems are used by the text. (In regard to the last point, the textbook introduces word problems after introducing symbolic subtraction.) Evaluate the reminder in the directions. What reminder might a teacher use instead?

Name _____

PROBLEM-SOLVING STRATEGY

Directions: Read the following story problems to the class. Have the students decide whether they should add or subtract. Remind them to look for the words *in all* or *left* to help them decide what they should do. Have them circle the correct sign.

1. Three little chickens were eating corn. Two more little chickens joined them. How many little chickens are there in all?

+ or -

2. Five little chickens were eating corn. Four little chickens went into the barn. How many chickens were left eating corn?

+ or -

page 88

THE MATH BOOK FROM HELL: Grade 1
Boring Books Publishing Co., Inc.

THE PROBLEM-SOLVING PROCESS

☞ Tackle Probe 2.3 (pages 2-27 to 2-28) before continuing with the text. Working in a group may be particularly helpful for this activity. Work out as many problems as you can; note how you solved a problem and where you encountered difficulties.

You may have found some of the problems in Probe 2.3 difficult. In some cases, you may not even know where to begin. This subunit discusses general problem-solving strategies using a four-phase approach for attacking genuine problems and some general problem-solving aids (heuristics) for facilitating problem-solving efforts. After reading these tips, retackle any problems you did not answer. You may also want to rethink those that you did answer. It may be interesting to discuss your group's efforts with the rest of the class.

A Four-Phase Approach

We should begin with a warning. The THE in the section title above is misleading: There is no one way mathematicians or others solve problems. Thus, it does not make sense to talk about *the* problem-solving process. Although there are various ways of solving problems, George Polya (1973) proposed a four-phase scheme for approaching problems in a systematic fashion. This scheme is now widely recognized as a useful tool for the problem-solving efforts of even primary-age children.

Phase 1: Understand the Problem. The first step in solving a problem is understanding what is being asked for. A clear understanding of the question and the unknown is essential for deciding what information is needed, which solution strategies are appropriate, and what answers are reasonable. Consider $7\frac{1}{2}$-year-old Arianne's response to a missing-addend word problem, Problem 2.11 below:

■ **Problem 2.11: Dolls Discovered.** Melissa was playing with five dolls. Then she found some more. Now, Melissa has eight dolls. How many dolls did she find?

After much mental effort, the girl finally used counters and responded "13." Like many young primary-age children, Arianne did not correctly identify the unknown as the amount added. As a result, she chose an incorrect strategy (adding 5 and 8) and felt perfectly satisfied with her impossible answer. Perhaps worse off than children who misunderstand a problem are students, who feeling overwhelmed by a problem, make no effort to comprehend it.

Phase 2: Devise a Plan. Once a problem is understood, it is time to consider how to determine the answer(s). Ideally, a thoughtful analysis will lead to considering alternative solution strategies and picking the most appropriate plan. Novice problem solvers, however, might use a relatively inefficient trial-and-error approach, which basically entails trying different strategies until something works. Perhaps worse, they may prematurely seize upon one strategy. Worst of all, if novices do not immediately recognize how to solve a problem, they throw up their hands and give up.

Phase 3: Carry Out the Plan. The third phase entails carrying out the plan devised in Phase 2 *and* carefully monitoring the solution procedure. This monitoring is important not merely to check whether the procedure is executed accurately but to gauge whether the plan is doing the job intended. Sometimes it becomes clear there were unanticipated complications or that more data need to be collected. Novices may not consider careful monitoring important and may even resist evaluating their course of action or—horrors—changing it.

Phase 4: Look Back. Once a solution is determined, it is important to check the results. Does the solution make sense? Does it answer the original question? Is there any other way the problem could be solved and does this solution method produce the same answer? Many students feel that once they have determined an answer, their job is done.

Some Problem-Solving Heuristics

How can a teacher help students effectively implement each of Polya's four problem-solving phases? Described below are some general problem-solving aids or heuristics that can help students with each of Polya's four phases. A teacher may wish to display a chart summarizing the heuristics for each phase, such as one shown in Figure 2.7. A teacher may wish to use a simpler summary for younger children and a more complete one for older students. In any case, a teacher may find it helpful to remind students of these problem-solving hints as they proceed through the problem-solving process. Note that some of the heuristics described below are techniques for helping problem solvers represent a problem or to transform the problem into one they can represent. Many of the aids serve as "metacognitive prompts"; they encourage problem solvers to reflect on their understanding of the problem, their progress in solving the problem, and the effectiveness of their chosen course of action (Silver, 1982).

Heuristics for Understanding the Problem. The following heuristics can facilitate a thoughtful analysis of a task or situation, which is essential for understanding genuine problems. Employing such strategies can get students involved in thinking about the problem rather than worrying about its difficulty. Taking these concrete steps can overcome the initial panic and sense of inertia many people feel when confronted with an unfamiliar problem. In a sense, these heuristics can serve to prime the problem-solving pump.

✚ **State the problem in your own words.** A teacher can prompt students with a question such as: "What do you think the problem is saying?" Restating the problem gets students to focus on what a problem is about and what needs to be found. It also allows a teacher or peers to check whether a student has the same interpretation of the problem. Conflict between interpretations may prompt students to re-examine the problem.

✚ **Decide what the unknown is.** An important question to consider when trying to understand a problem is: "What is the unknown in this problem?" This question helps students to focus specifically on deciding what needs to be found.

✚ **Decide what information is needed.** With some problems, particularly those stemming from the real world, students need to consider what information they need to collect. In many real-world situations, a person is confronted with a wealth of information and must decide what is relevant and what can safely be disregarded. With more sophisticated school problems, students likewise need to decide which data are needed and which are not. Useful prompts include: "What information was given?"; "Do you have enough information to solve the problem?"; "What additional information do you need?"; and "What information is *not* needed to solve the problem?".

Figure 2.7: Problem-Solving Heuristics for Each of Polya's Four Problem-Solving Phases

Some Problem-Solving Hints

PHASE 1: UNDERSTANDING THE PROBLEM. Did you try the following?

✚ State the problem in your own words.

✚ Decide what the unknown is.

✚ Decide what information is needed.

PHASE 2: DEVISE A PLAN. Might the following help?

✚ Draw a picture.

✚ Examine some examples and look for patterns.

✚ Organize the data in a list, table, or chart, and look for patterns.

✚ Simplify the problem and look for patterns.

✚ Relate the problem to familiar problems.

✚ Write a number sentence.

✚ Work backwards.

✚ Use logical reasoning to eliminate possibilities.

✚ Guess and check.

PHASE 3: CARRY OUT THE PLAN. Did you do the following?

✚ Decide whether or not the plan is working.

PHASE 4: LOOK BACK. Did you consider the following?

✚ Decide whether the solution is reasonable.

✚ Decide whether the solution answers the question.

✚ Decide if there are other solutions.

Heuristics for Devising a Plan. The following heuristics can help students think through how to solve a problem and/or develop solution methods. Nearly all of these strategies could *also* be used to understand the problem, carry out the plan, and/or look back.

✚ **Draw a picture, draw a diagram, make a model, or act out the problem**. The key here is to represent the problem pictorially or concretely so that a student has something to experiment with and to reflect on. In fact, such a representation can help a problem solver understand the problem, monitor the solution process, and check a solution as well as devise or choose a strategy. For example, encouraging children to draw a picture or create a model of Problem 2.11 above might help them conceptualize this missing-addend problem as well as devise a plan for solving it. By reflecting on a representation, a child might realize that the problem was different from familiar missing-sum problems and that adding the numbers would not be appropriate. By analyzing or experimenting with the representation, the child might be able to devise and carry out an appropriate strategy (see Box 2.5).

During any of Polya's four-phase approach to solving problems, creating a pictorial or concrete representation can help problem solvers notice important factors that otherwise may not have been considered. Take, for example, Problem 2.12:

Box 2.5: Using a Model to Understand and to Solve a Missing-Addend Word Problem

Encouraged to represent Problem 2.11 with pennies, Arianne (who, as mentioned earlier, initially failed the task) reconsidered the missing-addend problem and then devised a successful strategy like those illustrated below.

A. (1) Child counts out counters to represent the starting amount (5), leaves a space for the added amount, and counts out counters to represent the total (8).

   (2) Child recognizes that the total is comprised of the starting amount and amount added and reasons that eliminating the starting amount would leave the amount added

   (3) After counting five of the eight counters and setting them aside, child counts the remainder to determine how many were added.

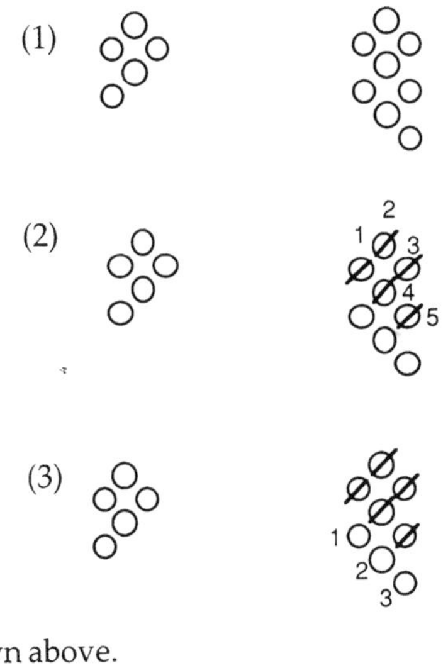

The following model basically shortcuts the one shown above.

B. (1) Child counts out five counters to represent the starting amount;

   (2) adds on counters to model until the total eight is represented;

   (3) counts how many counters were added on (three).

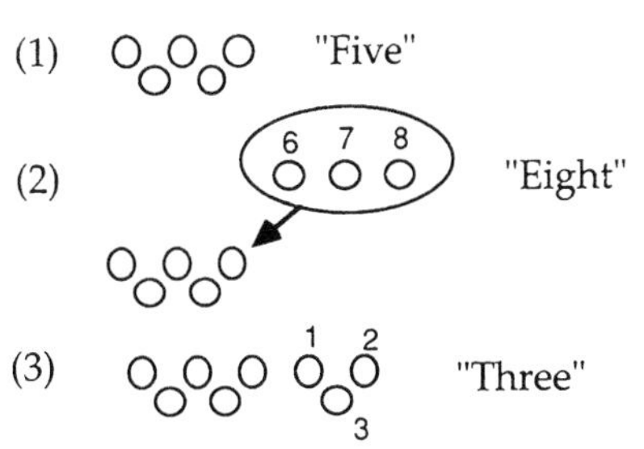

■ **Problem 2.12: The Rock Garden.** Mr. Xuan (pronounced Swan) wanted to create a rock garden along the length of his back porch. He wanted to surround his rock garden with a walkway made of square patio blocks 1 foot on a side. To keep weeds from growing, Mr. Xuan wanted to cover the area of his rock garden with a plastic weed barrier. If the outside length of the walkway was 10 feet and the outside width of this walkway was 6 feet, how much plastic weed barrier did Mr. Xuan need?

Some students might leap to the conclusion that the answer is 60 square feet. Examine Figure 2.8 below. What does the answer fail to take into account? How much plastic weed barrier does Mr. Xuan really need?

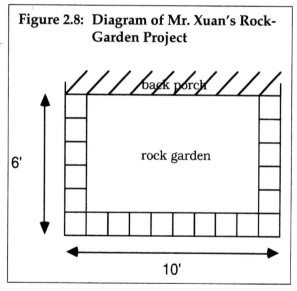

Figure 2.8: Diagram of Mr. Xuan's Rock-Garden Project

back porch

rock garden

6'

10'

As another example, carefully drawing a diagram to represent Problem 1 in Probe 2.3 can readily provide the answer. Hint: Consider representing the passage of time with a line segment. If for Problem 2 in Probe 2.3 you divided 128 by 8 and got an answer of 16 steps, draw a picture. Is there something you did not take into account? For Problem 3 in Probe 2.3, if you concluded that the second race ended in a tie, draw a diagram to check your answer. For further discussion of these and other problems in Probe 2.3, see Answers to Selected Questions at the end of the chapter (pages 2-137 and 2-138).

✦ **Look for a pattern by examining specific examples.** Solving a problem often entails noticing a pattern. One way to find patterns is to examine specific examples. Considering one example at a time can be more manageable than trying to analyze all the data at once. After a pattern or rule is detected with one instance, it should be checked out with other examples. If the pattern or rule does not hold across examples, a student needs to consider what other pattern or rule does fit the examples. Consider Problem 2.13 below.

■ **Problem 2.13: Case of the Predatory Partner.** Jeb and Slim formed a partnership. Jeb soon suspected there were some serious inequalities in the partnership. Not only did Jeb carve all the wooden ornaments, but he did all the selling too. Moreover, on Monday he turned in $12 to the treasurer (Slim) and received only $3 for his efforts. On Tuesday he sold $24 worth of ornaments and his commission was $7. On Wednesday he peddled $18 worth and received $5. On Thursday he registered sales of $9 and got $2. On Friday he hawked $4 worth and was paid $.33. On Saturday he sold $10 worth. How much could Jeb expect to receive for his efforts on Saturday?

To determine Jeb's Saturday commission, you must assume that Slim is determining his partner's commission in some systematic way. In other words you must assume there is a rule (a function) that transforms a specified earning into a specified commission. This rule can be determined by examining specific instances of an earning and the resulting commission. By examining the first example (12 ➜ 3), it appears that the rule is simply divide by four. Though this rule works for Monday's data, it does not work for those of the other days (e.g., for Tuesday, $18 \div 4 \neq 5$). Clearly, our initial guess must be modified or abandoned. Try to decipher Slim's devious rule. This problem is discussed further below. Looking for patterns, in general, is discussed further in the next unit: Mathematics as Reasoning.

✦ **Make a list, table, or chart.** Another way to facilitate looking for patterns is to organize your data in lists, tables, or charts. For Problem 2.13 above, listing the data *in order* can help in deciphering Slim's devious commission system:

4	9	10	12	18	24
.33	2	?	3	5	7

The usefulness of making an organized list is made especially apparent by Problem 2.14, which Ms. Wise posed to her class:

■ **Problem 2.14: Crack the Code.** The Keep the Cooties Away (KCA) Club had devised a secret alphabet code. Brenda was not allowed to join KCA because she was a girl. She sensed, from the flurry of secret messages her brother Bret received, that the club was planning something important and probably naughty for Halloween. "If I could crack the KCA code, I could sabotage their evil plans," mused Brenda. "That would show them they can't snub me." While Bret was out, Brenda searched through his room. She found plenty of secret messages and a paper with the alphabet, but no decoder. Bret noticed that someone had been pawing through his stuff and guessed it was Brenda. "You won't find a decoder," he taunted. "The code is simple enough that we don't need one, but even so, you'll never figure it out." "Oh yeah," Brenda responded feebly. Later that day, though, Brenda got a break when she overheard Bret identify himself on the phone as 1-9-16-10. Can you crack the code from the clues Brenda had?

Someone suggested putting the clues on the board, so Ms. Wise wrote:

B R E T
1 9 16 10

Darla suggested, "C could be 2, D would be 3, and.... No, wait. That's not possible," she concluded. Why? April further noted that Darla's answer would make J 9 and 9 was already assigned to R. Ms. Wise recorded a J and crossed out a 9 below it. Several other suggestions were made and discounted. Ms. Wise dutifully recorded each suggestion and crossed out those that were clearly not possible.

"This is getting very confusing," complained Logan. "We need to get organized." "It would help greatly," Darla suggested, "if we wrote the alphabet out in order." By making the list below the class soon saw a pattern and cracked the code.

A B C D E F G H I J K L M N O P Q R S T U V W X Y Z
1 2̶ 3̶ 16   8̶   9 10

Tables or charts are like lists but include labels to help categorize data. Consider the cow-fence problem described and illustrated in Box 2.6 on the next page. Labels may be helpful in communicating suggestions and solutions to other students.

Sometimes lists, tables, or charts can be used to delineate the various possibilities and to keep track of which have been checked and which need to be checked. Note that Ms. Wise recorded and crossed out incorrect suggestions above so that the class would not waste time repeating them.

Creating a chart and examining it for patterns can be most helpful in solving Problem 4 in Probe 2.3. Creating a table of possible answers and crossing out unworkable possibilities can help one focus in on the solution to Problem 5 in Probe 2.3.

✦ **Simplify the problem.** It sometimes helps to solve simpler versions of a problem. A pattern may emerge that can then be applied to the complex problem. Consider Problem 2.15:

■ **Problem 2.15: The Handshake Problem.** If each person in your class shook hands with everyone else in the class, how many hand shakes would occur?

For the sake of illustration, let's say there are 24 people in your class. Drawing a picture could help you solve the problem, but trying to represent such a large number of handshakes can get pretty messy and confusing. Let's consider a much simpler case, a class of two. Then examine a few somewhat more complicated cases. Organizing the data into a chart can also help here.

number of people	2	3	4	5
number of shakes	1	3	6	10

■ Box 2.6: Using a Table to Solve the Cow-Fence Problem†

Alexi, age 9, was told that it took 8 fence sections (white blocks) to surround 1 cow (colored block).

He was asked how many fence sections it would take to surround 2 cows. By extending the model, he quickly surmised it would take 10. He was then asked how many fence sections it would take to surround a row of 3 cows. Before extending the model, he decided to summarize his results in a table. (Not knowing how to spell fences, he simply labeled the second entry F.) After determining and recording an answer of 12, he was asked how many fence sections it would take to surround a row of 10 cows. To encourage the use of patterns, he purposely was not given enough blocks to determine the answer. Even if blocks were available, the prospect of working with so many blocks might prompt many children to consider a less concrete solution method. In fact, Alexi had no sooner recorded 12 in his table when he commented: "Oh, it [the number of fence sections] goes up by two." He then used this pattern to complete the table below up to 10 cows.

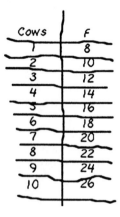

Cows	F
1	8
2	10
3	12
4	14
5	16
6	18
7	20
8	22
9	24
10	26

---

†The Cow-Fence problem was based on a problem described in the *Pattern Factory: Elementary Problem Solving Through Patterning* by Ann Roper and Linda Harvey, © 1980. It is described here with the permission of the publisher: Creative Publications, Palo Alto, CA.

Examine the data generated. Do you notice a pattern? The increase in the number of handshakes increases by one each time:

1 ⌢ 3 ⌢ 6 ⌢ 10
  +2   +3   +4

There are several ways to use this pattern to determine the solution to Problem 2.15. One, simply, is to extend the chart:

5	6	7	8	9	10	11	12	13	14	15
10	15	21	28	36	45	55	66	78	91	105

16	17	18	19	20	21	22	23	24
120	136	153	171	190	210	231	253	276

Like the Handshake Problem, Problem 6 in Probe 2.3 may seem overwhelming as posed. Consider the sums of much smaller series. Play with summing these series in different ways. Is there anything you notice?

✚ **Relate a new problem to familiar problems.** Even though problems may, on the surface, look different, some problems share the same underlying structure and solution. Because children may focus on superficial differences, it is important to encourage them to consider how new problems may be like familiar ones. For example, a teacher might prompt: "Does the new problem remind you of situations you can solve?" Consider Problem 2.16:

■ **Problem 2.16: The Tournament Problem.** The state sectionals were held at Chaos Middle School (CMS). Unfortunately, CMS did not qualify for the sectionals, because the team basically goofed off. Coach Krumb was so angry with the team, he decided they would have to sit through the whole tournament. If 20 teams participated in the tournament, each team played the other 19 teams, each contest lasted one hour, and only two teams played at a time; how long could the CMS players expect to be spectators?

Essentially the problem boils down to determining how many contests the 20 teams must play. Although the Tournament Problem does not appear to be similar to the Handshake Problem on the surface, it shares the same mathematical structure and solution. The first team would play 19 other teams (19 games). Discounting games already counted, the second team would play 18 games; the third team, 17 games; the fourth team, 16 games; and so forth. If 20 people were to shake hands with each other, the first person would shake hands with 19 other people (19 times). Discounting handshakes already counted, the second person would shake hands 18 times; the third person, 17 times; the fourth person, 16 times; and so forth. The solution for Problem 2.16, then, is the same for Problem 2.15 *with 20 people*. Using the chart generated to answer Problem 2.15, one can find that the answer for Problem 2.16 is 190. Does Problem 7 in Probe 2.3 remind you of a problem you have encountered before?

✚ **Write an equation.** It sometimes helps to write out the information given in a problem in the form of a number sentence or equation. A missing element can be denoted by a box or letter. If more than one element is missing, various shapes ($\square, \bigcirc, \triangle$, etc.) or letters can be used. Consider Problem 2.17 below:

■ **Problem 2.17: The Cookie Muncher.** Sophie had baked a large batch of cookies for the holidays. Her husband Jelko ate half the cookies while watching the Saturday college football games. He ate another quarter of the cookies while watching the Sunday pro football games. Jelko sat down to watch Monday night pro football and asked for some cookies. Sophie, who was concerned about her husband's weight, tactfully noted he had already consumed 54 cookies over the weekend. How many cookies had Sophie baked?

Letting N represent the unknown (the total number of cookies), the problem can be represented $\frac{N}{2} + \frac{N}{4} = 54$. Simplifying the expressions:

$$\frac{4 \bullet N}{2} + \frac{4 \bullet N}{4} = 4 \times 54$$
$$2N + N = 216$$
$$3N = 216$$
$$N = 72$$

Once an equation was written, the solution procedure was simply a matter of solving for the unknown.

Although Problem 8 in Probe 2.3 can be solved in several ways, a relatively straightforward method involves writing an equation. This heuristic is especially useful in solving algebra problems. However, it can also be useful as early as in the primary grades to solve, for instance, missing-addend problems such as Problem 2.11. A child could model the meaning of this word problem by noting 5 for the initial amount of dolls, $+\square$ for more dolls found, and $= 8$ for the resulting total: $5 + \square = 8$.

✚ **Work backwards.** Working backwards is particularly useful when a problem specifies the result of a sequence of events and the task is to determine the starting condition. Consider Problem 2.18 (Musser & Shaughnessy, 1980):

■ **Problem 2.18: A Winning Strategy for Force Out.** In Force Out, play starts with a total: a multidigit number such as 37. Two players take turns choosing a number from 1 to 9 and subtracting it from the total. The first player who reduces the total to 0 is the *loser*. Assuming you can go first, devise a strategy that would permit you to win nearly all the time.

The winning strategy can be determined by first considering the last move. Invariably, the last play of the game will find the loser subtracting 1 from 1. (If the total is between 2 and 10, a player could leave the total greater than 0 and, thus, avoid losing. For example, if the total is 8, a player could avoid defeat by subtracting any number between 1 and 7.) A winning strategy, then, involves being the first player to reduce the total to 1. How can you ensure this? Earlier, you must be the first player to get to 11. Why 11? Nothing your opponent can subtract from 11 will reduce the total to 1. If your opponent subtracts 9, for instance, that leaves the total 2. You can then subtract 1 and leave the total 1. To be the first to 11, you must even earlier be the first to reach 21. The same logic above applies. To ensure this, you must be the first to reach 31. Working backwards can be particularly useful in solving Problem 9 in Probe 2.3.

✚ **Use logical reasoning.** More concretely, this can be stated: *Use if-then reasoning to eliminate possibilities.* For example, with Problem 2.14 (Crack the Code) above, Darla proposed that the letters were numbered in sequence beginning with B. She quickly realized that *if* this were so, *then* E would be 4. Because E was, in fact, 16, her solution was clearly wrong. This was confirmed by April's observation.

If Darla's solution is correct, *then* J should be 9. However, 9 was already assigned to R. Similarly, with Problem 2.13 (the Predatory Partner), *if* the commission rate was 25% as suggested by the first example (12 → 3), *then* the commission for $18 in sales should be $4.50. Because, the commission was, in fact, $5, we can dismiss 25% as a plausible solution. Using if-then reasoning is discussed further in the next unit: Mathematics as Reasoning.

Often, making a chart to summarize the data can facilitate the process of using logical reasoning. Consider Problem 2.19 below:

■ **Problem 2.19: Dicey Arrangements.** The numbers on a die are arranged in a particular manner. Examine the dice shown below:

Example A   Example B   Example C

From these examples, can you determine how the numbers 1 to 6 are arranged on a die? No fair examining an already-manufactured die. Hint: (a) What can you conclude from the table below about what must be the opposite of 2? Note that from the information given, we know that 2 is adjacent to 4 and 6 (Example A), 3 (Example B), and 1 (Example C). (b) Fill in the table as much as you can. What conclusions can you draw?

Adjacent Numbers

Side	1	2	3	4	5	6
1	X					
2	yes	X	yes	yes		yes
3			X			
4				X		
5					X	
6						X

✦ **Guess and check.** A *random-guess-and-check strategy* is a trial-and-error approach to problem solving. It is particularly useful where there are only a few possibilities and a desired outcome is known or can be estimated. Consider Problem 2.20, which would be appropriate for primary children and which could be adapted for older students:

■ **Problem 2.20: The Unwanted Number.** Cross out one or more numbers in the number sentence below so that the sum is correct.

$$18 + 27 + 35 + 42 = 87$$

By fostering a guess-and-check strategy, a teacher can underscore the point that making mistakes is a natural part of the problem-solving process and that we can learn from our mistakes. Such a strategy is particularly important for primary children, because they have few problem-solving resources. Even children with more resources should be helped to recognize that if other methods fail, a trial-and-error approach can be useful. Although not efficient, it at least keeps a problem solver involved with a problem and may lead to the recognition of patterns and constraints that ultimately lead to a solution. Consider Problem 2.21 below. A trial-and-error strategy provides a straightforward method for attacking this problem. What do you notice as you try various solutions?

■ **Problem 2.21: Tower of Hanoi.** The disks on Peg A need to be moved to Peg C. Only one disk at a time may be moved, and a larger disk may not be placed on a smaller disk. What is the fewest number of moves in which this can be done?

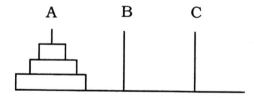

There are several things children can do to make a guess-and-check approach more effective or efficient (Musser & Shaughnessy, 1980).

1. *A systematic-guess-and-check approach* systematically *accounts for all the possibilities.* Such a strategy is useful for solving Problem 2.22 below.

Problem 2.22: Different Packs of Batteries. Ty bought a new electronic toy that required 52 AAA batteries. When he got to the store, Ty discovered that AAA batteries were sold in packages of 3 and 5. Because of a special sale, the three-packs had a lower unit price than did the five packs. What is the most economical way for Ty to buy exactly 52 batteries?

There is no point in trying more than 11 five-packs: 11 x 5 = 55. Constructing a table can help to systematically account for all the possibilities. In the table below, a student started with 10 five-packs and systematically worked down from there. Complete the table and determine the answer to Problem 2.22.

Five Packs	Three Packs	Total
10 x 5 = 50	1 x 3 = 3	53
9 x 5 = 45	2 x 3 = 6	51
8 x 5 = 40	4 x 3 = 12	52

2. *An inferential guess-and-check approach* narrows down the number of possibilities by taking into account *the information given.* (This basically represents an application of the use-logical-reasoning heuristic.) In Problem 2.23 below, it can help to approach the problem by systematically checking possibilities. However, because we are interested in scores in the range of 24 to 26, there is no need to consider all the possible ways four shots could be scored. Logically, we can infer that Ebb got at least one 9-point hit: Four 5-point hits is only 20 points, and everyone seems to agree that Ebb scored at least 24 points. Systematically examine the possibilities with at least one 9-point hit to see if scores of 24 and 26 are each possible.

Problem 2.23: The Disputed-Score. Mrs. White's second grade was having a bean-bag throwing contest. The three rings of the target were worth 9, 5, and

1. After his four shots, Ebb rushed to score his target. Before Mrs. White had a chance to record the score, the fire alarm rang. School was dismissed because of a fire in the kitchen. The next day, school and the contest resumed. Mrs. White realized that in all the commotion the previous day, she had not recorded Ebb's score. Ebb thought his score was 26 but wasn't sure. Fran, his main competitor, thought the score was 24. Is one score more likely than the other to be correct?

☞ Try the problems in Probe 2.4 (page 2-29) and then continue with the text.

Heuristics for Carrying Out the Plan. Children need to recognize the importance of monitoring their efforts and deciding whether or not their chosen plan is going to get them where they want to go. They need to understand that genuine problem solving can involve going up blind alleys (discovering that a solution procedure is completely wrong). It can involve finding oneself on an access road (discovering that a solution procedure is only part of the answer). Genuine problem solving can also involve detours (discovering that a solution procedure may work, but only eventually).

✦ **Decide if a new point of view is needed.** If children find themselves in a blind alley, perhaps the problem needs to be reconsidered and a new strategy devised. Solving the problems in Probe 2.4, for example, frequently requires problem solvers to change their perspective by overcoming an assumption. For Problem 1, the assumption that the lines cannot extend beyond the dots will prevent a solution. For Problem 2, it may appear that the answer is 8 x 8 or 64. What assumption is this *incorrect* answer based on? Problem 3 defeats many because they assume the constraint applies to all the lines in the diagram, including the line segments that form the houses A, B, and C. With these hints, reconsider any problems you did not solve on the first try.

✦ **Determine whether all the relevant information has been used.** If children find themselves on an access road, additional aspects of the problem need to be considered to complete the solution. A useful prompt at this time (or any time during the four-phase problem-solving process) is: "Did you use all the relevant information?"

✦ **Consider whether there are easier ways to solve the problem**. If students find themselves on a detour, particularly one that will take considerable time or effort, they might want to consider more elegant solution strategies.

☞ Try the problems in Probe 2.5 (page 2-30) and then continue with the text.

Heuristics for Looking Back. The following heuristics can facilitate thoughtful reflection on the solution to a problem. Once the following issues have been resolved and the answer appears acceptable, it can be useful for children to consider whether their solution method and answer to the problem at hand might apply to other problems.

✦ **Decide whether the solution is reasonable**. It is important that students get into the habit of gauging whether or not their answer makes sense. If you answered 5/6 or 15/32 pounds of hamburger for Problem 1 of Probe 2.5, consider whether this is plausible.

Problem 2 of Probe 2.5 (A Problematic Sports Problem) was modeled after similar problems in mathematics textbooks for elementary mathematics majors. When devised, though, the teacher did not pay attention to the fractions used (Civil, 1990): $2/3 + 1/2 = 7/6$. Although the sum is greater than one, unreflective students may simply record this impossible answer. More reflective students may be baffled by the answer but unsure what to do. Reflective and autonomous students may recognize that the teacher made an error. It may actually be a good idea for a teacher to purposely make errors on occasion to keep his students alert. If handled with humor, this technique could evolve into an instructive and motivating game of "Gotcha."

✦ **Decide whether the solution answers the question**. Sometimes a solution to a problem really isn't. If you answered 30 minutes for Problem 3 of Probe 2.5, consider whether this answer really addresses the question posed by the problem. What question does the answer 30 minutes really answer?

✦ **Decide if there are other solutions**. Sometimes reflection reveals that there is more than one correct answer to a problem. Drawing a picture can help facilitate reflection. If you answered 7 miles for Problem 4 of Probe 2.5, consider whether this is the only possibility. If you have not done so already, try drawing a picture for Problem 4.

➤ Probe 2.3: Sample Problems

↑ ▪ Problem 1: Rhythmic Drops[†]

Maggie was trying desperately to study for her final exams. Unfortunately, the faucet in her apartment kitchen leaked making a dripping sound. Worse, her roof leaked making a binging sound as the water dripped into a pan placed under the leak. The noise was about to drive Maggie crazy when she noticed the soothing rhythm made by the drips and bings. The drips and bings had started at exactly the same time. The drips occurred 3 times a minute, the bings 5 times a minute. What was the order in which Maggie heard the drips and bings?

↑ ▪ Problem 2: The Inexperienced Carpenter

A do-it-yourself carpenter wanted to build a stairway from ground level to the porch of his house. The height between ground level and the porch floor was 10 feet 8 inches (128 inches). The height of each step was supposed to be 8 inches. How many steps are needed to get from the ground to the porch floor?

↑ ▪ Problem 3: Rapid Rabbits[†]

Ralphie the Rapid Rabbit bet Quickie Karl Rabbit he (Ralphie) was the faster in the 50-yard dash. Ralphie won the race by 5 yards. Ralphie then bet Karl "double or nothing" that he could beat Karl in the 50-yard dash even if he started 5 yards behind the starting line and Karl started at the starting line. "If we tie," added Ralphie, "I'll give back what you lost in the first race."

"You're a real sport, Ralphie," replied Karl.

Is Ralphie a sport? Did he get carried away and make a bad bet? Who, if anyone, would win the second race? Assume the rabbits were tireless and both ran the second race at the same rate of speed they ran the first race.

↑ ▪ Problem 4: An Unhappy Couple[†]

Abby and Bartheleme were a military couple. Abby had every third day off; Bartheleme had every sixth day off. If during the week of January 1, Abby had Sunday off and Bartheleme had Monday off, how often during the course of a year would the couple get the same day off?

[†]These problems were inspired by similar problems described in *Mathematician's Delight* by W. W. Sawyer, © 1943/1971 by Penguin, Middlesex, England.

Probe 2.3 continued

■ Problem 5: Won't-Come-Out-Even Problem

Nyugen decided to count the pennies he had in his piggy bank. He decided it would be quicker to count by five. However, he ended with two uncounted pennies. So he tried counting by two but ended up with a remainder of one. He then tried counting by threes and finally by fours. In each case there was one remaining penny. Nyugen concluded that sometimes it just isn't worth taking short cuts. Though he knew he had less than $1.00 worth of pennies, he still did not have an exact count. How many pennies did Nyugen have in his bank?

■ Problem 6: Sum of An Arithmetic Series

Miss Brill decided to challenge her class with the following problem: What is the sum of the numbers from 1 to 100?

LeMar began to write out the problem but soon tired and simply noted:
$$1 + 2 + 3 + 4 + 5 + 6 + 7 + 8 + 9 + 10 \ldots 98 + 99 + 100$$

If writing out the problem made him feel tired, the prospect of adding the 100 numbers was down right depressing.

Noticing LeMar's reaction, Miss Brill coaxed, "Is there an easier way to solve the problem?"

"Like adding a smaller series?" asked LeMar.

"Yes," noted Miss Brill, "and then play with summing the numbers in different ways."

■ Problem 7: A Staircase Problem

Two children were building a staircase from wooden cubes. The first step consisted of one cube; the second step, two stacked cubes; the third step, three stacked cubes; and so forth. One of the children asked, "If we had 50 steps, I wonder how many blocks we'd need?" How many blocks would the children need?

■ Problem 8: Sum of Three Consecutive Numbers

Consider three consecutive pages in a book. The sum of the page numbers is 534. What are the three page numbers?

■ Problem 9: Golf Balls

A boy spent an afternoon in the woods surrounding a golf course collecting golf balls. On his way home, he was stopped by a Fleadirt gang member, who demanded half his golf balls plus two. After paying off the gang member, the boy encountered a second Fleadirt who made the same demand. After paying off the second gang member, the boy encountered a third Fleadirt who also demanded half his golf balls plus two. After paying off the last gang member, the boy had two golf balls left. How many golf balls did he begin with?

→ Probe 2.4: Problems with a Twist

Problem 1: The Nine-Dot, Four-Line Problem

Connect the dots to the right with four straight lines.
Constraint: Once started, you may not lift the pencil or
retrace a line.

Problem 2: The Checkerboard Problem

How many squares are there in the checkerboard below?

Problem 3: The Utilities Problem

Three new houses (A, B, and C) were built in a subdivision. Each needed electric (e), water
(w), and sewerage (s) service. Connect each house to each utility. Constraint: You may not
draw utility lines so that they cross.

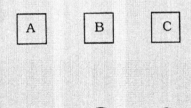

↗ Probe 2.5: Some Problems That May Be Worth Reconsidering

♀ ■ Problem 1: A Hamburger-Hungry Dieter

Hammond loved hamburger and ate 5/8 pounds of the meat a day. After testing revealed that his blood consisted mostly of cholesterol, he decided to alter his eating habits by cutting his hamburger consumption by 3/4 (75%). How many pounds of hamburger a day did Hammond eat on his new "low-cholesterol" diet?

♀ ■ Problem 2: A Problematic Sports Problem

If 2/3 of the boys in the seventh grade of Raucous Middle School played football only and 1/2 played baseball only, what fraction of the seventh-grade boys played neither?

♀ ■ Problem 3: Waiting for the Bus

Rosalie arrived at Campus Bus Stop Number 1 just as a bus was pulling away. To add to her frustration, she saw 72 students, visitors, demonstrators, and dope pushers in line in front of her waiting to take the next bus. If the maximum capacity of a campus bus was 24, and a bus left the stop every 10 minutes, how long before Rosalie could board a bus and leave for campus? Assume all arriving buses are empty and that no one else arrives at the bus stop before Rosalie leaves.

♀ ■ Problem 4: How Far the House?

Lacy, Marv, and Philippe all lived on the same straight road. Lacy's house and Marv's house were 3 miles apart, and Marv's house and Philippe's house were 4 miles apart. How far apart were Lacy's house and Philippe's house?

PROBLEM-SOLVING INSTRUCTION

This subunit examines the different ways problem solving can be incorporated into instruction, the keys to fostering problem-solving skill, types of problems and their uses, and how a teacher can create a desire to engage in problem solving.

Approaches to Using Problems

How should problem solving be incorporated into instruction?

Three Different Approaches. Instructionally, problems can be used in three very different ways (Schroeder & Lester, 1989; Stanic & Kilpatrick, 1989).

1. **Teaching *via* problem solving.** This approach focuses on using problem solving as a means for teaching subject-matter content. In addition to serving as a vehicle for practicing basic computational skills, problems are often used to show how content relates to the real world. They are also used to introduce and provoke discussion about a topic. Problems are sometimes used to motivate students to study and master content. One way this is done is to present a problem at the beginning of a unit to show students what they will be able to accomplish by studying the unit. Another way is to use recreational problems to show how school-learned skills can be used in entertaining ways.

2. **Teaching *about* problem solving.** This approach involves direct instruction about general problem-solving strategies. It commonly entails explaining and/or illustrating Polya's (1973) four-phase model of problem solving (or some variation of it) and specific heuristics for implementing the four phases. In effect, problem-solving techniques such as the heuristic of drawing a picture are treated as subject-matter content. Textbooks have only recently begun to use problems to teach children about general problem-solving strategies (see Box 2.7).

3. **Teaching *for* problem solving.** This approach focuses on *teaching general problem-solving strategies by actually giving children the opportunity to solve problems.* That is, children learn how to use Polya's four-phase problem-solving approach and problem-solving heuristics during the process of solving challenging problems.

An Integrated Approach. In practice, teaching about, via, and for problem solving often overlap (Schroeder & Lester, 1989). Indeed, it makes sense to use an integrated approach—to combine content instruction about problem-solving strategies and other subject matter with process-oriented instruction that focuses on how to solve genuine problems.

As Ms. Wise explained to the parents of her students at the first open house, "I use a problem-solving approach to mathematics instruction. Most of our time is spent solving problems. Typically, I begin a unit of instruction with a challenging problem. I don't show the children how to solve the problem. Instead, they usually work in small groups to devise their solution procedures and solutions. The discussion of our different solution procedures and solutions then provides a basis for introducing new content and problem-solving strategies. Additional problems are given to extend and practice the new material. Working on genuine problems creates a need to learn new concepts, computational strategies, and problem-solving strategies and, thus, helps children see why they are important to learn. Moreover, working on problems gives them the opportunity to apply and to practice concepts, skills, and strategies in interesting, meaningful, purposeful, and creative ways."

Extending Children's Problem-Solving Skill

How is problem solving learned? It is important for teachers to recognize that the answer to this question is: "SLOWLY AND WITH DIFFICULTY" (Kilpatrick, 1985b, p. 8). Some teachers overestimate how readily children can learn problem solving, become discouraged with the painfully slow and uneven progress, and give up on teaching problem solving.

Box 2.8 on page 2-33 illustrates a common mistake among teachers trying to teach problem solving for the first time: treating general problem-solving strategies simply as "stuff" to be memorized. Helping students become good problem solvers is like helping children learn how to ride a bicycle; tips can be helpful, but it's impossible to master the skill without actually trying it yourself. In brief, perhaps the most important factor in fostering problem-solving skill is regular practice solving problems.

Box 2.7: A Modern Use of Problems

Traditionally, textbooks have not discussed systematic problem-solving approaches such as Polya's four-phase method or heuristics such as the draw-a-picture heuristic. Only recently has interest shifted from presenting problems and prescriptions for solving particular kinds of problems to teaching general problem-solving strategies (Stanic & Kilpatrick, 1989). The example from the *Addison-Wesley Mathematics* (Grade 3) textbook shown below illustrates this new approach.[†]

Problem Solving
Draw a Picture

LEARN ABOUT IT

Some problems are easier to solve if you draw a picture. You can use the data in the problem to help you draw the picture.

> Four students were in the Spoon and Raw Egg Race. Amy finished ahead of Derek. Derek was between Emilou and Amy. Bill finished ahead of Amy. In what order did the students finish?

First I'll draw a line to show the race.

I'll show Amy ahead of Derek.

Then I'll show Derek between Emilou and Amy.

I'll put Bill ahead of Amy.

Bill was first. Then came Amy, Derek, and Emilou.

TRY IT OUT

At the basketball contest, students lined up from tallest to shortest. Kenji is taller than Michiko. Jeff is shorter than Michiko. Barb is taller than Kenji. Who is the tallest and who is the shortest?

1. Since Kenji is taller than Michiko, could Michiko be the tallest?

2. Who is shorter than Michiko?

3. Copy and finish drawing the picture to solve the problem.

38

[†]From Robert Eicholz et al. (Menlo Park, CA: Addison-Wesley Publishing Company, 1991), page 38. Reprinted by permission.

Box 2.8: The Case of the Problematic Problem-Solving Instruction

Although not sure how to proceed, Miss Brill was convinced her class needed problem-solving instruction. She checked her text and the District Curriculum Guide for Mathematics. Outlined in both was an explanation of Polya's four-phase problem-solving model and a number of problem-solving heuristics. She concluded it would be a great idea for her students to learn these general problem-solving strategies. Miss Brill described these problem-solving facilitators to her class in detail. To reinforce these ideas, she asked the class to read the section in their textbook about problem-solving strategies and to answer the questions at the end of the section. At the end of the week, she tested the class. One question entailed listing the four steps in Polya's model. The results of the test were very depressing.

Deeply disappointed that her students did not share her enthusiasm about learning problem-solving strategies, Miss Brill sought Ms. Wise's advice. Her co-worker allowed that children needed to learn *about* such strategies. She noted, however, "It's a mistake to treat Polya's four-phase problem-solving process and problem-solving heuristics merely as content to memorize. It's not enough for kids to learn about general problem-solving strategies; they need practice using them to solve genuine problems. In brief, the best way to learn about problem solving is to engage in problem solving."

However important, practicing solving problems is probably not enough by itself to become a good problem solver. Although children may learn some problem-solving strategies incidentally through "osmosis," practice alone will probably not help them to develop a wide array of strategies needed to tackle a variety of genuine problems. In other words, practice is a necessary, but not a sufficient, condition for learning problem solving (Kilpatrick, 1985b). This section discusses three ways of making this practice more profitable: (1) providing readiness experiences; (2) exploring problem-solving strategies; and (3) discussing the solutions of various types of problems (Charles & Lester, 1982).

Readiness Experiences. Many children need to be prepared to practice solving problems. The aims of readiness experiences are to foster (a) a positive disposition toward problem solving and (b) an ability to picture mentally the essential elements of a problem. An interest in problems and problem solving is essential for genuine problem-solving efforts. Forming a mental picture or representation of a problem is essential for understanding a problem. Charles and Lester (1982) recommend the following readiness activities for first and second graders:

🍎 Show students a picture and have them make up a story involving addition or subtraction.

🍎 Show students an addition or subtraction number sentence such as 5 + 3 = 8 and have them make up a story about it.

🍎 Read a word problem to children with their eyes closed and have them imagine the situation.

☞ Complete Probe 2.6 (pages 2-48 and 2-49) before reading on.

Exploring Problem-Solving Strategies. Children also need instruction to learn problem-solving strategies. They need to learn a systematic approach to solving problems (e.g., Polya's four phases) and problem-solving heuristics. General problem-solving strategies can be taught to even primary-age children, and they can have a real impact on students' problem-solving performance. Particularly with younger children, you will have to decide which heuristics your class will focus on. Better that children should feel comfortable with a few heuristics and use them effectively, than feel overwhelmed by many heuristics and use none effectively.

Moreover, *how* general problem-solving strategies are taught can make a big difference in whether or not students learn and use them. If taught in a mechanical manner (as illustrated in Parts I and II Probe 2.6), such strategies may not promote a thoughtful analysis of problems. (See pages 2-140 and 2-141 of Answers to Selected Questions for an analysis of the lessons in Probe 2.6). Perhaps the best way to help children appreciate the importance of looking back, for instance, is to suggest checking their results when this is needed. This is useful after solving a genuine problem, particularly if there are conflicting answers, or if the answer is incorrect or does not address the problem. Suggestions for teaching problem-solving heuristics are noted below.

✒ **Introduce heuristics in a purposeful manner, as a tool for overcoming blockage.** It is crucial to help students believe heuristics are ways of making sense of puzzling situations, not merely routines that can be used thoughtlessly. As Ms. Wise advised Miss Brill, "Always requiring children to draw a picture may be counterproductive [see Part II of Probe 2.6]. It may encourage thoughtless use of the strategy. Children need to understand that the purpose of such a problem-solving tool is to help them analyze and solve problems thoughtfully. Children need to see that drawing a picture is a means for helping them to understand a problem."

"How do you do that?" Miss Brill inquired.

"Basically, I try to create a genuine need for heuristics," replied Ms. Wise. "I begin by giving students a challenging problem for which a heuristic such as drawing a picture would be helpful. When students feel blocked and request help, I introduce them to the heuristic. Usually at least one group of students can use the hint to find a solution. Then, in the follow-up discussion, I have someone illustrate how the heuristic was helpful. In this way, students can clearly see the value of the heuristic." [Note that creating a genuine need to learn about heuristics was a key aim of Probe 2.3 on pages 2-27 and 2-28.]

✐ **Guided practice with challenging and interesting problems can help students master heuristics in a purposeful and motivating manner.** Ms. Wise noted that after introducing a heuristic, she presented her class with a number of additional problems for which it might be helpful. The heuristic can be posed as a hint, as in Probe 2.7.

☞ Complete Probe 2.7 (pages 2-50 to 2-52) before reading on.

✐ **In time, students should be given the opportunity to decide for themselves what heuristic(s) is (are) appropriate.** Once children are comfortable with a heuristic, the hint to use the strategy can be dropped.

✐ **Regularly model heuristics by thinking out loud.** "Moreover," added Ms. Wise, "I take every opportunity possible to model heuristics myself. I've gotten into the habit of talking out loud about my thinking processes when puzzling through a problem, and this often includes saying, 'A picture might help here.'"

✐ **Particularly at first, children may need help learning how to use a heuristic.** "I have found,"

added Ms. Wise, "that it is not enough to suggest using a heuristic. Many children don't know how to, say, draw a picture in a way that is helpful. Some make overly elaborate drawings, including unnecessary details; others make impoverished drawings, leaving out crucial details. It is important, particularly when a heuristic is first introduced, to monitor its use carefully and give tips on using it."

Discussing the Solutions of Various Types of Problems. "I reinforce the value of problem-solving strategies," continued Ms. Wise, "by discussing regularly assigned problems or problems that have come up. The focus of these discussions is not on the correct answer but on how to solve the problem. I give special attention to how an individual or group has used a heuristic successfully. This recognizes student accomplishments and further illustrates how heuristics can be used."

Types and Uses of Word Problems

What types of problems should be used in instruction and how? There are various kinds of word problems serving a variety of functions. Teachers should use an assortment of word problems, including routine word problems. This section discusses various types of problems and their roles in instruction. Because routine problems can become little more than practice exercises and not challenge children's thinking, this section focuses on nonroutine types of problems, which are more apt to require a thoughtful analysis. It also describes how a teacher can create nonroutine problems or convert routine problems found in textbooks into nonroutine problems.

It is important to keep in mind that the type(s) of problems you choose to emphasize depends on your goals as a teacher. If you set as your primary goal understanding content, you will want to choose more heavily from the first three types of problems listed below. If fostering problem-solving skill is your primary goal, you will want to choose more heavily from the last five types of problems listed.

Simple (One-Step) Translation Problems. Routine word problems are sometimes called *simple* or *one-step translation* problems, because (a) they involve a single operation and (b) they can be solved directly by translating the wording into a concrete model and/or a symbolic expression (number sentence). Such problems are particularly useful for introducing the arithmetic operations with whole numbers, fractions, and decimals. Before formal instruction on an operation, solving simple translation problems can be challenging to many children and provide a meaningful basis for later introducing the operation in symbolic terms. After symbolic arithmetic is introduced, it can provide a relatively meaningful and interesting way to practice basic computational facts and procedures.

Complex (Multistep) Translation Problems. This type of nonroutine problem entails the application of two or more arithmetic operations—either the repeated application of one operation or the combination of several different operations. These problems, such as Problem 2.24 below, can require a thoughtful analysis of the unknown, the data, and the solution method.

■ **Problem 2.24: Mary's Change.** Mary bought six cream-filled doughnuts for $1.80 and six glazed ones for $2.00. If she used a $5 bill to pay for the doughnuts, how much change should she get?

Other Modifications of Translation Problems. In addition to adding more steps, simple translation problems can be modified in other ways to require a more thoughtful analysis:

● **Problems that require finding a missing addend or factor.** Problems such as Problem 2.11 do not ask children for the sum, difference, product, or quotient of two numbers, but for one of the addends or factors. Although missing-addend or missing-factor problems can be translated into a concrete model or a symbolic number sentence and solved, they typically require a thoughtful analysis of the unknown by children and thus, can be relatively challenging.

● **Problems that require applying the answer.** Such problems require children to use the computed answer in a thoughtful manner, rather than simply to state it. Consider, for example, Problem 2.25:

■ **Problem 2.25: Disappearing Doughnuts—Take I.** Mary set out a dozen doughnuts for a party. Ruffus ate four doughnuts. Does Mary have enough left to serve nine people?

● **Problems with too much, too little, or incorrect data.** Problems with extra (see Problem 2.26), insufficient (see Problem 2.27), or incorrect information (see Problem 2.28) require children to analyze the

unknown and the data thoughtfully to determine what information is needed, what information is not needed, and what information needs to be replaced.

■ **Problem 2.26: Disappearing Doughnuts—Take II.** Mary set out a dozen doughnuts for her party of 6 children. Ruffus consumed 8. How many doughnuts did Mary have left?

■ **Problem 2.27: Disappearing Doughnuts—Take III.** Mary set out a dozen doughnuts for her party. Ruffus consumed some of them. How many doughnuts were left?

■ **Problem 2.28: Disappearing Doughnuts—Take IV.** Mary set out 12 doughnuts for her party. Ruffus ate 1/3 of them. Mary had a hunger attack before the party and ate 1/4 of the dozen. Ruffus returned and ate another 1/6 of the dozen. Mary's brother ate 1/12 of the dozen. Ruffus returned again and ate another 1/4 of the dozen. How many doughnuts were left for Mary's party?

● **Problems that can be solved in more than one way.** Problems that can be attacked in various ways can help children appreciate that many real-world problems have a number of solution methods. For example, Problem 2.29 below can be solved in two ways: (1) 7 + 4 = 11 and 11 is less than 12; or (2) 12 - 7 = 5 and 5 - 4 = 1 (She could buy the muzzle and chain and still have $1 left over).

■ **Problem 2.29: Ruffus Restrained.** Mary decided to buy some physical restraints for her dog Ruffus. She had saved $12; a muzzle cost $7 and a chain cost $4. Does she have enough to buy both?

● **Problems with more than one answer.** Problems with multiple answers can help children to recognize that real-world problems sometimes have more than one correct answer. Consider Problem 2.30:

■ **Problem 2.30: More Doughnuts for Mary.** Mary went to the store to buy some doughnuts. Sugar-coated ones cost 20¢ each. Cream-filled doughnuts cost 30¢ each. And cream-filled doughnuts with icing (called Diet Busters) cost 40¢ each. Mary has 100¢. What can Mary buy?

● **Problems that require an extended effort.** Such problems help children realize that not all problems can be solved immediately. For example, determining the class's most prolific "hitter" in kickball could entail collecting data over a number of games (days or even weeks).

Process Problems. Nonroutine problems that require the use of general problem-solving strategies (processes), such as those in Probe 2.3 on pages 2-27 and 2-28, are called *process problems*. Such problems can be used to illustrate the value of Polya's systematic approach and problem-solving heuristics. They can also provide children with real opportunities to practice these general problem-solving strategies.

Puzzle Problems. Nonroutine problems that involve a trick (e.g., a play on words) and require special insight (e.g., an unusual way of thinking about a situation) or luck are called puzzle problems. Problems with a Twist (Probe 2.4 on page 2-29) and riddles (Probe 2.8) fall into this category. Puzzle problems can serve to remind students of the importance of flexibility and remaining open to unusual suggestions. Such problems can also serve as a source of entertainment for those who feel challenged rather than frustrated by them.

☞ Try Probe 2.8 (page 2-53) before reading on.

Nongoal-Specific Problems. Nongoal-specific problems are a special kind of nonroutine problem. All the types of problems discussed so far are goal-specific or closed-ended in that they entail finding a *specific* answer or set of answers. Even nonroutine problems with insufficient or incorrect data have *a* correct answer: "No way Jose" (The solution to this problem cannot be determined). Nongoal-specific problems are open-ended in that they do not require finding a prescribed answer or answers. Such problems encourage students to explore their own questions and can involve answers unanticipated by a teacher. Probe 2.9 illustrates examples of nongoal-specific problems.

☞ Complete Probe 2.9 (pages 2-54 and 2-55) before reading on.

Research indicates that students who work on nongoal-specific problems are more likely to learn concepts and skills more effectively than those who work with the more traditional goal-specific prob-

lems (Silver, 1990). Nongoal-specific problems provide students an important opportunity to see relationships and reflect on their knowledge, and thus deepen and reorganize their knowledge. Fortunately, the goal-specific question found in typical textbooks can—with relatively minor modifications—be transformed into nongoal-specific questions.

Applied Problems. Nonroutine problems that stem from the real world or that are realistic are called *applied problems*. Consider Problem 2.31:

■ **Problem 2.31: Wasteful Waste?** What portion of the school's waste could be recycled rather than hauled to the landfill?

Note that such a problem would require students to use a host of mathematical concepts (e.g., percents), facts (e.g., measurement conversions), skills (e.g., adding and estimating), and processes (e.g., collecting and organizing data) in an integrated and purposeful fashion. Moreover, it illustrates how mathematics can be an integral aspect of other subjects (e.g., social studies and science) and everyday life (e.g., waste management)—a tool for solving "real" problems. Note that such a problem could also serve as an opportunity to practice general problem-solving strategies and, thus, could be considered a process problem. Note also that the problem is open-ended in that there is not a single way to measure the amount of waste that could be recycled. As a nongoal-specific problem, it could foster creativity and decision making.

Strategy Problems. These problems are another special class of nonroutine problems. Usually a problem is assigned with the aim that students will solve it. Although a discussion of the problem may concentrate on *how* to solve it, some students may tend to focus on whether or not their answer is correct (the product). To help students focus on strategies for understanding problems and devising a plan (the process), it may help to use a special kind of nonroutine problem we will call a strategy problem. Unlike problems that ask students for an answer or answers, strategy problems ask students for a solution strategy or strategies. Problem 2.32 illustrates such a problem:

■ **Problem 2.32: Bicycles and Tricycles.** In a neighborhood Fourth-of-July parade,

21 bicycles and tricycles passed in review. Hubie counted a total of 51 wheels. How many different ways could you find out how many bicycles there were in the parade?

Creating a Spirit of Inquiry

How can a teacher create a spirit of inquiry? Creating a climate conducive to problem solving should be a key aim of mathematics instruction at all levels. Creating a spirit of inquiry may not be easy for either students or some teachers, particularly those who are accustomed to a traditional skills approach (see Box 2.9, which begins in the next column and continues onto the next page). Not only may students have to break old habits and learn new ones, but so may teachers. Not only may students have to overcome entrenched beliefs and learn new ones, but so may teachers. Although easier to accomplish if efforts begin early, it is never too late to create a spirit of inquiry.

Central to creating a spirit of inquiry is Polya's (1981) first principle of teaching:

✐ **Encourage children to do and to discover as much for themselves as possible.** This implies giving children responsibility for their own learning and problem solving. This entails trusting children and sometimes being disappointed by them.

Creating a spirit of inquiry does not mean, however, that a teacher is passive. A teacher must actively work to create a climate conducive to problem solving. Box 2.10 on page 2-39 describes some actions a teacher can take before, during, and after students solve a problem. Note that with the possible exception of Action 1, the teacher acts as a facilitator, not an information dispenser. In effect, these actions model heuristics for each of the four phases of problem solving you hope your students will internalize and use on their own eventually. Box 2.11 on pages 2-40 to 2-44 describes a sample lesson that illustrates the teacher actions. Probe 2.10 discusses how problems can be modified to provide additional challenges (*extension*) for students who finish solving a problem before others, and for helping students generalize a solution strategy to new problems. Additional tips for creating a spirit of inquiry are noted below.

☞ Try your hand with Probe 2.10 (pages 2-56 and 2-57) before continuing with the text.

Box 2.9: The Case of the Tight Teacher and Tutees

Miss Brill was eager to introduce her class to genuine problem solving. She decided to give her students problems on a regular basis, using problems to introduce and practice content and problem-solving strategies whenever she could. However, the beginning teacher recognized that she would have to devote every waking moment and more to math to pull off a program like Ms. Wise's. Even with the more experienced teacher's help, it was going to take time to collect or devise suitable problems for the required content. Considering the other demands on her time such as preparing a reading program for four different levels of students, house chores, and a desperate need for rest, Miss Brill needed a stopgap measure for the near term. She would start by devoting one math class a week to problem solving. She dubbed this session: "The Freewheeling Friday Function."

Miss Brill was pleased with the idea of the Freewheeling Friday Function. It allowed her to quickly put more emphasis on problem solving while not overwhelming her. Miss Brill was reasonably sure she could come up with one challenging problem a week. The stopgap measure also gave her a comfortable way of beginning the new challenge of teaching problem solving. She felt secure devoting one day a week to her experiment. If things didn't work out, she still had four days to accomplish what was outlined in the textbook. Moreover, Miss Brill sensed that it would take time for her to adjust to a more open approach to teaching. She thought she could handle the uncertainties of an unaccustomed approach one day a week, but she was less confident of her ability to cope with a new approach for a longer period of time.

Although some students such as LeMar eagerly embraced the challenge of solving difficult problems, Miss Brill was disappointed that most students greeted the Freewheeling Friday Function with reluctance or even resistance. She was often greeted with panic-motivated questions like: "Will we have problems like this on our test?" Frequently, students complained, "Why can't you just tell us how to do this?"

2-38

Box 2.9 continued

Miss Brill was disappointed, moreover, by their problem-solving efforts. Frequently students raced to shout out an answer before group discussions had even begun. Many students tried to solve problems by blindly applying the mathematical procedure they had most recently learned—even when it should have been clear that the procedure was not relevant. When Miss Brill asked them if using the procedure made sense, students often looked confused or even betrayed. "That's what we learned about this week," was a common reply.

Reading the disappointment in Miss Brill's face, students would then launch into a barrage of questions in an effort to identify which previously studied procedure was appropriate. They scrutinized Miss Brill's face, gestures, and comments for clues as to the correct procedure. From a wince here, a smile there, students attempted to divine the correct method. Seldom did they analyze the problem as carefully as they did their teacher's reactions.

The students were not the only reason why the Friday Freewheeling Function did not live up to its name. Miss Brill could not resist a deeply ingrained impulse to control what her students were doing. When students asked for help, the teacher in Miss Brill frequently took control and she dutifully showed the students how to solve the problem. When students asked if their answer was right, Miss Brill instinctively praised them if they were right and often gave them the correct answer otherwise.

Miss Brill was stunned that the students seemed to be becoming even more passive. Exasperated, she went back to Ms. Wise.

Ms. Wise observed, "Unfortunately, your children have not had much instruction on problem-solving strategies or opportunities to solve genuine problems before. They are used to being spoon-fed and not thinking for themselves. They have become 'grade grubbers'; interest in getting grades has supplanted interest in learning and thinking for many. Their previous schooling encourages them to be impulsive. They've learned that the goal in mathematics is to respond quickly with something—anything [Kilpatrick, 1985b]. From past experiences, they assume that there is only one correct way to solve a problem and that way is most likely the procedure they have learned last. When that doesn't work, they turn to you—the authority—for the solution."

"I've tried giving them problems for a month now," complained Miss Brill, "and they don't show any signs of improving. Is there any hope for them?"

"Patience. All is not lost, even at this late stage of the game," counseled Ms. Wise. "You have to remember, they have been exposed to a very different way of teaching for many years now. It will not be easy breaking old habits and changing the whole way they view mathematics and mathematics instruction." The older teacher confided that it usually took her at least several months before most of her students felt comfortable with an approach that focused on problem solving instead of memorizing facts and routines: "It takes time to help them regenerate their curiosity and to get hooked on problem solving. I expect that as the primary teachers do more and more problem solving in the early grades, it will take less and less time for our students to become accustomed to the demands of problem solving."

"But what can I do now?" pleaded Miss Brill.

"You need to work on creating a spirit of inquiry," counseled Ms. Wise.

Box 2.10: Teacher Actions Before, During and After Students Solve Problems[†]

TEACHER ACTIONS BEFORE: UNDERSTANDING THE PROBLEM

1. To underscore the importance of reading problems carefully, read, or have a student read, the problem to the class. This is particularly important for children who may have difficulty reading a problem themselves. Discuss words that have special meanings in mathematics, other unfamiliar vocabulary, and settings, so that children can accurately comprehend the problem situation.

2. To help children focus on key data and to clarify the problem, ask the class what they think the unknown is and what data are needed to determine the unknown. You may want to suggest that students relate the problem in their words. It can be helpful to write out specific questions and hints before class begins.

TEACHER ACTIONS DURING: DEVISING AND CARRYING OUT A PLAN

3. (Optional.) To help students consider possible solution strategies, encourage the class to offer suggested solution methods. During this brain-storming effort, *do not criticize any suggestions*. Nor should you suggest there is a correct way to do the problem.

4. To evaluate students' progress and difficulties, monitor their work on the problem and ask them to justify their efforts.

5. To help students overcome blocks, give children hints, *not* the solution strategy. Needed hints can be in the form of a heuristic such as: "Why not consider a simpler problem?" or "Is this like any problems you have solved before?" In some cases, it may be necessary to help students reanalyze the problem (see Teacher Actions 1 and 2 above). Keep in mind that the goal is to have your students do as much thinking for themselves as possible.

TEACHER ACTIONS AFTER: LOOKING BACK

6. To encourage students to evaluate their answers, ask them to justify their answers (e.g., whether or not they are reasonable and answer the original question).

7. To challenge students who finish early and to help children generalize their solution strategies to new problems, pose extensions of the problem. For example, have them consider what would happen if one of the components in a problem had a different value. It is probably best to consider how you will pose extensions before class begins.

8. To illustrate the variety of solution methods, have students discuss their solution strategies with the whole class. To foster autonomy, have them also discuss their solutions, but *refrain from serving as the final judge*. Encourage students to justify their answers and solution procedures, to evaluate others' suggestions, and to arrive at a conclusion.

9. To demonstrate the generality of solution methods, discuss how the problem relates to other problems or situations: How is it similar and different from problems solved previously? How might a similar problem arise in different situations?

10. To help students consider the impact of special features, have students discuss important aspects of the problem. For example, was anyone misled by an accompanying picture (not an uncommon difficulty), a "key word," or extra information?

[†]This box is based on the Teacher Actions outlined on pages 42 and 43 of *Teaching Problem Solving: What, Why, and How* by R. I. Charles and F. K. Lester, © 1982 by Dale Seymour. Reprinted by permission.

2-40

Box 2.11: A Sample Problem-Solving Lesson

✐ The lesson begins with a problem—a single challenging problem.

☞ Before reading on, try solving this problem yourself or with the help of a group. Discuss your solution with your group or class.

Mrs. Stein, a third-grade teacher, handed out a sheet of paper with the following problem typed on it:

■ Rosa had four different-colored blouses: pink, yellow, green, and blue. She had three different-colored skirts: white, navy, and brown. In how many ways could Rosa combine four blouses and three skirts?

TEACHER ACTIONS BEFORE: UNDERSTANDING THE PROBLEM

✐ Mrs. Stein had the problem read to the class (Teacher Action 1), rather than having the students read it silently to themselves and plunge into solving it. This underscored the importance of reading problems carefully and thoughtfully, rather than simply performing some arithmetic operation with the numbers given.

✐ The terms *combination* and *skirts* were defined so that everyone would understand the context.

✐ Moreover, the children were encouraged to rephrase the problem in their own words.

Mrs. Stein asked Luis to read the problem out loud. Several students indicated they did not understand the question, particularly, the word *combine*. After a brief discussion, Luis rephrased the question: "How many different outfits could Rosa make with four blouses and three dresses?" Maxine corrected, "Three skirts, not three dresses." Because the boys in the class seemed bewildered by this distinction, Maxine noted that dresses have a top and a bottom and don't need a blouse, whereas a skirt is just a bottom and needs a top.

✐ Mrs. Stein used a whole-class discussion to help students better understand the problem (Teacher Action 2). Note that this helped to define what information was relevant to the problem (number of different blouses and skirts) and what information was irrelevant (e.g., the color of blouses).

Mrs. Stein asked the class if there were any questions before they began. Argus who had already misplaced his paper, asked, "What color were the blouses again?" Deter pointed out that knowing the specific colors was not important. All one needed to know was that Rosa had four different blouses and three different skirts.

✐ The teacher asked specific clarifying questions such as, "What is the unknown?"

Mrs. Stein then asked the class, "What is it you're trying to figure out?"

TEACHER ACTIONS DURING: DEVISING AND CARRYING OUT A PLAN

✐ Skipping a whole-class discussion of possible solution strategies (Teacher Action 3), Mrs. Stein observed and questioned students to gauge difficulties and progress (Teacher Action 4).

✐ Mrs. Stein provided a hint, but not a specific solution strategy (Teacher Action 4).

Mrs. Stein circulated among the groups to monitor their progress. At the first group, Sherard complained, "We don't know what to do."

"Might drawing a picture help?" suggested Mrs. Stein. The four members of the group then busily set about trying to represent the problem.

At the next group Abdullah said proudly, "Look Mrs. Stein, we found six ways Rosa can combine her blouses and skirts:

Box 2.11 continued

P+W, Y+N, G+Br, B+N, Y+W, and G+N

"Are there six, or are there more?" asked Mrs. Stein.

"There are probably more," offered Claiborne, "but it's so hard to figure out."

✐ Note that Mrs. Stein again gave the children a hint, but not a specific solution strategy or the answer (Teacher Action 5).

"Is there any way you could list the possibilities in a systematic way?" hinted Mrs. Stein.

✐ Mrs. Stein encouraged the students to evaluate their answers themselves (Teacher Action 6). Note that she did not criticize the students' answers but, instead, asked them to justify their answers.

One group excitedly called Mrs. Stein over. "Is the answer three?" they asked with eager anticipation.

Resisting the temptation to dismiss this apparently ridiculous answer and to take over the discussion, Mrs. Stein asked, "Why do you think it's three?"

Shanti explained, "Look [pointing to the diagram below], these three blouses match up with these four skirts to make three outfits. The last blouse doesn't have a shirt to match up with, so Rosa can only make three outfits. Is that right?"

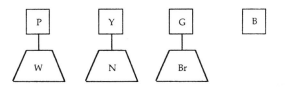

✐ Note that Mrs. Stein again resisted passing judgment. She responded to the common "Is this right?" question with questions of her own. Although students may find this disconcerting at first, they often become accustomed to it, particularly if they understand its purpose.

Mrs. Stein responded, "What do you think? Does everyone agree?"

Smiling at Mrs. Stein, Shanti remarked, "I should have known by now, she always answers a question with a question."

Sandy seized the opportunity to press her doubts. "I guess I don't understand the problem," she announced.

✐ Sandy experienced blockage. At this critical juncture, Mrs. Stein provided a hint (Teacher Action 5) by asking students to rephrase the question in more familiar terms (Teacher Action 1 again).

"Can you state the problem in your own words?" suggested Mrs. Stein.

Sandy offered, "How many ways could Rosa combine her blouses and skirts to make different outfits?" At this point, the other members of the group insisted their original solution of three had to be right. Sandy was still unconvinced, but could not offer an alternative solution.

Box 2.11 continued

Because Mrs. Stein sensed that the group could go no further, she offered another hint in the form of a question (Teacher Action 5 again). Note that the teacher again did not simply indicate that the solution strategy and solution were wrong or tell the students the correct strategy.

Pointing at their diagram, Mrs. Stein then asked, "Is there another way the blouses and skirts can be combined?"

Shanti drew a new diagram:

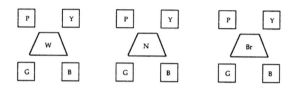

"So, four and four is eight, and four more is twelve," beamed Shanti.

Mrs. Stein encouraged the group to evaluate the new solution (Teacher Action 6).

"What do the rest of you think? Does Shanti's solution make more or less sense than an answer of three? Does it answer the question?" inquired Mrs. Stein, leaving the group to debate the merits of Shanti's solution.

TEACHER ACTIONS AFTER: CHECKING THE ANSWER(S)

Julie proudly showed Mrs. Stein the chart her group had developed.

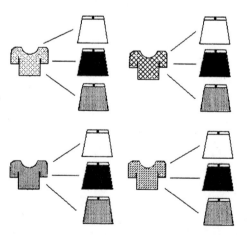

After Julie's group justified their answer, Mrs. Stein provided extension (Teacher Action 7).

When it was clear that everyone in the group was convinced of the answer, Mrs. Stein presented two new problems with the following challenge: "See if you can figure out a short cut for determining the total number of combinations."

■ For his party, Alexander had 5 flavors of ice cream and 3 toppings. How many different kinds of ice cream treats could be made if a child could choose combinations of one flavor and one topping?

Box 2.11 continued

■ Alina had 5 different-shaped cookie cutters and 4 different colors of icing. How many different-looking cookies could Alina make?

Mrs. Stein had the groups represent their solutions on the board. In addition to Shanti's and Julie's solutions already shown, two other methods were illustrated. Abdullah's group hit upon the following solution:

Pi + W	Y + W	G + W	B + W
Pi + N	Y + N	G + N	B + N
Pi + Br	Y + Br	G + Br	B + Br

Gualberto's group drew:

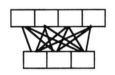

✐ Mrs. Stein then encouraged the groups to share their solution strategies and answers with the whole class (Teacher Action 8).

✐ Note that Mrs. Stein did not act as the final judge but encouraged the class to evaluate the groups' answers. Explanations from peers are often less threatening and more intelligible to children. Also note that Mrs. Stein encouraged reasoned arguments; an opinion held by a majority does not make it correct.

Pointing to a drawing of four blouses and three skirts, Shadawn noted their group had arrived at a different answer: Seven. Mrs. Stein asked the class what they thought. Stuart commented that seven had to be wrong because nobody else got it. After Mrs. Stein asked if Stuart's conclusion was necessarily true, and the class agreed that it was not, she asked, "Why do you think it's seven, Shadawn?"

"Because four and three is seven altogether," responded Shadawn.

"Why did you add?" asked Izzie.

"Adding doesn't make sense," commented Sreka. "That tells how many pieces of clothing Rosa had altogether, not how many outfits she can make."

Shadawn remarked brightly, "Oh, I see now."

✐ Mrs. Stein encouraged the children to relate the problem to other problems (Teacher Action 9).

Next, Mrs. Stein asked the class how this problem was similar and different to other problems they solved. Stuart offered that unlike previous problems that involved combining things, this problem did not involve adding the two numbers.

Box 2.11 continued

Questions for Reflection

1. What is the shortcut (arithmetic operation) for determining the number of possible combinations? Why is this operation applicable?

2. Mrs. Stein's problem-solving lesson was based on a lesson suggested by her textbook. How does the textbook lesson below use problems? That is, for what purpose are they used in the textbook lesson? In what ways is this purpose the same or different from Mrs. Stein's use of problems?

Enrichment Combination Meaning of Multiplication

Problem 1: Rosa had 4 blouses and 3 skirts. How many different outfits could she make?

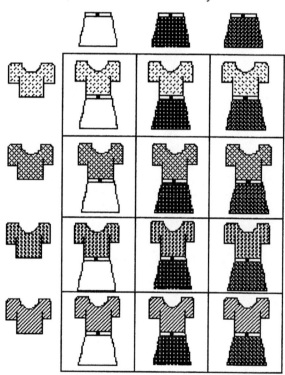

The number of different combinations Rosa can make is the product of the blouses and the skirts: 4 x 3 = ☐

Problem 2: If an ice-cream store sells 5 flavors of ice cream and 3 toppings, how many different combinations of desserts can it sell?

5 x 3 = ☐

Problem 3: If 4 boys and 3 girls are at a party, how many boy-girl dance pairs are there?

☐ x ☐ = ☐

THE MATH BOOK FROM HELL: Grade 3   page 128   Boring Books Publishing Co., Inc.

Build on Children's Understanding to Maximize the Chances of Success. Problem solving should build upon children's existing or informal knowledge.

✐ **Word problems should be used to** *introduce* **arithmetic operations.** Because word problems can be more meaningful to children than symbolic expressions, they should be an integral aspect of instruction from the start (see, e.g., Feinberg, 1988). This can promote the development of thinking skills and reduce the blind application of formally prescribed procedures.

✐ **Children's intuitive strategies should be encouraged.** For example, they should be encouraged to use their informal counting strategies to model and solve problems. Children will feel more comfortable solving problems if they know they can use their own, trusted methods.

✐ **The use of manipulatives should be allowed**. Young children, particularly, stand a better chance of devising a meaningful solution strategy and determining the answer if they can use real objects. This, in turn, breeds confidence.

✐ **Problems need to be selected carefully to match the developmental level of children**. To foster a spirit of inquiry, children need to have *success* solving *challenging* problems. If problems are too difficult for children, they will become discouraged. If problems are not sufficiently challenging, children may come to the conclusion that all problems can be solved quickly, without much thought. Moreover, they may lose interest in "problem solving."

Foster a Positive Disposition Toward Problem Solving. To foster the drive needed to solve genuine problems, a teacher needs to promote interest in problem solving, self-confidence, and perseverance. A key element in accomplishing these aims is to attack beliefs that undercut these qualities and to promote beliefs that support them.

✐ **Model interest in and excitement about problem solving.** The atmosphere a teacher inspires is crucial. An atmosphere of inquiry can be inspired by words but more effectively by deeds. Exhibit curiosity yourself by exploring problems that arise spontaneously as the by-product of assigned problems or other classroom activities. Welcome challenging questions from students. Even at the primary level, teachers can learn much by remaining open to unexpected problems and students' questions. Furthermore, teachers should exhibit excitement about students' problem-solving efforts, whether a problem or solution is familiar or not. Even when students simply rediscover what you already know, it is important to show your pleasure and excitement about *their* discovery. Such selfless interest in the growth of students is an important quality of good teachers.

✐ **Use a variety of problems, particularly nonroutine problems, to challenge students' thinking on a regular basis.** Problems can serve as the basis for introducing and applying content instruction. Japanese students, who are relatively successful problem solvers, regularly work on challenging problems. Such problems can inspire curiosity and creative solutions as well as help students better understand the need for concepts and procedures. In addition to using problems to teach content, create a "Problem Corner" on a bulletin board, chalkboard, or activity center. On a daily or weekly basis, pose nonroutine problems that are or are not related to ongoing instruction. Make sure that you take the time to discuss students' solutions to these problems.

✐ **Create a safe, nonthreatening atmosphere**. It is important that students feel they can pose their ideas, solution strategies, and solutions without the threat of humiliation and embarrassment. In addition to assuming a nonjudgmental stance yourself, you should insist that your students treat each other with respect. You need to make clear that disagreement is welcomed but put-downs are not.

✐ **Encourage risk-taking.** It is important to help children see that accomplishing many worthwhile things involves taking a risk. Play a game such as "Capture the Flag" and discuss how taking a risk is essential to winning the game. Discuss the risks involved in opening yourself up to someone and why it is important for emotional health to do so. To foster risk-taking, praise earnest and thoughtful efforts, even if students are unsuccessful. Treat errors as opportunities to learn what to avoid and what to do next, not as shortcomings.

✐ **Give children time to work on challenging problems**. In contrast to the U.S. where students often spend considerable time completing numerous exercises or routine problems, Japanese students spend much of their class time working on one or two challenging problems. If children regularly solve problems that require an extended effort, they may develop perseverance.

✐ **Foster beliefs conducive to problem solving**. Instruction needs to cultivate a better understanding of the nature of problem solving. It is important for children to understand, for example, that genuine problems are not something that can usually be solved quickly, but that they often require time. Although discussing such beliefs is important, even more convincing is tangible evidence of their truth (e.g., regular experience with problems that require extended effort).

Moreover, "no instructional program can be successful that does not deal with the effects of students' negative attitudes and beliefs about themselves as problem solvers" (Kilpatrick, 1985b, p. 9). Children need to recognize that problem-solving skill is not innate but can be learned—that all of us, with effort, can improve our problem-solving skill. Students need to realize that they already have the resources to solve many problems, if only they would use their hidden strengths.

Foster Self-Regulation or Autonomy. It is essential that teachers help students "take charge of their own learning" (Campione et al., 1989, p. 94). Central to achieving this is the fostering of metacognitive skills: awareness about one's own thinking processes and self-monitoring strategies.

✐ **Encourage children to write their own word problems and share them**. This can serve to increase their interest in problem solving and their sense of mathematical power. Another strategy is to have children rewrite problems (e.g., add extra information or change the contexts) (Kilpatrick, 1985b).

✐ **Try student diaries**. Have students record their reflections on their problem-solving efforts including which strategies they use, where they get stumped, how they feel, and what lessons they have learned. This can help students become more aware of their own thinking processes and may prompt them to monitor these processes more carefully.

✐ **Encourage children to take responsibility for monitoring themselves**. Initially, a teacher may have to assume the lion's share of directing the problem-solving process. A teacher may need to

model and prompt self-monitoring skills (e.g., ask whether anything the students know applies or if the answer makes sense). In time, children should take over more and more of the responsibility for directing the problem-solving process (Campione et al., 1989).

✐ **Encourage children to evaluate their own answers**. To foster autonomous thinking, a teacher should generally avoid serving as the final authority. Children frequently ask, "Is this right?" Instead of noting whether the answer is correct or incorrect, a teacher can ask, "Tell me, what do you think?" A common response to such a question is: "I don't know. (You're the teacher)." At this point a teacher can reply, for example, "Does the answer make sense to you?" Asking children to justify their solution procedures or answers helps develop a sense of self-reliance. Asking them to evaluate each others' solution procedures or answers can further diminish a teacher's role as *the* final authority. By discussing an idea and coming to a conclusion themselves, children take ownership of the learning process and the mathematics.

✐ **Avoid overprotecting children**. Teachers should help children learn how to make use of errors, not protect them from making errors. They should also help children learn how to resolve conflicts in socially acceptable ways, not protect them from conflict. Allowing children to take charge of their thinking and learning means allowing them to make mistakes and to disagree with each other. Both can prompt children to reflect carefully on their knowledge, strategies, or solutions and provide the basis for further growth.

In an effort to protect children from humiliation, many U.S. teachers either prevent children from making errors (e.g., by providing the answer), or minimize errors (e.g., by saying, "It wasn't important," or "It's okay, I'm sure you'll get the next one"). This stems from their beliefs that errors reflect stupidity and that stupidity is bad—beliefs that children sense and then adopt for themselves. Japanese teachers, in contrast, welcome errors as a basis for discussion and opportunity to learn (Fuson, in press). It is important that teachers and students view errors as a natural consequence of learning—a natural result of extending (incomplete) knowledge.

Many teachers and children feel uncomfortable about conflict. Taught to be "nice" and to avoid disagreements, they consider conflict as socially unacceptable or even threatening. In fact, conflicts are an inevitable fact of intellectual (or everyday) life. It is important to help students understand that conflicts themselves are neither good nor bad; *how* they are resolved is what matters. Resolving conflicts fairly is desirable; resolving them unfairly is undesirable.

Encourage Flexibility. Teachers should encourage critical and creative thinking.

✎ **Encourage students to continually examine their assumptions**. To encourage flexibility, present students regularly with problems that require them to overcome assumptions. Problems like those in Probe 2.4 on page 2-29 and Activity File 2.1 can be useful for this purpose. Questioning one's assumptions can also be done in other content areas (e.g., Is it true only light things float?; Why don't you associate with members of the chess club?; If we didn't have highways, what impact would that have on our lives?)

✎ **Foster an openness to novel or different ideas**. By word and deed, a teacher should help students see that it is important not to dismiss new, unfamiliar, or even strange ideas. Instead, a teacher should encourage tolerance for and curiosity about ideas (things, people, and places) that are different. Children must learn to balance openmindedness and skepticism (critical thought), which is not an easy task.

 Activity File 2.1: Identifying Planers[†]

◆ Fostering Problem-Solving Flexibility
◆ Grades 3-8 ◆ Whole Group

Read the following instructions to your class: *A point we'll call point A lies in the plane of a piece of paper. Mark this point on your piece of paper. Now go 2 inches in any direction. Next go 3 inches in any direction. Lastly, go 1 inch in any direction. Where are you?*

This activity demonstrates the power of habits and assumptions. Once students are given paper and pencils, nearly all naturally assume the answer must appear *on* the paper. Thus once they make a point on a piece of paper, most get locked into this plane. Although the instructions say they can move in *any* direction, they assume the instructions restrict them to the two-dimensional space of the paper's surface and end up somewhere on the paper. Unlike "planers," "free spirits" may move up above the plane of the paper or even pierce the paper to move below it.

[†]Source unknown.

➤ Probe 2.6: Practicing General Problem-Solving Strategies

Part I: Is This What Polya Had in Mind?

Illustrated below is a first-grade workbook lesson on Polya's four-phase approach to problem solving and heuristics. Evaluate the lesson.

Name_____

PROBLEM-SOLVING STRATEGY

Directions: Read the following story problem to the class. Have the students follow the 4-step problem-solving process.

Six kittens were playing. Four got sleepy and took a nap. How many kittens were left playing?

Step 1. Understand the problem: Does the problem ask *in all* or *what's left*? *Draw a picture.*

Step 2: Devise a plan: *Write a number sentence for the problem.*

Step 3. Carry out the plan: Find the answer of the number sentence.

Step 4. Check your results: Count the kittens in the picture (for addition) or add what is left to what was taken away (for subtraction).

page 89

THE MATH BOOK FROM HELL: Grade 1

Boring Books Publishing Co., Inc.

---

1. What approach to problem solving does the lesson take?

2. What is commendable about the lesson?

3. What are its limitations?

4. How might a teacher modify this lesson to make it more effective?

Probe 2.6 continued

Part II: A Case of Unhelpful Heuristic Instruction

   Miss Brill decided she would first teach her class the heuristic of drawing a picture. Without really considering if drawing a picture would be helpful in solving the problems, Miss Brill assigned her class problems with the instructions, "Solve this problem by drawing a picture." An example is illustrated below. Initially, most of Miss Brill's students did not find the heuristic helpful. A number of them wondered, "How do I use a drawing to find the answer?" The heuristic was, in general, used ineffectively, if at all. Some children drew pictures that were totally irrelevant to the problem (some appeared to be gross caricatures of a young teacher doing very bizarre things). Some drew pictures that were relevant but only after they had figured out the answer (see comments on Probe 2.6 in the *Answers to Selected Questions* section, pages 2-140 and 2-141). Others regularly forgot to make a diagram or resisted drawing a picture. "Why isn't this instruction on problem-solving strategies working?" wondered Miss Brill.

Name _____

Draw a picture to solve the following problem: How many halves are there in four-thirds?

---

1. Solve the problem above by drawing a picture. Discuss how you solved the problem with your group or class. Did most people find the suggestion to draw a picture helpful?

2. Why do you suppose Miss Brill's heuristic instruction was not more successful?

3. What could she do to make her instruction on heuristics more profitable?

↗ Probe 2.7: Problems to Practice Using Heuristics

■ Problem 1: The Long Elevator Ride

Absent-minded Professor Trumble got on the elevator at the first floor of his hotel. Unfortunately, he forgot to push the button for the 14th floor. The elevator went up 12 floors, went up another 5 floors, went up another 6 floors, down 9 floors, up 4 floors, up 7 floors, and down 8 floors. Sensing something had gone awry, and thoroughly confused, Professor Trumble got off the elevator. How many floors away from the 14th floor was he? Assume that the ground floor is the first floor and that the building has a 13th floor.

> ✦ **Hints:** Might the heuristic of *drawing a picture* be helpful? *Look back:* What's wrong with an answer of 3?

■ Problem 2: Sluggish Progress

A slug fell into a ditch 18 inches deep. Each day the slug moved 6 inches up the wall of the ditch, only to slip back 3 inches at night. How many days will it take the sluggish slug to reach the top of the ditch wall?

> ✦ **Hints:** Although the answer seems readily apparent, *draw a picture*. Is there anything you overlooked?

■ Problem 3: Costly Cuts

Mr. Tilden needed a board cut into 8 equal pieces. When he had another board cut into 4 equal pieces, the lumberyard had charged him $1.20 to make the cuts. How much could Mr. Tilden expect to pay now?

> ✦ **Hints:** Although the answer may seem obvious, try *drawing a picture*. What does a picture reveal?

■ Problem 4: Stamp Tetrominoes

Mr. Ki, the new postmaster, wanted very much to please his customers. When Mrs. Vogel asked for four stamps, Mr. Ki surprised her by asking, "Attached or unattached?" Not wanting loose stamps in her handbag, Mrs. Vogel indicated attached. Mr. Ki's next question was even more surprising: "In what shape do you want your four attached stamps?" Mrs. Vogel wondered—with some irritation—how many shapes could four attached stamps have? What is the answer to Mrs. Vogel's question? (Note that such stamps would form a tetromino: four squares joined at a side. Consider the example and nonexample below.)

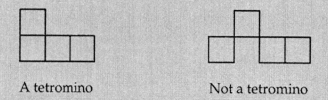

A tetromino   Not a tetromino

> ✦ **Hint:** Try to *draw all of the possibilities in a systematic fashion*.

Probe 2.7 continued

■ **Problem 5: A Train of Toothpick Triangles**

If toothpicks are arranged as a row of triangles as shown below, how many toothpicks will be needed to make a row of 100 triangles?

✦ **Hints:** *Examine simpler cases* of the problem (e.g., the number of toothpicks needed for 1, 2, and 3 triangles). *Organize the data in a table*, and *look for a pattern*.

🔑 ■ **Problem 6: The Fifteen-Penny Triangle**

Thirty-six pennies are arranged in the form of a triangle. (The first fifteen pennies of the triangle are shown below.) What is the fewest number of moves it would take to turn the triangle upside down? Constraint: Only one penny may be moved per turn.

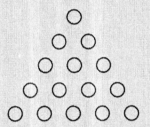

✦ **Hint:** *Examine simpler cases* (e.g., triangles made of 3, 6, 10, 15, and 21 pennies). *Organize the data in a table* and *look for a pattern*.

■ **Problem 7: Spoke Addition**

Write the numerals 1 to 19 in the 19 circles below so that any three numbers in a row have the same sum.

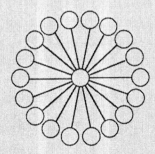

✦ **Hints:** *Solve a simpler problem* (e.g., fill in a 5-circle version with the numbers 1 to 5) and *look for a pattern*.

Probe 2.7 continued

■ **Problem 8: An Uneven Effort**

Three friends, Gif, Harvey, and Iagnacio earned $320 for a trip. Gif earned eight times the amount Harvey earned. Iagnacio earned the difference between Gif and Harvey. How much did each earn?

✦ **Hint:** *Express the information given as a number sentence.*

■ **Problem 9: The Big Loser**

A gambler took his paycheck (all the money he had) for a weekend fling at the racetrack. On each day, he had to pay $3 for parking and another $10 for lunch. On Saturday morning he lost one-fourth of his money left after paying for the parking. On Saturday afternoon he lost one-fourth of his money left after paying for lunch. The same thing happened Sunday morning and afternoon. By the time he got home Sunday night, the gambler had only $60. How big was the gambler's paycheck?

✦ **Hints**: *Draw a picture* and *work backward.*

■ **Problem 10: Poison**

Poison is a two-person game, in which any number of objects (e.g., blocks) are put out (or drawn). A player may take (cross out) one or two items on his or her turn. The object of the game is not to be the player who takes (crosses out) the last item. Find a winning strategy for playing Poison with 26 objects.

✦ **Hints:** *Examine particular examples* of the game with small numbers of items. *Organize the data in a table,* and *look for a pattern.*

■ **Problem 11: A Homework Mystery**

Three of Miss Su's students did not put a name on their homework. The grades on the papers were A, B, and C. Joy, Kiwane, and Lola were the only children for whom Miss Su had not recorded a grade. The B paper, the shortest of the three, was an intriguing autobiographical account of the advantages and disadvantages of being an only child. The next day, Joy and Kiwane were absent, and so the teacher asked Lola about her paper. Lola noted she had written about her skiing adventure with Kiwane's sisters. After the teacher handed Lola her paper, she complained, "Rats, my paper was twice as long as anyone's, and I still didn't get an A." Which paper belonged to which student?

✦ **Hints:** *Make a table* and *use logical reasoning to eliminate possibilities.*

■ **Problem 12: Misleading Labels**

Little Feather put two nickels in a box, a nickel and a dime in another, and two dimes in a third box. She then applied labels 10 cents, 15 cents and 20 cents to the *wrong* boxes and challenged her friend Javier to correctly identify the contents of all three boxes by taking a single coin from one of the boxes.

✦ **Hints:** *Make a table* and *use logical reasoning to eliminate possibilities.*

↗ Probe 2.8: Some Classic Riddles

Riddle 1: The Mahomet Bulldog Baseball Team A scored 6 runs without a single man crossing homeplate. How is this possible?

Riddle 2: Two U.S. coins have a total value of 30¢. One is not a nickel. What are the two coins?

Riddle 3: Two children played seven games of checkers. Each won the same number of games; there were no ties. How could this be?

Riddle 4: Take three apples from five apples and what do you have?

Riddle 5: A farmer had 16 sheep. All but seven died. How many does the farmer have left?

Riddle 6: A plane crashed on the U.S.-Canadian border. Where did they bury the survivors?

Riddle 7: How much dirt could you remove from a hole that is 6 feet long, 3 feet wide, and 4 feet deep?

Riddle 8: Exhausted, Hollis went to bed early to get a good night's sleep. Because he needed to get up at 9 A.M., he set his mechanical alarm clock for that time. If Hollis went to bed at 8 P.M., how much sleep did he get?

Riddle 9: A man built a house with a southern exposure on all four sides. He saw a bear walk by his living room window. What color was the bear?

Riddle 10: There are 12 1¢ U.S. stamps in a dozen. How many 2¢ U.S. stamps in a dozen?

Riddle 11: If a doctor gave you three pills and told you to take one every half hour, how long would the pills last?

Riddle 12: Do they have the fourth of July in England?

Riddle 13: Some months have 31 days. Some have 30. How many have 28 days?

Riddle 14: If you have only one match and enter a dark, cold cabin with an oil lantern, a gas stove, and some kindling, what do you light first?

Questions for Reflection

1. Did you find the riddles amusingly challenging or frustratingly irritating?

2. Do you suppose all children react to such puzzle problems in the same way? What instructional implications does this suggest?

→ Probe 2.9: Nongoal-Specific Problems

Examine the examples of goal-specific and nongoal-specific questions below. Then answer the questions that follow.

Goal-Specific	Nongoal-Specific

Ruffus managed to get into the Bradley house one afternoon. He chewed up 4 of Amy's shoes and 5 of Brad's shoes. How many shoes did Ruffus the dog demolish?

Ruffus managed to get into the Bradley house one afternoon. He chewed up 4 of Amy's shoes, 3 of her toys, and 6 of her socks. He also chewed up 5 of Brad's shoes, 7 of his toys, and 2 of his socks. Write and solve as many problems as you can about the damage that Ruffus wrought.

Ruffus made off with 12 biscuits. He buried 8 of them before Mrs. Xu discovered him. How many unburied biscuits did Ruffus have?

Mrs. Xu baked 2 dozen biscuits. Ruffus made off with 12 biscuits. He buried 8 of them before Mrs. Xu discovered him. Think of questions you could ask using the data given. Write out your questions and your answers.

Howard wanted to buy a case for his keys. To find out how big a case he needed, he took an inch ruler and measured his biggest key, shown below. How long a case did Howard need to buy?

Howard wanted to buy a case for his keys. To find out how big a case he needed, he decided to measure his biggest key, shown below. In what ways could Howard measure the length of the key?

Tiu and Mario each ride their bikes to school. Tiu lives 6 blocks from school; Mario lives 9 blocks away. It takes Tiu 12 minutes to ride his bike to school. How long does it take Mario to ride his bike to school if he rides at the same rate of speed as Tiu?

Tiu and Mario each ride their bikes to school. Tiu lives 6 blocks from school; Mario lives 9 blocks away. It takes Tiu 12 minutes to ride his bike to school. Write and solve as many different problems as you can.

Find the area of the shaded sector of the circle shown. Use $\pi = 3.14$ and round to the nearest hundredth.

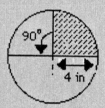

Find out all you can about the shaded and unshaded parts of the circle shown. Round to the nearest hundredth.

Probe 2.9 continued

Evaluate the following efforts to transform a goal-specific problem into a nongoal-specific problem. Consider whether the transformed problem is really open-ended in nature. Consider whether it could be substituted for the goal-specific problem. That is, does the revised problem involve roughly the same level of mathematical knowledge as the goal-specific problem, or knowledge that is far more advanced than the textbook example? Justify your choice to your group or class.

Routine Word Problems	Transformed Word Problems
1. Gene colored 9 eggs. He colored five blue and he colored the rest red. How many eggs did Gene color red?	Gene has 9 eggs to color. He has red and blue paint. If each egg is painted one color, find all the different ways he can paint the eggs.
2. Ruffus got loose and did $30 damage to the Bradleys' lawn, $45 damage to the Clintons' garden, $35 damage to the Chins' lawn decoration, and $28 damage to the Whites' fence. How much damage did the renegade Ruffus do in all?	Ruffus got loose and did $30 damage to the Bradleys' lawn, $45 damage to the Clintons' garden, $35 damage to the Chins' lawn decoration, and $28 damage to the Whites' fence. Think of questions you could ask using the data given. Write out your questions and answers.
3. Ana had 75¢. She bought two pencils for 28¢. How much money did she have left?	Ana had 75¢. She bought two pencils for 28¢. Did she have enough money left to buy a candy bar costing 45¢?
4. Jenifer earned $16 babysitting. She spent 25% of this on junk food. How much did the junk food cost?	Jenifer babysat for $1.25 per hour. She earned $220 over the course of a year. She spent 25% of this on CDs, 40% on clothes, and 10% on junk food. Jenifer saved the rest. Did she save enough to buy the new bicycle she really wants?
5. The E-Team consisted of Brandie, Deedee, Missie, and Tracie. Brandie won a 1st place prize, three 2nd place prizes, and no 3rd place prizes. Deedee won two 1st place prizes, no 2nd place prizes, and one 3rd place prize. Missie won no 1st place prizes, five 2nd place prizes, and no 3rd place prizes. Tracie won four 1st place prizes, one 2nd place prize, and one 3rd place prize. Complete the table below:	The E-Team consisted of Brandie, Deedee, Missie, and Tracie. Brandie won a 1st place prize, three 2nd place prizes, and no 3rd place prizes. Deedee won two 1st place prizes, no 2nd place prizes, and one 3rd place prize. Missie won no 1st place prizes, five 2nd place prizes, and no 3rd place prizes. Tracie won four 1st place prizes, one 2nd place prize, and one 3rd place prize. Make a table summarizing this information. Then write and solve as many problems about the table as you can.

	1st	2nd	3rd
Brandie	1	3	0
Deedee			
Missie			
Tracie			

Routine Word Problems	Transformed Word Problems
6. Oranges cost 33¢ each. Doreen bought two oranges. How much did she spend?	Two oranges cost 66¢, four apples cost 92¢, and three pears cost 84¢. Doreen has $2. Write and solve as many problems about this as you can.

➤ Probe 2.10: Providing Extension

In any classroom, there are bound to be significant individual differences in children's abilities to solve problems. Frequently, one child or group will finish before the others. It is important, then, that a teacher be prepared to provide extension (additional challenges) to keep such individuals or groups from becoming bored and restless. Extension is also helpful because it can help students see that a solution strategy can apply to a broad class of problems—even to problems that on the surface look different. This valuable lesson can prompt children to look for similarities between new and familiar problems even when they appear to be quite different. This is an essential step in the development of a mathematical way of thinking.

Two ways of providing an additional challenge are (1) asking children to consider additional solutions (for problems with multiple solutions) and (2) asking them to devise alternative solution methods. Another way is to modify a problem. The table below (based on Charles & Lester, 1982) illustrates some ways this can be done.

■ **Perimeter of Squares.** What is the perimeter of 100 1' x 1' square blocks placed side by side?

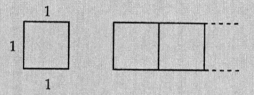

1.	*Change the context.*	How many *chairs* are needed if 100 *card tables* are lined up end to end and one chair will fit each side of a card table?
2.	*Change the numbers.*	What is the perimeter of *500* 1' x 1' squares placed side by side?
3.	*Change the number of conditions.*	What is the perimeter of 100 1' x 1' square blocks placed in *two rows* side by side?
4.	*Reverse the given information and the unknown.*	One-foot square blocks were placed side by side. *The perimeter was 202 feet; how many blocks were used?*
5.	*Change a combination of elements.*	How many *chairs* are needed if *500* card tables are lined up in *two rows* side by side?

1. What are some other ways a problem can be modified to provide extension? Consider, for instance, how translation problems can be modified. Are any of those suggestions applicable here?

Probe 2.10 continued

2. (a) Solve the following extensions of problems from Probe 2.7 on pages 2-50 to 2-52. (b) In each case, indicate how the problem was extended.

- ◆ **Extension of Problem 1 (The Long Elevator Ride):** How far would absent-minded Professor Trumble be from the 14th floor if he started on the first floor and if the elevator went up 19 floors, went up another 12 floors, went down 6 floors, went down another 15 floors, and then went up 19 floors?

- ◆ **Extension of Problem 7 (Spoke Addition):** Once you have found a solution, try finding two more solutions. (Note that the same hint for the original problem is applicable to the extension: Examine a simpler case.)

- ◆ **Extension of Problem 10 (Poison):** What would the winning strategy be if the rules for Poison were changed so that players could take (cross out) one, two, or three items on their turn?

3. Use the five techniques outlined in the table above to write extensions of the following problem:

- ■ Mr. Dense bought stock in Downer, Inc., for $80 per share. Concerned about its plummeting value, Mr. Dense sold the stock when it was worth $60 a share. Assuming the value of Downer stock had bottomed out, he bought some again when it was worth $30 a share. Unfortunately, Mr. Dense was wrong, and the stock continued to lose value. At $20 a share, Mr. Dense finally decided to unload his Downer stock once and for all. How much a share did Mr. Dense gain or lose on his Downer stock investments?

Discuss your effort to modify the problem above with your group or class.

MATHEMATICS AS REASONING

Figure 2.9: A Case of Unreliable Reasoning

Reasoning is an essential tool for mathematics and everyday life. However, like any tool, it can be used effectively or ineffectively and for worthy or unworthy purposes. As Quote 1 in Box 2.12 implies, learning about the art of logic can provide you with a powerful tool for evaluating your own and others' reasoning. Consider, for instance, Figure 2.9. Despite the fact that Lucy had on all previous occasions tricked Charlie Brown, he concluded that this time he could trust her. If poor Charlie Brown had been conversant in the art of logic, he would have recognized that his reasoning was flawed and could have avoided suffering the consequence of making a groundless conclusion.

Unfortunately, many people would rather not get entangled in the art of logic. As Quote 2 in Box 2.12 implies, they feel that logic is arcane, tricky, and confusing—something better not pondered or discussed. Alice, for example, ignores Tweedledee's logic by politely changing the subject. Perhaps you too feel uncomfortable about the topic of logical reasoning. If so, hang in there; we will try to be clearer than Tweedledee. With any luck, you might even find yourself enjoying the topic.

The unit begins by identifying the three main types of reasoning. It then addresses why each is important for mathematics and everyday life. Next,

Box 2.12: Two Views of Logic

Consider the very different attitudes toward logic captured by two quotes below. Which corresponds more closely to your attitude?

Quote 1: "[Logic provides] the power to detect fallacies, and to tear to pieces flimsy illogical arguments which you so continually encounter in books, in newspapers, in speeches, and even in sermons, and which so easily delude those who have never taken the trouble to master this fascinating Art. Try it. That is all I ask you" (Lewis Carroll in *Symbolic Logic and the Game of Logic* published in New York by Dover Publications, 1958).

Quote 2: *"Contrariwise, . . . if it was so, it might be; and if it were so, it would be; but as it isn't, it ain't. That's logic"* (Tweedledee in *Through the Looking Glass* by Lewis Carroll).

it discusses children's natural reasoning strengths and weaknesses. The last subunit describes how instruction can foster mathematical reasoning in developmentally appropriate and interesting ways.

REASONS FOR FOCUSING ON REASONING

This subunit describes types of reasoning that are relevant to mathematics, how the topic of reasoning is relevant to students and everyday life, and common misconceptions and problems with reasoning.

Types of Reasoning

☞ *What are the differences among intuitive, inductive, and deductive reasoning?* Complete Probe 2.11 (page 2-64), Activity 2.1 (pages 2-65 to 2-67), and Probe 2.12 (pages 2-68 to 2-71) and then continue.

As noted in Probe 2.11, intuitive reasoning entails a ready insight or playing a hunch. Frequently we do not have all the information necessary to make a decision and so we base our decision on what is obvious or on a gut feeling. For instance, we may decide to stand in Aisle C at the check-out counter, because it appears to be the shortest line.

Inductive reasoning involves perceiving a regularity. (The heuristic of looking for a pattern discussed in the previous unit on problem solving involves this type of reasoning.) Finding (inducing) a commonality among diverse examples is a basis for concept formation and greatly reduces what we have to remember. For instance, the meaning of "dodecagon" can be determined by finding what the following examples share in common:

Deductive reasoning may sound daunting to many. In fact, it is simply a matter of drawing a conclusion that necessarily follows from what we know. In other words, "given certain information, we can be sure of other things," which we may or may not be able to check directly (Donaldson, 1978, p. 36). For example, given the knowledge that we can always add one more to a number, we can conclude that there is no largest number—that the numbers do not end but extend on infinitely. Although beyond their means to confirm directly, even 8- and 9-year-olds deduce that the number sequence is inexhaustible (Gelman, 1982). (The if-then reasoning discussed in the unit on problem solving is a form of deductive reasoning.)

Applications

What types of reasoning do mathematicians use when doing mathematics? What relevance does the study of reasoning have for children and everyday life?

The Reasoning Needed to Do Mathematics. Intuitive, inductive, and deductive reasoning all play an important role in the development and application of mathematics. Since the early Greeks, mathematicians have used deductive reasoning to prove geometric theorems. In a traditional skills-approach, memorizing geometric proofs in middle or high school may constitute the only formal instruction on mathematical reasoning students receive. Not surprisingly, many people are aware of this logical side of mathematics but not its exploratory side.

In fact, mathematical inquiry often begins with a conclusion drawn from intuitive or inductive reasoning called a conjecture. (*A conjecture is a guess, inference, theory, or prediction based on uncertain or incomplete evidence.*) Deductive proofs are a means of *checking* conjectures.

The Need for Reasoning in School Mathematics. According to the NCTM (1989) *Curriculum Standards*, major goals of mathematics instruction should be fostering children's belief that mathematics makes sense and cultivating their sense of mathematical power (a feeling of control over their learning, confidence in their ability to think and to learn, and autonomy). Classrooms that value and promote reasoning are essential for achieving these goals. Developing reasoning competencies is essential to help children go beyond the level of merely memorizing facts, rules, and procedures. A focus on reasoning can help children see that mathematics is logical and supposed to make sense. It can foster children's beliefs that mathematics is something they can comprehend, think through, justify, and evaluate. Moreover, children develop a sense of mathematical power by *doing* mathematics—actually solving problems themselves. Students cannot be involved in *doing* mathematics without reasoning (Silver, Kilpatrick, & Schlesinger, 1990). Activity 2.1 (on pages 2-65 to 2-67) and Probe 2.12 (on pages 2-68 to 2-71) describe a number of activities and games that can be used with elementary-age children to examine and practice reasoning.

Reasoning Involved in Other Content Areas. Reasoning skills can be applied to other content areas. For example, finding patterns in data (inductive reasoning) and using if-then (deductive) reasoning can be central to science activities or experiments. In Social Studies, what was the reasoning, for example, behind the restrictive immigration law passed in the 1920s, and was this reasoning reasonable (see Box 2.13)? Why did the framers of the U.S. Constitution *conclude* that church and state should be separate? (This question is addressed on page 2-62 in the section titled Limitations and Misuses).

Reasoning Needed for Everyday Life. Intuitive, inductive, and deductive reasoning are essential tools for coping with a complex world and solving everyday problems. For example, your #@✻! car won't start. What's the source of the difficulty? *If* the battery is dead, *then* the headlights will not come on. The headlights turn on, *so* the battery is not dead. *If* the gas tank is empty, *then* the gauge should continue to register "E" after the key is turned to accessories. The gauge moves when the key is turned to accessories, *so* the car has gas. Perhaps the problem is with the starter.

Evaluating others' reasoning is an important survival skill. Any form of persuasion—a lawyer pleading a case before a jury, an advertiser pitching a product, a politician seeking votes, a journalist writing an editorial, a child trying to get permission from a parent to engage in some activity, students trying to dissuade a teacher from enforcing a rule or giving an assignment, a young man trying to convince a young lady of the virtues of romance—involves reasoning of some kind. Does the persuader's argument make sense? Are his or her conclusions logical and reasonable? These are essential questions if we are to make everyday decisions effectively—if we are to avoid being hoodwinked.

Box 2.13: Unintelligent Thinking About Intelligence

The *Science and Politics of I.Q.*, (Kamin, 1974) chronicled key misconceptions about I.Q. testing. In 1923, Carl Brigham of Princeton published a book, *A Study of American Intelligence*, in which he noted that the I.Q.s of more recently arrived immigrants were generally lower than those of immigrants who had arrived earlier. This correlated with changes in immigration patterns. At the time, there were recent influxes of immigrants from southern and eastern Europe (e.g., Italians, Poles, and Russians), including many Jews. Earlier immigrants had largely come from northern Europe.

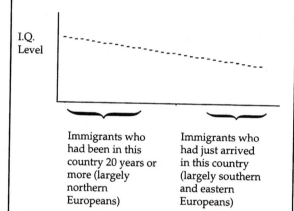

Immigrants who had been in this country 20 years or more (largely northern Europeans) / Immigrants who had just arrived in this country (largely southern and eastern Europeans)

The following logic was used to justify the Immigration Act of 1924, which restricted immigration from southern and eastern Europe, including that of many Jews who later would try to escape Nazi repression.

Premise 1: The I.Q. test measures innate intelligence.

Premise 2: The I.Q. level of recently arrived immigrants (largely southern and eastern Europeans) is lower than that of immigrants who have been here longer (largely northern Europeans).

Conclusion: The more recently arrived immigrants are inferior in native intelligence and should be prevented from entering the country and diluting the intelligence of our country. Therefore, we should restrict immigration from southern and eastern Europe.

Limitations and Misuses

☞ Try Probe 2.13 (page 2-72) and then read on.

To evaluate their own and others' reasoning and conclusions effectively, students need to be able to answer the following question: *What are the limitations and common pitfalls of each type of reasoning?*

Intuitive Reasoning. As noted earlier, intuitive reasoning is based on appearances or assumptions. Unfortunately, appearance can be misleading and assumption can be wrong. Thus, while intuitions may turn out to be correct, they may also turn out to be incorrect. For example, Question 1 of Probe 2.13 illustrates a classic illusion. Intuitively, it appears that Line B is longer than Line A. However, measuring the lines reveals that, in fact, the lines are equal in length.

Inductive Reasoning. Like intuitive reasoning, inductive reasoning cannot by itself prove a conclusion true. A rule induced by examining some examples may be true for those specific examples but not for all cases. In psychology, for example, a conclusion may be valid about the sample studied but may not apply to the whole population. The sample may be special in some way and, thus, not representative of the whole population. It turns out this is a major problem with medical research, which traditionally has studied male rats and male humans, and then made conclusions about rats and people, in general. Now consider Question 2 in Probe 2.13. The rule, "choose an odd number," certainly applies to the cases shown. However, would this induced rule apply if more cases, such as 2, 7, and 11, were examined? In brief, induction may produce a conclusion that is true about the specific examples studied, but it does not guarantee generalizable results—a conclusion that applies to all cases.

Deductive Reasoning. Deductive proofs can determine whether or not an insight or conjecture (intuition or induction) is logically consistent and whether it applies only to the cases examined or more generally. Although deductive reasoning is a powerful technique for demonstrating that an intuition or induction applies generally, it nevertheless has limitations or can be misapplied.

Are conclusions proven by deductive reasoning necessarily and universally true? Deductive reasoning guarantees a true conclusion if (a) the premises of the argument are true and (b) the argument is valid (logical). Even so, the conclusion may be true for only certain situations.

• **A house built on shifting sands will not stand.** Deductive reasoning, like a house, needs a firm foundation. The foundation of a logical argument is the premises (ideas demonstrated *or assumed* to be true). If a premise is untrue, then the conclusion may be untrue. Consider Argument I in Question 3 of Probe 2.13. *If you accept the premises, then the conclusion logically follows: If teachers are grossly overpaid and Winnie is a teacher, then it necessarily follows that Winnie is grossly overpaid.* Logically, the argument is valid, but is it true? Most people, particularly educators, would claim that the first premise is untrue and, hence, the conclusion is untrue. In brief, if a premise is not true, then a conclusion may be logical, but it may not be reasonable.* This is important for children to understand because, as Examples 2.1 to 2.3 below illustrate, logical but unreasonable conclusions are unnervingly common in everyday life.

Example 2.1: *Smart people take advantage of this once-in-a-lifetime offer* (Premise 1). *You look like a smart person* (Premise 2). *You should take advantage of this once-in-a-lifetime offer* (Conclusion). Such a salespitch is convincing to many people because they cannot resist the flattery of Premise 2 and the force of such a logical argument (the argument is valid because the conclusion necessarily follows from the premises). Note that as soon as you agree with the salesperson's first premise, turning down the once-in-a-lifetime offer implies that the second premise is *incorrect*.

Example 2.2: *A brave person wouldn't be afraid to go out on that pond of ice* (Premise 1). *Billy is a brave person* (Premise 2). *Billy will go get the ball* (Conclusion). If Billy agrees with Premise 1, refusing this dangerous challenge casts doubt on Premise 2 and his masculinity.

Example 2.3: In Box 2.13, the conclusion that served as the rationale for the Immigration Act of 1924 was based on a faulty premise: that *I.Q. tests measure innate intelligence.* Because the

---

*Untrue premises do not guarantee an untrue conclusion. Consider Argument II of Question 3 in Probe 2.13. The first premise (Teachers are slaves) is not true in any real sense, yet many people would agree that the conclusion is true.

premise was generally accepted as a fact, psychologists, politicians, and many others overlooked a more obvious interpretation: that the I.Q. test was culturally biased and that the longer immigrants were in this country (the more culturally assimilated they were), the better their test performance.

Another historical example likewise illustrates the pitfall of a questionable premise. The founding fathers of the U.S. faced a divisive situation. Should there be a state-sponsored religion or should state and church be separate? Consider the logic for the first position.

Premise 1:	People should be governed by the higher law of a true faith.
Premise 2:	Religion A is *the* true faith.
Conclusion:	All people should be governed by Religion A.

This conclusion does not pose much of a problem assuming everyone agrees on Premise 2—assuming everyone has the same faith. It is highly problematic in a pluralistic society where people have many different beliefs, including those who do not hold to any religion. In such a society, there would be little agreement about Premise 2 (and some people might even argue with Premise 1). In a society dominated by a particular religion but with minority religions, the majority of people would agree with both Premise 1 and 2 and would endorse the conclusion. Moreover, the majority might even try to enforce the conclusion by requiring members of minority religions to convert, leave the country, or face other unpleasant consequences (e.g., imprisonment, torture, or death). From the dismal experiences of religious (and political) persecution in their ancestral countries, the founding fathers recognized that the rights of minority groups (e.g., minority religions) needed to be protected. They recognized that a state-sponsored religion led too easily to the dangerous conclusion that everyone should believe the same thing and that any means were justified to ensure this homogeneity of belief. As a result, the United States was founded on the principle of tolerance for others' religious (and political) beliefs. (Consider whether you would feel comfortable living in Iran, with its state-sponsored religion.)

☞ *Isn't illogical reasoning easy to spot?* With the aid of Table 2.2 on page 2-63 and group discussion, evaluate your answers to Question 4 of Probe 2.13. Did any of the items cause you difficulty?

Anonymously share your results with your group or class. Tally the data. Which items (arguments) caused the most difficulty?

• **There's a right way and a wrong way to do most things.** Like most things, deductive reasoning can be done properly or improperly. A valid argument can lead to a true conclusion; an invalid argument can lead to a questionable conclusion (see Table 2.2). Unfortunately, invalid arguments can be seductively plausible.

Indeed, advertisers, sales representatives, lawyers, politicians, and others whose business it is to persuade people sometimes resort to slippery logic with great success. Note that Example 2.4 below is analogous to Argument Type 3 in Table 2.2: The premise (If you're popular, then you use Exhorbitant) is twisted into the invalid claim that if you use Exhorbitant, then you will be popular. Whereas Example 2.4 promises popularity by association, Example 2.5 below implies guilt by association. Although there may be some merit to the homilies, "Birds of a feather flock together," and "Chose your friends wisely because they reflect on you," strictly speaking, the conclusion in Example 2.5 is not logical. (The argument is invalid because the conclusion does not necessarily follow from the premises.) Lawyers oftentimes use such "logic," because of its psychological impact on jurors.

Example 2.4: Popular people like actress Gloria Glamorous use Exhorbitant Beauty Aids. If you use Exhorbitant Beauty Aids, then you will be popular too.

Example 2.5: Baby Face Bokoski is a known mobster. Mr. Riccutti associated with Baby Face Bokoski. Ladies and gentlemen of the jury, Mr. Riccutti is therefore a mobster.

• **Good looks will get you only so far.** Good logic, like good looks, is helpful up to a point. Consider the geometric theorem noted in Question 5 of Probe 2.13: The shortest distance between two points is a straight line. Is this truth applicable to all situations? Many people believe the answer is yes. Does the theorem apply to the surface of a sphere (e.g., when traveling from one point on the earth's surface to another)? In fact, it does not. The shortest distance between two points in such a situation is an arc. A theorem, then, is true for a certain, well-defined context. Outside this context, the theorem may not apply.

Table 2.2: Examples of Valid and Faulty If-Then (Deductive) Reasoning[3]

	If A, then B (A implies B)	Premise (Accepted as True)	If it rains, then the ground will be wet.	All members of the Kitty-Cat Club (KCC) are girls.*
1.	A, so B (Detachment)	Valid Argument, True Conclusion	It is raining, therefore the ground is wet.	Jamie is a member of KCC; therefore, Jamie is a girl.
2.	Not B, so not A (Contrapositive)	Valid Argument, True Conclusion	The ground was not wet, therefore it did not rain.	Chick is not a girl; therefore, Chick is not a member of the KCC.
3.	B, so A (Converse)	Invalid Argument, Questionable Conclusion	The ground was wet, therefore it rained.	Melanie is a girl; therefore, she is a member of the KCC.
4.	Not A, so not B (Inverse)	Invalid Argument, Questionable Conclusion	It did not rain, therefore the ground is not wet.	Dalia is not a member of KCC; therefore, Dalia is not a girl.

Note that this table holds for situations in which A is a sufficient condition for B. A sufficient condition is enough to produce a result (e.g., rain is sufficient to produce a wet ground). Of course, there may be other conditions that may precipitate the same result. For example, an activated sprinkler is sufficient to make the ground wet. This is why the conclusion to Argument 3 (the converse) or Argument 4 (the inverse) may or may not be true. Wet ground is insufficient information to determine if it rained. Moreover, knowing that it did not rain is insufficient information to determine if the ground is wet.

(The table does not hold for situations in which A is a necessary or a necessary and sufficient condition for B. A necessary condition is one of several prerequisites for a result. For example, clouds are one requirement for rain but by themselves not enough to produce rain. A necessary and sufficient condition is the *only* prerequisite for a result. For example, lightning by itself causes thunder.)

---

*This could be rephrased: If a person is a member of the KCC, then that person is a girl.

2-64

→ **Probe 2.11: Patterns and Reasoning**†

1. In 1514, Albrecht Dürer made an engraving entitled "Melancholy." In the background of this depiction of a depressed woman is the interesting grid of numbers shown at the right. Two cells appear to be missing numbers. Can you determine what they are?

16	3	2	13
5	10	11	8
9	6		12
4	15	14	

2. Inferences or conclusions can stem from intuitive, inductive, or deductive reasoning.

Intuitive reasoning involves basing a conclusion on appearances or what feels right (an assumption). The following is an example of a child's (accidentally correct) intuitive reasoning: "If I multiply 5 and 3, I guess the product would be odd because 5 and 3 are odd."

Inductive reasoning begins with examining particular instances and leads to drawing a general conclusion. In other words, it entails observing specific examples and discerning (inducing) an underlying pattern or rule. The following is an example of a child reasoning from particulars to the general: "When I multiplied the odd numbers 1 and 9, 3 and 3, 5 and 9, 7 and 3, and 9 and 7, all the products were odd [observation about particular instances]; therefore, the product of any two odd numbers is odd [general inference]."

Deductive reasoning begins with *premises* (general propositions) that lead inescapably to a *conclusion* about a particular instance. *Deductive reasoning* is different from other types of reasoning, because it involves drawing a conclusion that *necessarily follows* from what is given (Ennis, 1969). In contrast to inductive reasoning that goes from specific cases to a general rule, deductive reasoning goes from general rules to a conclusion about a specific case. The following is an example of reasoning from the general to the particular: "Multiplying two odd numbers always results in an odd product [general premise]; 5 and 3 are odd numbers [second premise]; therefore, the product of 5 and 3 *must* be odd."

a. What kind of reasoning was involved when you concluded that it was possible to determine what the missing numbers were?

b. What kind of reasoning was involved when you determined a rule for figuring out the numbers?

c. What kind of reasoning was involved when you used the rule to figure out the missing numbers?

3. There are a number of interesting patterns in Dürer's number grid (Jamski, 1989). Consider the four numbers in the corners. What do you notice about them? Does this four-number pattern appear elsewhere in the number grid?

†Probe 2.11 was adapted from page 44 of *Mathematics: A Human Endeavor* by H. R. Jacobs, © 1982. The adaptation is used with permission of the publisher: W. H. Freeman, San Francisco.

✍ Activity 2.1: Magic Squares

◆ Inductive and deductive reasoning ◆ K-Adult ◆ Any number

1. The 4x4 grid you completed in Question 1 of Probe 2.11 on the previous page is called a magic square. The following are examples of 3x3 magic squares:

Based on the examples and nonexamples of magic squares you have seen so far, explicitly define a magic square.

a.

1	6	5
8	4	0
3	2	7

b.

25	30	29
32	28	24
27	26	31

c.

243	248	247
250	246	242
245	244	249

d.

120	130	160
190	150	110
140	130	180

e.

5	6	7
8	6	4
5	6	7

f.

-3	2	1
4	0	-4
-1	-2	3

g.

$\frac{1}{2}$	$1\frac{3}{4}$	$1\frac{1}{2}$
$2\frac{1}{4}$	$1\frac{1}{4}$	$\frac{1}{4}$
1	$\frac{3}{4}$	2

h.

0.8	1.8	1.6
2.2	1.4	0.6
1.2	1.0	2.0

The following are <u>not</u> examples of magic squares:

0	1	2
3	4	5
6	7	8

2	7	6
5	1	9
8	3	4

3	6	9
10	4	2
5	8	7

4	11	6
5	7	9
8	3	10

2. Magic squares are engaging puzzles. Can you fill in the missing numbers in the square below to make it a magic square? Hint: Examine the examples in Question 1 to determine if the numbers making up a magic square *must* form an arithmetic sequence. If so, could the magic square below be solved? If not, what numbers are missing?

1	2	3

Activity 2.1 continued

3. Magic squares are versatile teaching tools (see, e.g., Sherrill, 1987), which can be used to implement a number of the NCTM (1989) standards. They can be used to encourage pattern searching (K-4 Standard 13 and 5-8 Standard 8: recognize a wide variety of patterns). Questions 1 and 3 of Probe 2.11 illustrate how they can be used to practice different types of reasoning (K-4 Standard 3: draw logical conclusions about mathematics). Question 2 of this probe illustrates an exercise in identifying types of reasoning (5-8 Standard 3: recognize and apply deductive and inductive reasoning). Magic squares can also provide practice of addition computation and recalling sums to 18 (K-4 Standard 8: develop reasonable proficiency with basic facts and algorithms). Moreover, magic squares can be designed to practice multidigit addition (see Examples b, c, and d in Question 1) or addition with negative numbers, fractions, or decimals (see Examples f, g, and h in Question 1) (Wood, 1989).

"Subtraction Magic Square" can provide practice with both addition and subtraction computation. With such a magic square, sum the numbers on the end and subtract the middle number. Complete the subtraction magic square to the right.

5		
6		
9		

♀ 4. Below Magic Squares A_1 to A_7 were all derived from Example A_0. How was each derived? What does this suggest once you have constructed a single Magic Square?

A_0 .

1	6	5
8	4	0
3	2	7

A_1 .

5	10	9
12	8	4
7	6	11

A_2 .

11	16	15
18	14	10
13	12	17

A_3 .

-3	2	1
4	0	-4
-1	-2	3

A_4 .

4	24	20
32	16	0
12	8	28

A_5 .

.01	.06	.05
.08	.04	0
.03	.02	.07

A_6 .

110	160	150
180	140	100
130	120	170

A_7 .

.3	.8	.7
1.0	.6	.2
.5	.4	.9

♀ 5. How can you construct your own magic squares tailored to your grade level or your specific objectives? You could, of course, try a trial-and-error method. Try it.

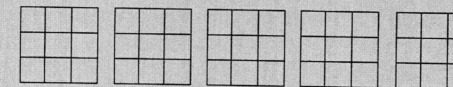

Activity 2.1 continued

Unfortunately, a trial-and-error approach does not work very well. It can waste a great deal of time and be very frustrating. Fortunately for your blood pressure, there are systematic methods for designing 3x3 magic squares involving an arithmetic sequence. The following activity is intended to help students discover how nine numbers in an arithmetic sequence can be arranged to make a 3x3 magic square.[4] Complete and compare the four magic squares below. Do you see a pattern? The pattern should provide you with an algorithm for constructing your own 3x3 magic square for nine numbers in an arithmetic sequence.

2	7	6
9	5	1
4	3	

3		7
	6	2
5	4	

4		
		3
6	5	

5		
		4

There are other algorithms for creating 3x3 magic squares or magic squares with any number of odd squares per side (see, e.g., Pappas, 1989; Sovchik, 1989). Wood (1989) also describes a computer program for generating such squares. Templates for converting an arithmetic sequence into 3x3 or 5x5 magic squares are shown below.

Second Term	Seventh Term	Sixth Term
Nineth Term	Fifth Term	First Term
Fourth Term	Third Term	Eighth Term

Seventh Term	Twenty-fourth Term	First Term	Eighth Term	Fifteenth Term
Twenty-third Term	Fifth Term	Seventh Term	Fourteenth Term	Sixteenth Term
Fourth Term	Sixth Term	Thirteenth Term	Twentieth Term	Twenty-second Term
Tenth Term	Twelfth Term	Nineteenth Term	Twenty-first Term	Third Term
Eleventh Term	Eighteenth Term	Twenty-fifth Term	Second Term	Ninth Term

6. Miss Brill asked her class to complete the two magic squares to the right. Is there more than one solution for each?

x.

		10
		5
		13

y.

		6

7. For introducing magic squares, particularly to younger students, a teacher might better use a relatively simple design. What is the smallest magic square that would make sense to use, a 2x2 or 3x3? Briefly justify.

➤ **Probe 2.12: Drawing Conclusions and Identifying Types of Reasoning**

Word Problems

Word problems can be an entertaining way to practice reasoning and to encourage reflection about it. Consider the problem below.

■ **Tom, Dick, and Harry.**[†] Three golfers named Tom, Dick, and Harry are walking to the clubhouse. Tom, the best golfer of the three, always tells the truth. Dick sometimes tells the truth, while Harry, the worst golfer, never does.

a. Can you figure out who is who? Explain how you know. (Hint: First, figure out which one is Tom.)

b. What type of reasoning did you use to identify the characters above? Briefly justify your answer.

Some Games and Activities that Involve Reasoning

Many upper-elementary and college-level students have difficulty distinguishing among the types of reasoning and need practice doing so. For each of the following activities or games, indicate what type of reasoning is required. After trying an activity or game with older students, you may wish to have them identify the type of reasoning required. In any case, the activities and games described below are an entertaining way for both primary and upper-elementary children to practice reasoning skills.

[†]This problem is based on a problem appearing on page 45 of *Mathematics: A Human Endeavor* by H. R. Jacobs, © 1982. The problem and accompanying graphic are used with the permission of the publisher: W. H. Freeman, San Francisco.

Probe 2.12 continued

🍎 **Guess My Rule.** In this game, children are shown some examples of a pattern (see Example A below) or a relationship (see Example B below) and must decipher the underlying rule. Children can be asked to describe the rule and/or to make a prediction based on the rule. Does figuring out the rule involve the same kind of reasoning as making the prediction?

Example A: Can you tell what comes next? Why? ΔOΔΔOΔΔOΔ__
Example B: What function is represented by the following pairs of numbers and what is the value of x? (-1,-1)(0,0)(1,1)(2,8)(3,x)

🍎 **In-Out (Function) Machines.** A function machine is another Guess-My-Rule Activity. It takes an input and uses a particular rule to translate it into an output. Does determining the rule of a function machine involve the same kind of reasoning as filling in the blank spaces in the table?

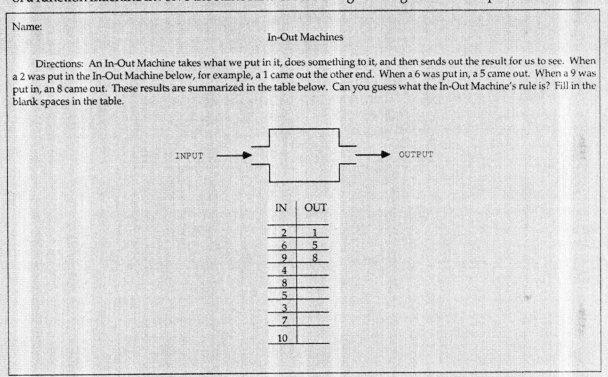

Name:

In-Out Machines

Directions: An In-Out Machine takes what we put in it, does something to it, and then sends out the result for us to see. When a 2 was put in the In-Out Machine below, for example, a 1 came out the other end. When a 6 was put in, a 5 came out. When a 9 was put in, an 8 came out. These results are summarized in the table below. Can you guess what the In-Out Machine's rule is? Fill in the blank spaces in the table.

INPUT →   → OUTPUT

IN	OUT
2	1
6	5
9	8
4	
8	
5	
3	
7	
10	

🍎 **Am I?** This activity involves starting with a definition and asking children to identify whether specific examples fit this definition. The following example involves two definitions:

An even number is an integer that is divisible by 2; an odd number is an integer that is not even. (a) Is 0 an even number? (b) Is -4 an even number? (c) Is -3 an odd number?

🍎 **Who Am I? Riddle** As illustrated by the example below, this activity involves using a number of propositions to logically determine an answer.

I am an even number.
I am more than 100 and less than 120.
The sum of my digits is 6.
What is the number?

Probe 2.12 continued

 20 Questions. In this popular children's game, the host picks an example from the categories animal, plant, or mineral. The contestants pose questions that can be answered yes or no. For example, "Is it an animal?" Contestants have 20 questions to guess the identity of the selected example. If the answer to a contestant's question is no, has the turn been wasted?

 Clue.® This popular children's game is published by Parker Brothers, Beverly, MA 01915. Each player is a detective who collects clues to solve a murder mystery. Solving the mystery entails identifying the perpetrator, the location of the crime (the room), and the murder weapon. For example, there are six possible murder weapons: knife, candlestick, revolver, rope, lead pipe, and wrench. If a player is dealt the cards representing the knife and candlestick and finds that his or her opponents have the revolver, rope, and lead pipe, then the murder weapon must be the wrench. In a junior version of the game, children serve as detectives trying to find a lost pet.

 Clues. This is a game in which players must decipher a mystery number from clues. The host picks a number within a prescribed range (e.g., 72 from between 1 and 100). The host then shows contestants clue cards. For example, from a card showing 2, 4, 6, 8, 10, 12..., contestants should figure out that the mystery number is even. From a card, showing 9, 18, 27, 36..., they should conclude the number is a multiple of 9. From a card showing 60, 61, 62...78, 79, 80, the students might infer that the mystery number is between 60 and 80. Does drawing a conclusion from a card (deciphering a single clue) involve the same kind of reasoning required to draw a conclusion from all the clues?

 Number-Guess Game. One child or team picks a number within a specified range of numbers. The other child or team is given a specified number of guesses. After each guess, feedback is provided: correct, smaller, or larger. For example, Abdul and Ben agreed to use the range 1 to 10 and give the guesser three chances. After guessing 8, Abdul said, "Larger." Ben then guessed 10. Abdul said "Smaller." With glee that comes with certain victory, Ben announced 9. Abdul dejectedly admitted, "Correct." (You and your students may find the following questions worth considering: Ben determined the correct answer this time, but in the long run, would starting with 8 be a good idea? Should he randomly choose the first number for each new game, or is there a more efficient strategy for maximizing his chances of winning?)

 Mastermind.®—This game—published by Pressman Toy Corporation, 200 Fifth Avenue, New York, NY 10010—can be played by two children or teams. One player or team creates an arrangement of four marbles. Each marble can be red, yellow, green, blue, white, or black. The other player or team, who cannot see the arrangement, attempts to determine the arrangement in the fewest turns possible. After setting out an arrangement, the first player or team must indicate how many correct colors were chosen and how many items are in the correct position. For example, in the game illustrated below, the feedback for the first try would be two correct colors (red and yellow), and one in the correct position (red).

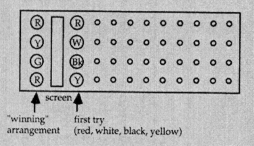

"winning" arrangement   first try (red, white, black, yellow)

Probe 2.12 continued

If the second player or team put out a black, black, white, white arrangement, the feedback would be no correct colors, and none in the correct position. Note that though incorrect, the second player or team has gained valuable information from the "mistake": The "winning" arrangement does not contain white or black marbles; it must contain at least one red marble, which may be in the first position, and at least one yellow marble, which may be in the fourth position.

Arianne's first three turns are illustrated below. Can you determine the winning arrangement from the clues shown? Why or why not? What type of reasoning is involved in trying to determine the answer?

Arrangement				*Feedback*
Bk	Y	R	G	one correct color
B	Bk	B	W	two correct colors, each in the correct positions
B	B	B	Y	no correct colors

Guess the Number. This place-value game is a variation of Mastermind. One player picks a multidigit number. The opponent tries to guess what the number is. The first player must indicate if a guessed number includes a correct digit and if the correct digit is in the correct position. For example, a player may pick 34. The opponent might guess 23. The player would announce: "One correct digit; no digits in the correct place." The opponent might then guess 31. The player would then announce: "One correct digit; one digit in the correct place." Play the game with a partner. What strategies can facilitate winning?

Discovery-Learning Activities. Assignments can be set up to make a pattern or relationship more evident. The assignment below, for example, is set up to encourage the discovery of the commutativity principle of addition: The order in which addends are added does not affect the sum.[†]

Name _____ Date _____

8.17 Math Detective

Murray was glum. His mother said he had to finish his math homework before he could play baseball. It was already 3:30 P.M., and his game was supposed to begin at 4 o'clock. Murray looked at his homework sheet again and groaned. "There's so many problems here I'll never figure them all out in time for my game. If I just guess, mom will just make me do it over again, and I'll be sure to miss the game." Murray then looked closely at the problems and smiled. "No problem! I know a trick that will let me get this work done quickly. This won't take half as long as I thought it would!"

What was Murray's trick and how did it cut in half the amount of finger-counting he would have to do? Discuss these questions with your group or class. Then try out Murray's shortcut by filling in the answers below.

2	1	1	8	7	3	4	6
+1	+2	+8	+1	+3	+7	+6	+4

5 + 4 = ____   4 + 3 = ____   2 + 6 = ____   3 + 9 = ____

4 + 5 = ____   3 + 4 = ____   6 + 2 = ____   9 + 3 = ____

[†]From *Elementary Mathematics Activities: A Teacher's Guidebook* by A. J. Baroody and M. Hank. © 1990 by Allyn and Bacon. Reprinted with permission.

➔ Probe 2.13: Evaluating Reasoning

1. Which straight line below is longer? Consider how children might respond to this question. What kind of reasoning would they probably use to draw their conclusions? Would their conclusions be correct?

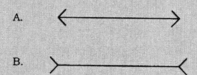

2. Can you guess the rule used to choose the following numbers: 3, 5, 7? What kind of reasoning was involved in drawing a conclusion from these examples? How sure can you be about your conclusion?

3. Consider the following arguments. Is each valid? Is the conclusion of each true?

   Argument I: Teachers are grossly overpaid. (Premise 1)
                  Winnie is a teacher. (Premise 2)
                  Winnie is grossly overpaid. (Conclusion)

   Argument II: Teachers are slaves. (Premise 1)
                  Slaves are underpaid. (Premise 2)
                  Teachers are underpaid. (Conclusion)

4. Evaluate each of the arguments a to d in Items I and II below. Indicate whether each conclusion is true, false, or whether there is not enough information to tell.

𝙸 I. The premise for each of the following arguments is: If George makes his sister cry, then he is sent to his room.

   a. George did not make his sister cry, so he was not sent to his room.
   b. George made his sister cry, so he was sent to his room.
   c. George was sent to his room, so he must have made his sister cry.
   d. George was not sent to his room, so he did not make his sister cry.

𝙸 II. A rhombus is an equilateral (equal-sided) parallelogram. The premise for each of the following questions is: All rhombuses have equal sides.

   a. Figure A has equal sides; therefore, it is a rhombus.
   b. Figure B does not have equal sides; therefore, it cannot be a rhombus.
   c. Figure C is a rhombus; therefore, all the sides of Figure C must be equal.
   d. Figure D is not a rhombus; therefore, all the sides of Figure D must not be equal.

5. The theorem below is commonly taught in plane geometry. Is it true in all possible situations?

   Theorem: The shortest distance between two points is a straight line.

CHILDREN'S NATURAL STRENGTHS AND WEAKNESSES

This subunit describes Piagetian research, which underscored the limitations of children's reasoning ability. It notes that children are not as illogical as they are sometimes portrayed or seem. It goes on to discuss why children may have difficulty with deductive-reasoning tasks and describe some problems they have with reasoning in general.

Piagetian Research

The psychologist Jean Piaget believed that with age, children's ability to reason logically changed dramatically. More specifically, he suggested (e.g., Inhelder & Piaget, 1964) that school-age children go through three stages of development, each marked by distinctly different ways of reasoning. Children younger than about 7 years of age (the "age of reason") were thought to be in a preoperational stage of thinking and, thus, incapable of thinking logically (deductively). Many parents and teachers of young children might be inclined to agree with this characterization. Young children can appear to be astoundingly unreasonable and illogical to adults at times.

According to Piaget, children in the concrete-operational stage (approximately 6 to 12 years of age), are capable of limited or elementary logical reasoning. He presumed they could reason about the concrete (objects or things they had experienced), but not about propositions (abstract verbal statements or ideas). Moreover, he found that such children could not systematically consider all the logical possibilities of a problem. According to Piaget, the capacity to think hypothetically (abstractly) and systematically about all logical possibilities is not possible until children have achieved the formal-operational stage of thinking at about the age of 12.

☞ Try Probe 2.14 (page 2-78) before reading on.

Ordering. To support his model, Piaget pointed out that children younger than about 7 years old had difficulty with tasks that required putting something in order. He took this as evidence that children could not reason logically about relationships. For example, Piaget found that young children were incapable of transitive reasoning: deducing a logical conclusion from several related premises called a "conditional chain." (Probe 2.14 illustrates a transitive-reasoning task.) A simple transitive-reasoning task would be as follows: If Stick A is larger than B and Stick B is larger than C, which is larger, Stick A or C? Although older ("operational"), children—those inferred to be in the concrete-operational stage—could reason that A had to be larger than C, young ("preoperational") children could not consistently answer such questions successfully. Piaget concluded that young children lacked the mental facility to apply their knowledge about the relationships between Sticks A and B and Sticks B and C to determine the relationship between Sticks A and C.

Classifying. Piaget also concluded that young children lacked the logical ability to sort (classify) things into groups (classes) systematically. Asked to sort blocks with different attributes into groups (see Box 2.14 on page 2-74), a preoperational child might make a "graphic collection" (e.g., make a "house" by placing a triangle on a square), use an idiosyncratic criterion (e.g., "I like them all mixed up because it's pretty"), or switch criteria in midstream (e.g., begin sorting by color and switch to sorting by shape). A concrete-operational child, on the other hand, can sort according to a criterion: a systematic rule or set of rules. When asked to sort the objects in a different way, such a child could also consider a new criterion and resort the objects. Unlike a child in the formal-operational stage, however, a concrete-operational child might not be able to consider all the possibilities.

Piaget concluded, moreover, that preoperational children cannot grasp the hierarchical nature of classification, the notion that a set (class) is the sum of its subsets (subclasses) and is larger than any one subset (subclass). As evidence, he noted that young children have difficulty with class-inclusion tasks. Such a task might entail showing a child three daisies and two violets and asking, "Are there more daises or more *flowers*?" Piaget found that younger children typically picked daisies (the subclass), not flowers (the class).

Children's Hidden Strengths

Research suggests that Piaget underestimated children's logical abilities. For example, it appears that many children before the age of 7 fail transitive-reasoning tasks because they do not remember the given relationships. If children cannot remember if Stick A is bigger or smaller than Stick B, knowing

Box 2.14: A Sorting (Classifying) Task Using Attribute Blocks

Attribute blocks in a set of 60 blocks have four attributes: size (small or large), shape (triangle, square, hexagon, or circle), color (red, yellow, or blue) and thickness (thick or thin). Note that the large, thin, blue (B) triangle can differ from other attribute blocks by a single attribute such as size, two attributes such as size and shape, three attributes such as size, shape, and color, or all four attributes.

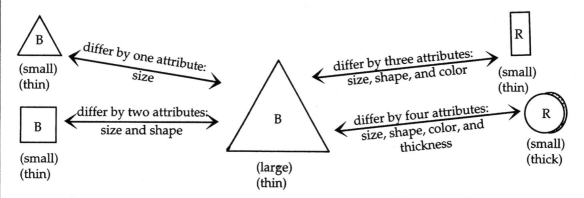

Sorting Task: Give a child a set of attribute blocks and ask, "What blocks belong together? Show me." A partial solution is illustrated below:

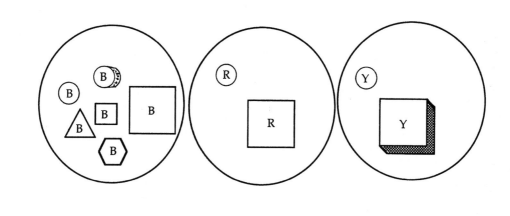

that Stick B is bigger than Stick C will not help them to determine the relationship between Sticks A and C. When young children were helped to remember the premises (original relationships), they were successful in the transitive-reasoning task (Bryant & Trabasso, 1971). Even kindergartners, then, appear to be capable of an important form of deductive logic.

Observations in natural settings also indicate that children younger than 7 can make deductive inferences before they can do so about unfamiliar, contrived situations. Consider the example of a 5-year-old described by Donaldson (1978). Three months after her school was visited by a research worker named Mr. (Robin) Campbell and four week after hearing a news report of the death of Mr.

(Donald) Campbell, who was trying to break the world water speed record, the child inquired if Mr. (Robin) Campbell were dead. Told no, the child concluded, "Well, there must be two Mr. Campbells then, because Mr. [Donald] Campbell's dead" (p. 83).

Moreover, contrary to Piaget's view, preadolescents may be capable of engaging in relatively abstract (propositional or hypothetical) reasoning, such as reasoning from a premise they know to be untrue. Consider the case of Alison, age $9\frac{1}{2}$. After reading a story about a colonial girl, she asked her father, "What's a colonist?"

Her father answered, "A colony is a place owned and settled by another country. Colonists are the people from this other land who settle the place."

Alison rejoined, "Oh, so if Germany owned the [Colonies]—I know that's *not* true—then [the characters in the book] would have been German colonists."

In brief, it is not clear that school-age children actually go through three qualitatively different stages of logical thinking or that preadolescents' reasoning ability is severely constrained (e.g., Ennis, 1975). How well elementary children can reason may depend largely on what learning opportunities they have and the difficulty of the task.

Factors Affecting the Difficulty of Deductive-Reasoning Tasks

Three factors can affect the difficulty of a deductive-reasoning task: (a) the logical principle involved, (b) the content of the problem, and (c) the complexity of the problem.

Difficulty Varies with Principle. In general, children perform better on logic tasks that involve valid arguments (Argument Types 1 and 2 in Table 2.2 on page 2-63) than those which involve invalid arguments (Argument Types 3 and 4) (Sutton & Ennis, 1985). Tasks involving valid arguments, however, are not equally easy for children. While children gradually improve on tasks involving detachment (Argument Type 1) without the benefit of deliberate logic instruction, little spontaneous improvement is seen on tasks involving contraposition (Argument Type 2) after third grade (Sutton & Ennis, 1985).

The recent Fourth NAEP testing further confirmed these two observations. Sixty-two percent of the third and the seventh graders correctly responded to Problem 2.33 below by concluding, "Tom is not on the team." This involved making a valid (Type 2 or contrapositive) argument. In contrast, only 13% of the third graders and 38% of the seventh graders responded correctly to Problem 2.34 by concluding, "There is not enough information to tell if Jane is on the team." (Even if Jane is tall, it does not guarantee that she is on the team. Perhaps she is uncoordinated or lacks interest in the sport.) Over half of the third and seventh graders made the invalid (Type 3 or converse) claim that "Jane is on the team." Note that seventh graders did no better than third graders on Problem 2.33, requiring valid reasoning.

■ **Problem 2.33: The Short of It.** Everyone on the team is tall. If Tom is short, then...?

■ **Problem 2.34: The Tall of It.** Everyone on the team is tall. If Jane is tall, then...?

Difficulty Varies with Content. Research indicates that reasoning ability is highly content-dependent (e.g., Evans, 1982). Children (and adults) typically reason more effectively about things they are familiar with and understand than those they are unfamiliar with or do not understand (see Box 2.15 on the next page). Put differently, we're all inclined to give illogical explanations about things that we are ill-informed about. Consider, for example, giving a child a coherent explanation of how a television works. A child (or an adult) may reason in a perfectly logical fashion in one domain but in an utterly illogical fashion in another. As they gain more understanding about a domain, their reasoning about the domain may improve dramatically—may move to a qualitatively different level. The key implication of this is that a teacher should not have children practice new reasoning skills or evaluate their reasoning with unfamiliar topics.

Difficulty Varies with Complexity. One factor affecting the complexity of a problem is the number of conditions or constraints. Problem 2.35 below has two constraints: the number of coins found, and the total value of the coins. Increasing the number of constraints in a problem increases its difficulty (LeBlanc et al., 1980). Consider how much easier it would be to come up with an answer if Problem 2.35 did not specify the number of coins found.

Box 2.15: Different Contexts, Different Performance

On the Fourth NAEP, only 55% of the eleventh graders were correct on the following transitivity problem set in an abstract mathematical context, while nearly 90% were successful on a transitivity problem involving age or an "older-than" relationship (Silver & Carpenter, 1989).

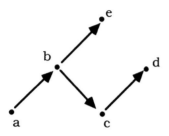

The letters in the diagram above represent numbers. If x → y means x > y, which of the following is NOT necessarily true?

$$b > d$$
$$e > d$$
$$a > d$$
$$a > c$$

■ **Problem 2.35: Found Money.** Aggie found an envelope with 11 coins in it worth $1.25. What coins and how many of each type did Aggie find?

Some Difficulties and Barriers

Whatever their strengths, children (and adults) often fall victim to common reasoning pitfalls or hold unhelpful beliefs. Some of these are noted below.

Generalizing from a Small Sample. Children often draw a general conclusion from a single example or a few examples. Not infrequently, adults fall into the same trap. How many times have you heard something like, "Gross, someone from Gamma Rho Omega Sigma asked you out? I went out with Fred Fern from Gamma Rho, and he was a real jerk. You don't want to go out with anyone from Gamma Rho. Call this guy back and tell him you have a terminal case of jerkaphobia." (Note that such rea-

soning can be a basis for prejudging—either overestimating or underestimating—a whole class of people.)

Not Appreciating the Value of Errors. In a remarkable book, *How Children Fail*, John Holt (1964) noted that children do not understand that an incorrect answer can be as valuable as a correct answer. For example, in playing 20 Questions, he—like Miss Brill below—found that children routinely were disappointed if the feedback to their question was, "No."

Anton: "Is it a person?"

Miss Brill: "No."

Anton (sadly): "Rats."

Even though he had eliminated a whole category of things (people) from further consideration, Anton was dejected, *because he was wrong*.

Dismissing a Constraint. Many children are baffled by problems involving multiple constraints and often simply disregard one or more of the constraints. Less than a third of the third graders and less than half of the seventh graders were able to correctly determine the answer to Problem 2.36, below, a problem on the Fourth NAEP. The most common error was to ignore the second constraint (the blue car is next to the red or first car) and select blue as the last car.

■ **Problem 2.36: Cars in a Line.** Four cars were in a single line at a traffic light. The red car is first in line. The blue car is next to the red. The green car is between the white car and the blue car. Which color car is at the end of the line?

Adding Unwarranted Constraints. The opposite of overlooking a constraint specified by a problem is reading into the problem constraints that are not there. Children and even adults commonly make assumptions about problems that are misleading, and so reduce their flexibility in solving a problem. Recall that a common stumbling block to solving the problems in Probe 2.4 (Problems with a Twist on page 2-29) involved making unwarranted assumptions (imposing constraints not specified by the problem). Consider Example 2.6 and Problem 2.37 on the next page:

Example 2.6: A Number Riddle. If you add my digits, you get 9. My tens digit is more than my ones digit. What number am I?

    a.   45
    b.   62
    c.   342
    d.   none of the above

■ **Problem 2.37: Cake Cuts.** What is the largest number of pieces that can be obtained by cutting a cake with 4 straight lines?

For Example 2.6, some students assume that because the riddle mentioned only the ones and tens digits, the answer should be a two-digit number. This would lead them to discount choice c and answer with choice d. In fact, the question does not place a constraint on the number of digits. Similarly, many students read into Problem 2.37 the unspecified constraint that all four cuts must go through the center of the cake and answer, "Eight." Consider how many pieces can be obtained if this unwarranted assumption is not made.

Confusing If with Only If. With if-then statements, children often misinterpret *if* as meaning *if and only if* (Donaldson, 1978; Shapiro & O'Brien, 1970). Consider following the proposition: "If you pull the cat's tail, then it will scratch you." Many children—rather dangerously—interpret such as a warning as, "Kittycat will scratch if and only if I pull its tail." Of course, there are many other reasons why a cat might scratch a child (e.g., poking a finger in kitty's eye might well prompt feline retribution).*

Confusing *if* with *only if* helps explain why converse arguments (Type 3 arguments in Table 2.2 on page 2-63) are relatively difficult for children to evaluate. For example, they interpret "*If* it rains, then the ground will be wet" as "*If and only if* it rains, then the ground will be wet." As a result, the converse ("The ground was wet, therefore it rained") makes perfect sense to them.

———

'In technical terms, children interpret the if statement of an if-then proposition as a necessary and sufficient condition for the then statement, not merely as a sufficient condition. That is, they interpret the if portion as the *only* condition to produce the then portion.

➤ Probe 2.14: A Complicated Love "Octagon"

Geraldo was the heartthrob of the sixth-grade girls of Minutiae Middle School. Bonita, who had hung out with Geraldo since kindergarten, wanted to clarify her position in his love life. She asked Geraldo point blank which girl he cared for the most.

Geraldo replied, "I care for you very much."

Sensing a smoke screen, Bonita pressed Geraldo for specifics, "Do you care for me more than Junice?"

To which Geraldo replied with a broad smile, "Most definitely."

At that moment Mercedes happened to walk by and caught the drift of the conversation. "What's this about caring for other women?" she demanded. "Just where do I stand with you, Mr. Romance?"

To prevent a violent attack, Geraldo said soothingly, "Mercedes, Mercedes, I much prefer your company to Loni whom I dearly care for."

Still not satisfied, Mercedes pressed on with, "Why did you ask Junice instead of me to go to the fun-fair with you last Saturday?" When Geraldo stopped for a brief moment to think, Mercedes had her answer. "So you also like Junice more than me, and after. . .after all that I've done for you," she sputtered. Spotting the approach of the principal, Mercedes lowered her 10 long razor-sharp fingernails. Summoning her dignity, Mercedes trooped off in a huff, never again to speak to Mr. Romance.

Almost satisfied, Bonita asked, "Do you like Gabrielle and Sara better than me?"

Temporizing, Geraldo said, "I like Gabrielle a little bit more than Sara."

Just then, Loni stormed up the hall exclaiming, "Mercedes said you like someone better than me." In an inspired effort at damage control, Geraldo proclaimed, "What would a big-mouth like Mercedes know anyway? Surely I care for you more than I care for Azure."

No sooner had he bought a moment of peace, when Sara walked down the hall. Geraldo interrupted Bonita's next question and quickly excused himself. Falling over himself, he engaged Sara in conversation.

"So, he likes Sara more than me. I guess that pretty much tells me where I stand," sighed Bonita. "I don't see any point in playing second fiddle. I'm dumping this creep."

1. Whom did Geraldo like more, Bonita or Mercedes?
2. Did he like Bonita more or less than Loni?
3. Which girl was at the top of Geraldo's hit parade?
4. Where did Bonita stand in relationship to Geraldo's top choice? Was she really a second fiddle, a third fiddle, or what?
5. Where did Azure stand in Geraldo's affections?

REASONING INSTRUCTION

This subunit discusses the part reasoning instruction should play in the elementary curriculum and how instruction can meaningfully introduce sorting and classifying, exploring patterns, deductive reasoning, and evaluating logic.

The Role of Reasoning and Conjecturing

What types of reasoning should instruction foster at the primary and intermediate level? What should elementary students understand about the roles of intuitive, inductive, and deductive reasoning in mathematics?

In the Elementary Curriculum. Schoolchildren of all ages are capable of using intuitive and inductive reasoning and of making conjectures. Moreover, even primary-age children are capable of making simple deductions such as using if-then reasoning to eliminate cases. Elementary schoolchildren can also at least begin to evaluate the logic of others.

✐ **Children need ample and regular opportunities to practice using reasoning skills and making conjectures.** As noted earlier in this chapter, children should learn the processes of mathematics as well as its products, and this should include using reasoning of all kinds and conjecture-making. Actual experiences in looking for patterns (inductive reasoning), formulating conjectures about these patterns, evaluating the conjectures by logical (deductive) reasoning, and collecting more information, helps children better understand both the processes involved in doing mathematics and the exploratory side of mathematics (Silver et al., 1990). "When students are given the opportunity [to engage in intuitive, inductive, and deductive reasoning and] to make mathematical conjectures, they come in contact with mathematics in the making, with mathematics as it is practiced" (Silver et al., 1990, p. 12). Furthermore, such process skills are especially important to foster in this day and age when creative problem solving is increasingly becoming essential in the workplace.

✐ **Encourage educated guessing.** A fear of being wrong also makes children afraid to make educated guesses (propose conjectures) in class (Silver et al., 1990). Students of all ages fear exposing their ignorance or confusion. This fear is often compounded by their previous experience with

mathematics, a subject where you are either correct and therefore smart, or incorrect and therefore dumb. It is essential to create a class environment where children are not afraid to be wrong.

Teachers often discourage or even ridicule guessing (e.g., "You're just guessing"). Although thoughtless and groundless guessing is not desirable, care needs to be taken not to discourage educated guessing: a guess based on the information at hand, however uncertain or incomplete. A teacher needs to help children see that incorrect answers are a part of the process of learning and that making educated guesses or conjectures is important:

> "Students need to know that it is only by making a good guess, probing and improving it, and supporting it with evidence, that anyone can do mathematics at all. Anything else is just memorizing. Mathematics in the making requires a willingness to take risks by offering a guess" (Silver et al., 1990, p. 12).

✐ **Help children understand the value of negative feedback in deducing an answer.** Children need to understand that incorrect guesses can eliminate certain possibilities from further consideration and, thus, provide invaluable information. They also need to appreciate that the effectiveness of a guess depends on how many possibilities it eliminates. For example, in playing 20 Questions, it is better to begin by asking about general categories.

In Mathematics. Children should understand that intuitive reasoning, inductive reasoning, and conjecturing, as well as logical proofs (deductive reasoning) play a vital role in mathematics.

✐ **Underscore the importance of intuitive thought and why and how it should be checked.** Children need to understand that intuitive thought plays an important role in problem-solving efforts. They should be made aware that intuitions have been the basis of many advances in mathematics, science, and other fields. Children should also be helped to understand that an intuition needs to be substantiated by, for example, collecting data or using deductive logic.

✐ **Underscore the importance of inductive reasoning and why and how it should be checked.** Children need to understand that the search for patterns, regularities, relationship, and order is the heart of mathematics. They need to understand that a mathematical rule must apply across all examples. Thus, before a discovery can be considered a rule, it must be tested against a wide range of problems, situations, or examples. If it does not survive the test, then its limits or exceptions need to be defined, or the discovery cannot be considered a rule.

Moreover, children need to recognize that even if a pattern holds up over a wide range of examples, there is always the possibility of finding an exception (see Box 2.16). Thus, patterns must be justified by more certain means, such as by deductive reasoning.

Sorting and Classifying

Children should be introduced to *concrete* sorting and classifying activities from the time they begin school.

🖉 **Concretely foster the language of logic.** The development of logical reasoning is closely linked to children's understanding of certain important words such as *all, some, not, and, or,* and *if.* Concrete sorting and classifying activities can be invaluable in helping children to construct an understanding of such terms and, thus, further their reasoning ability (see Activity File 2.2 on the next page).

🖉 **Exploit opportunities where concrete sorting and classifying serve a real purpose.** Ideally, many sorting and classifying activities would grow out of a real need for such activities. There are numerous everyday situations that require sorting and classifying. A teacher might, for example, ask students to sort toys, games, and other classroom materials into usable or not usable (e.g., broken, missing a key part, torn, and so forth), or to sort a bin of crayons into boxes by color or sets of needed colors. The study of other content areas also presents many opportunities to practice sorting and classifying concretely and purposefully (see Activity File 2.3.)

🖉 **Use Venn diagrams to foster classification skill and reasoning ability.** By the time children enter school, they have had numerous informal classification experiences. Nevertheless, children need to master such formal classification skills as knowing systematic and explicit ways of categorizing things. Venn diagrams—used in conjunction with real objects or attribute blocks—are useful for this purpose (see Activity 2.2).

Box 2.16: Encouraging Children to Evaluate Additional Examples

Mr. Adams introduced his third-grade class to the game Poison (see Problem 10 of Probe 2.7 on page 2-52) and challenged them to find a winning strategy. He encouraged them to work with relatively simple cases (small numbers of items), and to make a table and look for a pattern:

Number of items	1	2	3	4	5	6	7	8
Player who wins			1	2	1			

Several groups concluded that if there were an even number of items, then a player should choose to go second; if there were an odd number of items, then a player should choose to go first. Instead of indicating that this observation was right or wrong, Mr. Adams asked, "Who do you think will win if there are six items?" The students predicted that the second player should win. Mr. Adams then encouraged them to check out their prediction and systematically examine larger and larger cases.

Questions for Reflection

☝ 1. Was the students' prediction about six items correct or not?

☝ 2. What lessons about inductive reasoning was Mr. Adams trying to help his students appreciate by prompting them to make a prediction and check it?

☝ 3. Below is Tara's description of the pattern her group found. Is this pattern entirely correct?

Number Pattern Tara

The number pattern that we got is 2 1 1 2 1 1 2 1 1 2, from one to ten. 1 you want to be first, 2 you want to be second and so on. I figured it out with some wonderful friends.

☝ 4. For a 20-item game, should you choose to go first or second? To win, how many items should you leave your opponent on each turn?

Activity File 2.2: Classifying Our Class†

◆ Sorting & Classifying ◆ K-4 ◆ Whole group

Ask the class, "How could we split the class up into two groups?" Students may offer various criteria such as girls or boys, left-handed or right-handed, and tall or short. The last example leads naturally to a discussion of "What is tall?" and underscores the importance of defining a criterion clearly.

Some students may suggest criteria such as wearing green or *not* wearing green, wearing glasses or *not* wearing glasses, 9-years-old or *not* 9-years-old. Note that criteria such as girls or boys can also be expressed in the same manner: girls or *not* girls. In formal terms, *not* indicates the *negation* of a characteristic.

Have the class sort themselves according to one criterion. For example, have the girls stand and go to one side of the room, and have the boys stand and go to the other side. Note that *all* the children are either girls *or* boys, that *some* children are girls and the rest are boys, and that *none* of the children remain in their seats. Ask whether *all* who are *not* girls are boys. This demonstrates that in the case of a characteristic and its negation, every element (child) in a set (the class) must necessarily be in one subset (girl) or the other (boy). It also concretely demonstrates that a set is the sum of its subsets.

Have the class consider other criteria. Do two mutually exclusive characteristics always completely partition a set or class? Consider the following criteria: Youngest in the family or oldest in the family; has brown hair or blond hair; and walked to school this morning or rode the bus to school this morning. Have the class consider, for example, whether all children who did not walk to school this morning rode the bus.

Are two characteristics always mutually exclusive? Consider the following criteria: Have a cat or have a dog; have a brother or have a sister; walk to school or take the bus. Does having a cat necessarily mean a child does not have a dog?

Note how important precise wording is when considering a criterion. Consider the difference between walk to school and walked to school this morning. In the first case, a child might use some other form of transportation on some days. Walking to school would not necessarily exclude other forms of transportation. In contrast, walking to school on a given day probably would exclude using other forms of transportation.

†Based on a lesson in the Nuffield Mathematics Project described in *Logic*, © 1972 and published for the Nuffield Foundation in the U.S. by John Wiley and Sons, New York.

Activity File 2.3: Integrated Categorizing Lessons

◆ Sorting & Classifying ◆ K-8 ◆ Any number

There are numerous opportunities in other content areas to sort and classify. In science, students might sort things into two categories, such as things that roll or don't roll, magnetic or non-magnetic things, things that float or sink, or high (> 3 grams) cholesterol foods or low cholesterol foods. Examples with three or more categories include classifying rocks as igneous, sedimentary, or metamorphic, and sorting foods into food groups. In language arts, students could sort characters into heroes and villains; words into nouns and verbs; or grammatical examples into those requiring a comma, those where a comma is optional, and those where a comma is not required.

☞ Try Activity 2.2 (pages 2-90 and 2-91) now.

Initially, a teacher may wish to have young children use (colored) strings to form Venn diagrams. With guidance, primary children typically have no difficulty drawing Venn diagrams on construction paper (see Activity File 2.4 on the next page). Activity File 2.5 on page 2-83 describes a game that can be used to practice interpreting Venn diagrams.

☀ Activity File 2.4: Diagramming Our Class

◆ Using Venn diagrams to classify and reason ◆ K-6 ◆ Whole Class

After children have been introduced to the various ways Venn diagrams can be used (see Activity 2.2 on pages 2-90 and 2-91), they can be challenged to create their own diagrams. "Diagramming Our Class" is essentially "Classifying Our Class (Activity File 2.2 on page 2-81) using a Venn diagram. A teacher could note or ask for various criteria on a chalkboard: age (e.g., over 8, over 9, over 10), illnesses (e.g., had chicken pox or not), pets (cats, dogs, other), siblings (brother, sister), and so forth. With primary-age children, particularly, it can be helpful to discuss how to set up each Venn diagram, including how many loops are necessary and whether or not the loops interlock or are concentric.

The teacher can then ask which teams would like to do what diagrams. After the various diagrams have been apportioned, each team can set about drawing a Venn diagram on construction paper and then canvassing the class to see where each class member fits into the diagram. Afterward, the teams can embellish their diagrams with color (e.g., the sister loop can be colored in with yellow magic marker, the brother loop, with blue—resulting in a green intersection). Each team could also summarize their findings to the class. The diagrams then could be hung up as a display: "Our Class." This would be ideal before a Parents' Visitation Night. Diagrams from a second and a third grade[5] class are shown below:

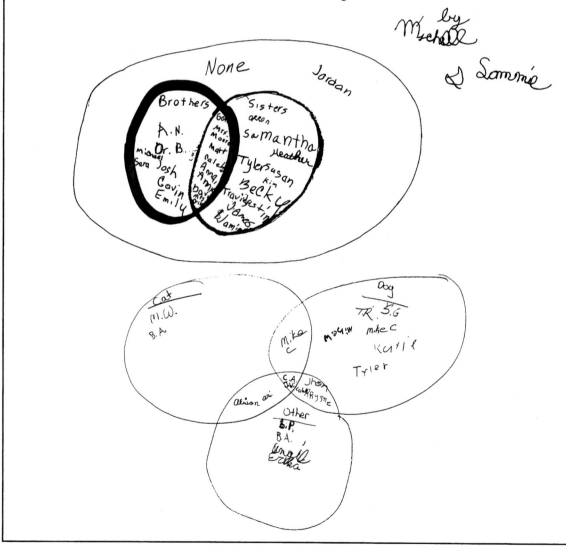

Activity File 2.5: Where Do I Go?

◆ Classifying and Sorting
◆ K-3 ◆ Two or more teams of 1 to 5

This game provides practice in interpreting Venn diagrams. Each team needs a set of Attribute Blocks, a copy of a Venn diagram with each section of the diagram labeled with a letter, and letter placards. The diagram shown below, for example, can be used with children as young as second grade. With younger children, a teacher may wish to use simpler diagrams.

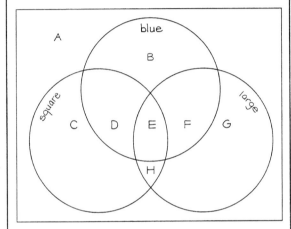

The teacher or other game host selects and shows an attribute block (e.g., a large red square). Each team decides where the block should be placed in the diagram. After reaching a consensus, the team then selects the appropriate letter placard. When the game host calls for a vote, a team member holds up the placard of the letter chosen by the team. The host can record each vote next to the team's name on the chalkboard. Discrepancies can be discussed and answers justified. After the correct answer is determined, teams with the correct answer are awarded a point.

Patterns

Children should work with patterns throughout the elementary years. As a rule, instruction should begin with concrete patterns and gradually introduce more abstract patterns.

✐ **Help children to see a wide variety of patterns.** Children should appreciate that they are surrounded by patterns of all types. There are regularities in events (e.g., the class eats lunch at 12:15 P.M. every day), everyday things (e.g., designs in wall paper, rugs, or quilts), space (e.g., things "grow" smaller with distance), and numbers (e.g., four groups of three and three groups of four both make twelve). Visual patterns are a good place to begin with primary children. Auditory patterns (e.g., rhythmic beats or music) and motion patterns (e.g., stand, squat, sit patterns) are also appropriate for young children. Number and arithmetic patterns can be introduced in time.

✐ **Children should be encouraged to copy, find (analyze, recognize, extend, describe), and create patterns.** Young children can be introduced to copying, finding, and creating patterns, in that order (DeGuire, 1987). Copying a pattern is a relatively simple task and could be done in the context of an art or a crafts project (see Activity File 2.6). Identifying or finding a pattern actually requires a child to analyze and recognize a pattern and, thus, is more demanding than simply copying a pattern. To ensure that children have, in fact, identified a pattern, they can be asked to extend or describe it. Finding patterns can be practiced by a wide variety of activities and games (see Probe 2.12, pages 2-68 to 2-71). Pattern Prediction (see Activity File 2.7), for instance, entails discerning a pattern to determine what comes next. Creating their own patterns can be a big step for some children and may require encouragement.

Activity File 2.6: Replicating Patterns for an Art or Crafts Project

◆ Copying patterns ◆ K-8 ◆ Any number

Young, primary-age children can replicate relatively simple patterns to make necklaces or decorations (see illustration below). Older children can be challenged to replicate more complicated and intricate designs.

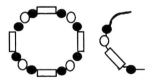

🍎 Activity File 2.7: Pattern Prediction

◆ Analyzing, recognizing, and extending patterns ◆ K-8 ◆ Any number

The object of Pattern Prediction is to predict what comes next. The answers can be placed on the back of cards to facilitate individual or small-group play.

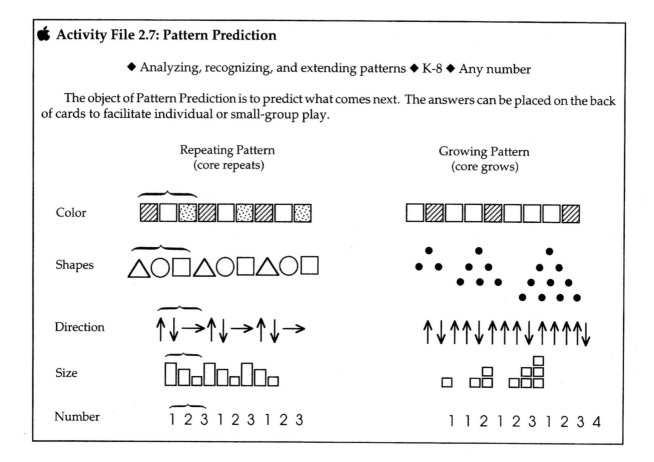

To help children find patterns, encourage them to identify the "core" pattern. There are basically two types of patterns: (a) repetitive or repeating patterns and (b) sequential or growing patterns. As the diagram in Activity File 2.7 illustrates, *"repeating patterns" consist of a repeating core,* whereas *"growing patterns" have a core that grows.* To avoid ambiguity, complete rather than partial cores are used in the examples. Moreover, in repeating patterns, a core should be repeated at least three times to provide a good example of a pattern. Identifying simple repeating patterns can be introduced in kindergarten. Although some growing patterns are readily recognizable (e.g., a staircase pattern of one interlocking block, two interlocking blocks, three interlocking blocks, and so forth), such patterns are generally more difficult for children to discern than are repeating patterns. As a rule, then, growing patterns should be introduced later than repeating patterns.

Particularly at first, pattern activities involving physical materials are preferable to pattern activities in workbooks. Work with physical materials more readily lends itself to a trial-and-error approach. Moreover, some children greatly enjoy continuing a repeating pattern at length—something more easily done with manipulatives than on a workbook page.

☞ Try Activity 2.3 (pages 2-92 to 2-94) and then continue with the text.

Labeling patterns can help children find repeating patterns and discover commonalities among such patterns. As Part I of Activity 2.3 illustrates, using letters can help students analyze and identify patterns. Moreover, coding patterns with letters gives children a convenient way of explicitly describing patterns. As Part II of Activity 2.3 illustrates, such letter codes can help children see that patterns constructed of different materials can share the same structure. Understanding that a pattern can be embodied in various, even different-looking ways represents an important advance in children's mathematical thinking. There comes a dawning recognition that mathematics is a search for *underlying structure* that transcends appearances.

✐ **Elementary-age children should be encouraged to relate physically or pictorially represented growing patterns to numerical patterns and to make predictions based on numerical patterns.** Helping children to translate physical or pictorial patterns into numerical patterns is an important step in their mathematical thinking. Not only does it help children to see connections between more concrete and symbolic representations, it more readily allows them to extend patterns and to make predictions. See, for example, Box 2.6 on page 2-22 and Part III of Activity 2.3 on page 2-93.

✐ **Older children should be encouraged to summarize growing patterns as a general formula.** A table summarizing a pattern can be used to make predictions either in an informal or in a formal way. To illustrate, consider again the problem of determining how many handshakes a class of 24 will make (Problem 2.15). The data for the simplest cases are summarized in the table below:

number in the class	2	3	4	5
number of handshakes	1	3	6	10

Elementary students will naturally be inclined to use the relatively apparent relationship among the number of handshakes:

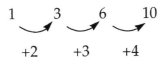

By using this relationship, they can extend the table and informally solve the problem.

Older students need to understand, though, that there is another formal and more powerful way to use a table to make predictions: determine the relationship (rule) *between* the two sets of numbers in a table.

☞ Before reading on, try to decipher the rule for transforming the number in a class to the number of handshakes in the table above.

In the Handshake Problem, for instance, the rule for transforming the number in a class into the number of handshakes is as follows: Multiply the number of people (n) by n - 1 and divide by 2 (e.g., for 5 people: $[5 \cdot 4] \div 2 = 10$). Although deciphering a relationship in the formal manner is frequently more difficult

than doing so in the informal manner, the necessity for discovering a general rule can be established by asking students to predict very large cases (see, e.g., Part IV of Activity 2.3 on page 2-93). For instance, after students have determined the number of handshakes for a class of 24 students, ask them what it would be for a class of 240, or a class of 2,400 students.

Deductive Reasoning

Even primary-age children can be encouraged to engage in activities and problems that involve deductive reasoning.

✐ **Encourage children to represent reasoning problems using their own concrete or pictorial models.** Creating an informal representation may help some children solve reasoning problems (see Box 2.17 on page 2-86). Although some elementary-age children can mentally determine the answers to such problems, a concrete or pictorial representation is a useful way of justifying their answer to others.

✐ **Encourage children to solve problems by the process of elimination.** Probe 2.12 on pages 2-68 to 2-71 lists a number of games and activities that entail using the process of elimination: Who Am I? Riddles, 20 Questions, Clue, Clues, Number-Guess, Mastermind, and Guess the Number. Children need to learn that they should try to eliminate as many possibilities as quickly as possible. For example, when playing 20 Questions, primary-age children frequently advance very specific questions such as, "Is the answer Mickey Mouse?" or "Is it someone in this room?". Unfortunately, such questions eliminate only one or a few of the infinite possibilities. Children should be encouraged to begin with general questions, then proceed to more and more specific questions. For instance, "Is it an animal?" is a good first question because, whether the answer is yes *or* no, a huge number of possibilities are eliminated from further consideration.

Problems can also provide opportunities to reason by the process of elimination. Consider, for instance, the Tom-Dick-and-Harry Problem described earlier in Probe 2.12 on page 2-68, or Brandi's solution to the transitive reasoning (The Richest Child) problem described in Box 2.17 on the next page.

☞ Try tackling the problems in Probe 2.15 (page 2-95) before reading on.

Box 2.17: Informal Representations of a Deductive-Reasoning Problem

Third graders[6] were presented the transitivity problem below:

- **The Richest Child**: Ty has more money than Guy. Ni has more money than Di. Di has more money than Ty. Can you tell (a) who has the most money and (b) who has the least money?

Sam devised the following pictorial representation. Initially, he put two dollars under Ni and one under Di to show that Ni had more than Di. After reading that Di had more money than Ty, he adjusted his diagram by adding two dollars to Di's column and three more dollars to Ni's column.

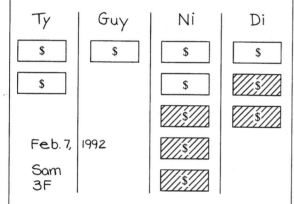

Brandi drew and labeled four circles to represent each child. She then crossed out Guy's circle (because Ty had more than Guy) and Di's circle (because Ni had more than Di). She then proceeded to cross out Ty (because Di had more than Ty), leaving Ni (the person with the most money). To figure out who had the least money, Brandi reversed the process. For example, she crossed out Ty because he had more than Guy.

Brandi
Perry
3G Feb. 7, 1992

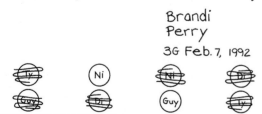

✏ **Help students see that Venn diagrams can be an aid in solving problems.** Encourage students to solve problems like Problems 2.38 and 2.39 in any way they wish. Such problems may well seem overwhelming and unsolvable to them.

- **Problem 2.38: An Unhealthy Cookout.** Mr. Stanley left his scouts with the instructions to plan a nutritious dinner for their campout. When he got back, he discovered that his scouts had a peculiar understanding of nutrition: 18 had voted to have candy bars as the main course and 12 had voted for potato chips. There were only 24 boys in the troop, so apparently some health-nuts had voted for both candy bars and potato chips. How many had done so?

- **Problem 2.39: Election Confusion.** A ballot for faculty representative listed three names, Ms. Rose, Mr. Stuben, and Mrs. Trykowski, and the instructions: "Vote for no more than two candidates." Ms. R got a total of 19 votes; Mr. S, a total of 22; and Mrs. T, a total of 27. One faculty member voted for Ms. R only, two voted for Mr. S only, and 3 voted for Mrs. T only. Six faculty members voted for both Ms. R and Mr. S, 10 voted for both Ms. R and Mrs. T, and 12 voted for both Mr. S and Mrs. T. How many faculty members did not read the ballot instructions carefully and voted for all three candidates? If there are 42 teachers on the faculty, how many did not vote?

Encourage students who experience blockage to represent the problems with Venn diagrams. For Problem 2.38 above, such a diagram can help make clear the number of boys who voted for both snacks (B):

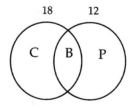

C = scouts voting for candy
B = scouts voting for both candy and potato chips
P = scouts voting for potato chips

C + B + P must equal 24. C + B must equal 18, and B + P must equal 12. Pre-algebra students can solve the problem by trial and error. For example, if C is arbitrarily assigned the value of 8, then B must be 18 − 8 or 10. If B is 10, then P must be 12 − 10 or 2. However, 8 + 10 + 2 = 20, not 24. Therefore, C must have some value between 0 and 18 other than 8.

The amount of data in Problem 2.39 may seem unmanageable. A Venn diagram is an invaluable aid in sorting the information out:

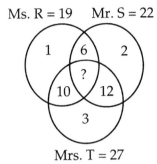

Ms. R = 19   Mr. S = 22

Mrs. T = 27

The diagram makes clear that 17 of the 19 votes for Ms. R are accounted for. The remaining two must have come from ballots in which all three candidates were checked off. Note that the answer 2 makes Mr. S's total 22 and Mrs. T's total 27. The completed Venn diagram indicates how many faculty members voted, which can be subtracted from 42 to determine how many did not vote.

If you had difficulty solving the problems in Probe 2.15 or came up with an answer of 25% or 35% for Problem 1, consider using a Venn diagram. For Problem 3 of Probe 2.15, the following Venn diagram may help in finding the solution:

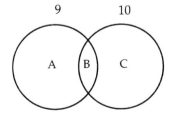

9   10

A = Conscious the first half but not the second.
B = Conscious both halves.
C = Conscious the second half but not the first.

13 = number of games conscious for one half.

If you need additional hints, see Probe 2.15, Answers to Selected Questions, page 2-144.

Informally Evaluating Reasoning

From the beginning of their schooling, children should be encouraged to evaluate conjectures informally (see Box 2.18 on the next page). Intermediate-grade students can be encouraged to check conjectures further by devising informal deductive proofs. Older students should also have experience in informally evaluating deductive arguments. Although intermediate-level students typically do not need deliberate instruction to evaluate detachment arguments (Argument Type 1 in Table 2.2 on page 2-63), many do need it to evaluate contrapositive, converse, and inverse arguments (Argument Types 2, 3, and 4 in Table 2.2).* Two methods for informally evaluating reasoning are discussed below.

✒ **Encourage children to use counterexamples to identify invalid conjectures or deductive arguments.** *A counterexample is an example that shows a statement is false.* Such examples force us to reject a general statement altogether or to amend it (make it more specific) (see Figure 2.10 on page 2-89). Consider, for instance, the statement, "The product of any two whole numbers is even." This statement is not true because the product of 3 × 5 (or any other pair of odd numbers) is not even. The statement could be revised to read, "The product of any two *consecutive* whole numbers is even." Is this statement true? Can you produce a counterexample to disprove it? Why or why not? Children at all levels should be encouraged to search for examples that might be inconsistent with an intuition, an induced rule, or a deductive inference.

---

*Although formally evaluating arguments is not introduced until high school, the use of Table 2.2 might be appropriate for more advanced middle-school students or students interested in logic. Instruction could begin by a teacher posing such questions as, "Do you think it is easy to spot illogical arguments?" "Is it as easy as spotting logical arguments?" Students could individually evaluate the conclusions of various types of arguments (e.g., the items in Question 4 of Probe 2.13 on page 2-72). The teacher could anonymously tally how the students responded on each item and point out the degree of disagreement on each item. In small groups, the students could then discuss the validity of each conclusion using Table 2.2 as an aid. This could be followed up by a whole-class discussion at which time the data tallied earlier could be evaluated.

Box 2.18: Helping Students Evaluate Their Conjectures

Mrs. Song presented her third-grade class with the following problem on the chalkboard:

■ **The Tallest Child.** Alton is taller than Brittney, who is taller than Cameron or Dot. Can you tell (a) who is the tallest of the four children and (b) who is the shortest?

A student made a conjecture based on what appears to be intuitive reasoning.

Akiko commented, "I can tell just by looking that it can't be answered."

✐ The teacher encouraged the child to reflect on her (incorrect) conjecture and consider how she could defend it.

Mrs. Song responded, "Are you saying there is insufficient information to answer either question? How could you convince others? Would drawing a picture help?"

A child overlooked one of the constraints specified by the problem.

The class quickly reached a consensus that Alton was the tallest child. Davis then spoke up enthusiastically, "Oh, I know who the shortest is: It's Brittney."

Mrs. Song inquired, "How do you know that?"

"Because," answered Davis, "Alton is taller than Brittney."

✐ The teacher helped the child to consider whether his answer fit all the facts.

"Does that by itself make Brittney the smallest?" questioned Mrs. Song.

"No," replied Davis.

"What other information in the problem either supports or refutes your conclusion?" asked Mrs. Song.

Quickly assessing that his conjecture was ill-founded, the child adjusted his reasoning.

"No, wait," commented Davis, "Brittney is taller than Cameron or Dot, so she can't be the smallest."

Perhaps accustomed to questions that can always be answered, a student made a guess.

Avraham offered, "Dot must be the smallest."

✐ The teacher asked the child to consider the implications of his answer and whether the information given was consistent with it.

"If so, what else does this imply, and does the problem support your claim?" asked Mrs. Song.

Avraham reasoned, "If Dot was the smallest, then Cameron would be bigger than her. The problem doesn't really say. I guess we can't tell who is smallest."

Figure 2.10: An Overstated Case

YOUNG ONES' VIEW

Conjecture

Counterexample

Amendment

✏ **For intermediate-grade children, Euler diagrams can be useful.** Leonhard Euler (pronounced "oiler"), a Swiss mathematician who lived from 1707 to 1783, developed a system using circles to teach deductive logic to a German princess (Ennis, 1969). Activity 2.4 describes how Euler diagrams are constructed and how they can be useful in evaluating the validity of an argument. This activity also illustrates how counterexamples can be used to evaluate reasoning.

☞ Try Activity 2.4 on pp. 2-96 to 2-98 before reading on.

🖳 **Sidelight**

After they have had some programming instruction, intermediate children can be challenged to devise a program for the Number-Guess Game. A program written in BASIC is delineated below. Note that students may need to be given line 20—the instructions for randomly selecting a number.

```
10   PRINT
20   LET R = INT (RND (10) * 100) + 1
30   PRINT "THE SECRET NUMBER HAS BEEN SELECTED."
40   PRINT
50   PRINT "WHAT IS YOUR GUESS?"
60   INPUT G
70   IF G > R GOTO 130
80   IF G < R GOTO 150
90   PRINT "YOU GUESSED IT. CONGRATULATIONS!"
100  PRINT
110  PRINT "PLAY AGAIN...."
120  GOTO 30
130  PRINT "LOWER"
140  GOTO 60
150  PRINT "HIGHER"
160  GOTO 60
170  END
```

Primary teachers can use the program above to create a computerized version of Number Guess for their students.

🍎 Activity 2.2: Guiding Learning About Venn Diagrams

◆ Classifying and reasoning ◆ K-4 ◆ Any number

Venn diagrams can consist of a loop made of string or drawn on construction paper.

A. Classifying things according to a single characteristic and the absence of that characteristic.

Tell the children you need, for instance, blue attribute blocks. Ask them to pile blue blocks inside the loop. Note that all blocks outside the loop are *not blue* ("nonblue"). You may want the children to label their Venn diagram as shown to the right.

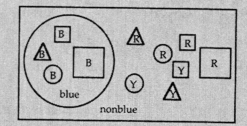

B. Classifying things in terms of two mutually-exclusive characteristics.

Next, ask the children how they sort things in terms, for instance, of two colors. Children typically should have little difficulty suggesting two loops. Again, it might be helpful to label each area of the Venn diagram as shown to the right. This will provide a basis for understanding the next step.

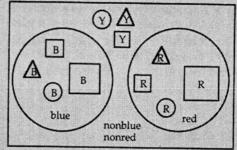

C. Representing two nonexclusive characteristics.

1. The following example is patterned after the discovery-learning approach used in *Mathematics Their Way* (Baratta-Lorton, 1976):

Mrs. Dumplings regularly tore out her hair, because she could not find needed classroom materials. This was largely due to the fact that her storage closet was a complete mess. Finally, Mrs. Dumplings had had enough; she resolved to organize her storage closet. She enlisted her classes' help, and together they set about the task of sorting through the materials in the closet, labeling the containers, and putting the containers on shelves in a systematic manner. This process led to some interesting questions and problems.

Ricardo took on the job of sorting through the box of rulers. He found rulers with inches and rulers with centimeters. To help him with the sorting task, he got two jump ropes, one to encircle the rulers with inches and one to encircle the rulers with centimeters.

Activity 2.2 continued

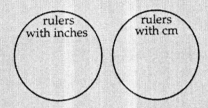

Toward the bottom of the box, Ricardo discovered a bunch of rulers that had *both* inches and centimeters. "Where should I place these?" he wondered. (a) What could Ricardo do to take into account the dual-purpose rulers if there were no more jump ropes? (b) Ali, a third grader, suggested putting the rulers with both inches and centimeters in a pile between the two existing loops. Evaluate this suggestion in light of the logic portrayed by Venn diagrams. (c) Where should a "Zork ruler" be placed? (The basic unit of measurement on the planet Zork is the width of an average Zorkian finger—about 3/4 of an inch).

2. Construct a Venn diagram that would allow you to sort a set of attribute blocks into square blocks, blue blocks, and other. Label each part of the diagram. Spencer, a third grader, suggested using three loops. Is this necessary? Why or why not?

D. Representing three nonexclusive characteristics.

Construct a Venn diagram that would allow you to sort a set of attribute blocks into square blocks, blue blocks, large blocks, and other. (a) Indicate where a small, thin, blue square would go. (b) Indicate where a large, thick, blue square would go. (c) Indicate where a large, thick, yellow square would go.

E. Using Venn diagrams to illustrate a hierarchical relationship.

Show how a Venn diagram could be used to sort blocks into the following categories: triangles, blue triangles, and large blue triangles.

Questions to Consider

1. A third-grade class was asked to make a Venn diagram to show those children with a brother and those with a sister. Before the class could decide on a representation, Jaime noted, "But I have both a brother and a sister." (a) How might a teacher respond to this comment? (b) How should the Venn diagram be constructed, and where should Jaime's initials be placed in the diagram? (c) Jaime's comment prompted the teacher to ask, "What about an only child?" Where should an only child be placed in the diagram?

2. A Venn diagram was used to illustrate the two nonexclusive characteristics: *red* and *triangle*. (a) Where would a block that is red *and* triangular be placed in the diagram? (b) Where might a block that is red *or* triangular be placed? (c) The union of two sets is represented by what situation above (a or b)—by what term, *and* or *or*? (d) The intersection of two sets would be represented by what situation above (a or b)—by what term, *and* or *or*?

☁ Activity 2.3: Generalizing Patterns

◆ Finding and describing patterns ◆ K-8* ◆ Any number

Part I: Using Letters to Find Repeating Patterns

Illustrated below is a repeating pattern that could be made using interlocking blocks. Note that each different element (color) is given a different letter. The core of the first display (ABBB) is obvious even without a letter code.

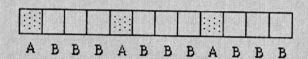

A B B B A B B B A B B B

However, many repeating patterns may be less obvious. Use letters to identify the cores of the following repeating patterns.

1. Clapping of hands and snapping of fingers: Clap, snap, clap, clap, snap, clap, clap, clap, snap, clap, clap, snap, clap, clap, clap, snap, clap, clap, snap, clap, clap.

2. Paper shapes: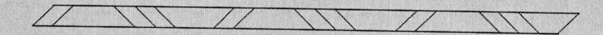

3. Patternblocks:

4. Toothpicks: | | / | | \ | | — | | | | / | | \ | | — | | | | / | | \ | | — | |

Part II: Using Letters to Identify General Repeating Patterns

1. Use letters to code the repeating patterns illustrated in Activity File 2.7 (Pattern Prediction on page 2-84). What do you notice? How might using letters to code repeating patterns help children extend their thinking about patterns?

2. Which of the following music patterns is most similar to the repeating color pattern illustrated in Activity File 2.7?

(a) do, re   (b) do, re, do   (c) do, re, mi   (d) do, re, mi, fa   (e) do, do, do

---

*Parts I & II would be appropriate for children as young as kindergarten. Part III would be appropriate for children as young as second grade. Part IV would be appropriate for intermediate-level children.

Activity 2.3 continued

Part III: Translating Growing Physical Patterns into Number Patterns

Successively larger Ts can be made by adding a counter to each of the three ends of the previous T:

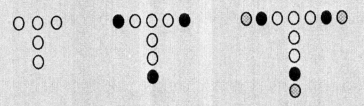

(Note that this pattern could also be represented pictorially on grid paper.) How many counters will be needed to make the next (the fourth) T? How many would be required to make the tenth T?

Although the questions above could be answered by using counters to make concrete models of the fourth and tenth T, considerable effort could be saved by making a table and looking for a pattern. (A teacher could encourage this more abstract approach by supplying students with only 11 counters needed to make the third T.)

Triangle Number	1	2	3	4	5	6	7	8	9	10
Number of Blocks Needed										

1. What number pattern does the table make evident?

2. How many counters would it take to make the tenth T?

Part IV: Generalizing Growing Patterns

Consider the following visual pattern, which can be thought of as making successively larger rectangles by adding 1 to the length and 1 to the width.

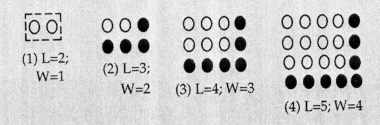

(1) L=2; W=1   (2) L=3; W=2   (3) L=4; W=3   (4) L=5; W=4

This pattern can be summarized as numerical data in a table:

Rectangle Number	1	2	3	4	5	...	500
Number of counters	2	6	12	20	?		?

Activity 2.3 continued

As suggested earlier, one way to determine the number of counters for the fifth rectangle is to examine the relationship among the number of counters:

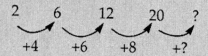

From the pattern that readily emerges (4, 6, 8...), it appears 10 should be added to the previous number of counters, 20, to determine the number of counters in the fifth triangle.

Consider, though, how tedious and time consuming this approach would be if you had to determine the number for (good grief!) the five hundredth rectangle in the sequence. Fortunately, there is another more powerful method for using a table to make a prediction: determine the *relationship between* the two sets of numbers in the table. In the table above, for instance, this means determining the rule for transforming the number of a rectangle into the number of counters: the rule that transforms 1 into 2, 2 into 6, 3 into 12, as well as 4 into 20. Although deciphering this relationship is more difficult than deciphering the relationship among the number of counters alone, once found, the rule can be used to determine the counters needed for *any* rectangle in the sequence, including the five hundredth one.

1. (a) What is the relationship between the rectangle number and the number of counters needed? Express your answer as a general (algebraic) formula. (b) How many counters are needed to construct the five hundredth rectangle in the sequence?

2. In some cases, one way to decipher a rule is to consider what remains constant from case to case, and what changes. For successive Ts, described in Part III above, a core of 5 counters remains constant; the second T added 3 counters to the core; the third T added 6 counters; and so forth. Algebraically, this could be expressed as $5 + 3(n - 1)$ where n is the number of the T. This expression can be simplified: $5 + 3(n - 1) = 5 + 3n - 3 = 3n + 2$. (a) Use this approach to determine the relationship between the number of cows and the number of fence sections in the Cow-Fence Problem in Box 2.6 on page 2-22. (b) How many fence sections would be needed to enclose a row of 100 cows?

➤ Probe 2.15: Some Reasoning Problems

⦿ ■ Problem 1: Foreign-Language Instruction at Chaos Middle School

Chaos Middle School offers French and Spanish to its eighth graders.

40% of the eighth graders are enrolled in French
25% of the eighth graders are enrolled in Spanish
10% of the eighth graders are enrolled in both

What percent of the eighth graders are taking neither?

⦿ ■ Problem 2: A Botched Science Experiment

Siegfried was conducting a probability experiment. He flipped two coins 20 times and recorded the number of heads (23) and the number of tails (17). "I can't answer these questions," he complained to his neighbor Rashard.

After looking at Siegfried's notebook, Rashard observed, "Of course you can't. You recorded the data of your experiment wrong. You were supposed to record how many trials came up heads-heads, head-tails, and tails-tails."

"I do remember there were only three times both coins came up tails," mused Siegfried.

Without redoing the experiment, can Siegfried use the data he has to generate the data he needs? Justify your answer.

⦿ ■ Problem 3: Sacked Zack or the Unconscious QB

Zack, the quarterback for the Durham Dolts, was sacked and knocked unconscious in 13 games. Fortunately for Zack, this happened only once a game—either in the first half or in the second half. Zack was conscious for 9 first halves and 10 second halves. How many games did Zack play total? How many times did his offensive line afford him the luxury of remaining conscious for the whole game?

⚜ Activity 2.4: Using Euler Diagrams and Counterexamples to Check Conclusions

◆ Informally evaluating deductive reasoning ◆ Intermediate ◆ Whole class

Using Euler Diagrams to Evaluate Deductive Inferences

Euler diagrams are useful for confirming valid arguments (true conclusions) or for spotting invalid ones (untrue conclusions).

Example 1: A True Conclusion About an Example. Euler diagrams use a circle to represent a class. Consider the class of numbers that are multiples of 4. All multiples of 4 are numbers that have a ones digit of 4, 8, 2, 6, or 0. Now, not all numbers that have 4, 8, 2, 6, or 0 are multiples of 4 (e.g., 14, 18, 22, 26, and 30). These observations can be summarized in the Euler diagram below:

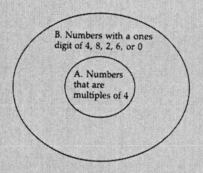

Now consider the following argument: "The product of 2495.25 and 16 is a multiple of 4, therefore this product must end in 4, 8, 2, 6, or 0. Is this a valid conclusion or not? Place a dot labeled p within Circle A, the circle representing numbers that are multiples of 4. Note that the p is also inside Circle B and, thus, must have a ones digit of 4, 8, 2, 6, or 0.

Example 2: A True Conclusion About a Nonexample. Consider the number 39,927, which does not have a ones digit of 4, 8, 2, 6, or 0. Show this number in the diagram above with a point labeled q. Can 39,927 be a multiple of 4?

Example 3: An Untrue Conclusion About an Example. Consider the following argument: "The product of 1826.9 and 20 has a ones digit of 8, therefore it is a multiple of 4." Clearly the point labeled r representing this product should go inside Circle B, but can you be sure whether this point should go inside Circle A or outside it?

Example 4: An Untrue Conclusion About a Nonexample. Consider the following argument: "The product of 2851 and 14 is not a multiple of 4, therefore it cannot have a 4, 8, 2, 6, or 0 in the ones digit." Can you be sure whether the point labeled s representing this product should go inside Circle B or outside it?

Activity 2.4 continued

1. Example 1 above illustrates what type of argument in Table 2.2 on page 2-63? What about ' Example 2? Example 3? Example 4?

2. Consider the following argument: "If a number is a multiple of 8, then it is a multiple of 4 [Premise 1]. The product of 2984 and 15 is a multiple of 8 [Premise 2]." What conclusion can you draw about the ones digit of this product? Construct an Euler diagram and indicate the product with a point labeled t.

3. One of the biggest difficulties students have in using Euler diagrams is setting up the diagram properly. Evaluate each of the following Euler diagrams. Is it set up correctly? That is, does the outer circle represent the larger class? If not, draw a correct Euler diagram.

   a. Premise: If you are 16 years old, then you are eligible for a driver's license.

   b. Premise: If a restaurant fails its health inspection, then it is closed down.

   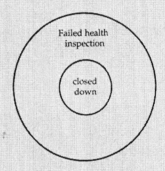

   c. Premise: If it rains, then Lorraine takes the bus.

   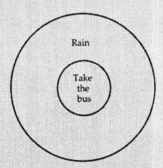

   d. Premise: If Hank gets an A on his report card, then he gets a dollar.

   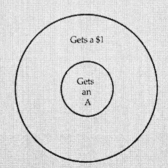

4. After examining several examples of Euler diagrams, Jennifer asked, "Is the if-part of a premise always represented by the inner circle and the then-part of the premise by the outer circle?" Is Jennifer's observation always correct, sometimes correct, or never correct? Why?

Activity 2.4 continued

⚡ 5. (a) Show how an Euler diagram could demonstrate whether the following arguments are valid or invalid. (b) Give a counterexample to show that an invalid argument is not necessarily true.

A. If you are 16 years old, then you are eligible for a driver's license. Samir is not 16 years old, so he is not eligible for a driver's license.

B. If a restaurant fails its health inspection, then it is closed down. Stu's Septic Diner is closed down; therefore, it must have failed its health inspection.

C. If it rains, then Lorraine takes the bus. Lorraine is taking the bus; therefore, it must be raining.

D. If Hank gets an A on his report card, then he gets a dollar. Hank did not get a dollar, so he must not have gotten an A on his report card.

⚡ 6. (a) Draw an Euler diagram to represent the following premise: If two triangles are congruent, then a side and an adjacent angle of each triangle must be equal. (b) Use the Euler diagram to evaluate each of the following arguments. (c) For invalid arguments, cite a counterexample to show that it is not necessarily true.

A. Triangles A and B are not congruent; therefore, no side and its adjacent angle of each triangle is equal.

B. Triangles C and D have a side and an adjacent angle that is equal; therefore, Triangles C and D are congruent.

Using Counterexamples to Evaluate Conjectures

Questions 5 and 6 above involved using counterexamples to evaluate the validity of a deductive inference. The questions below ask you to use counterexamples to evaluate conjectures. Can you come up with a counterexample to disprove the conjecture? Revise any false statements to make them true.

1. The sum of any four whole numbers is even.

2. The sum of any two whole numbers can be evenly divided by two.

3. The sum of any four whole numbers can be evenly divided by two.

4. The sum of any three whole numbers can be evenly divided by two.

MATHEMATICS AS COMMUNICATION

Figure 2.11: What We Have Here Is a Failure to Communicate

PEANUTS reprinted by permission of UFS, Inc.

In a traditional skills-approach to mathematics instruction, communication is largely a one-way affair. Teachers and textbooks provide a torrent of words and written symbols that often—as Figure 2.11 illustrates—have little meaning to children. Student communication is largely restricted to providing short verbal answers to teacher-posed questions and concise symbolic answers to written exercises—answers which they may not understand. Students are rarely asked to explain their ideas in any form. Nor are they encouraged to share their questions and ideas with peers. (In Figure 2.11, note that Sally sits alone as she tries to decipher the mathematical jargon.) Indeed, talking among students is often viewed as disruptive, as an impediment to learning.

This unit begins with a discussion of why it is important to open up the channels of communication in a classroom. It then discusses how to build a community that fosters open communication. Last, the unit turns to a discussion of how instruction can foster the following key aspects of communicating: representing, listening, reading, discussing, and writing.

REASONS FOR FOCUSING ON COMMUNICATING

This subunit offers two reasons why mathematics instruction should focus on communicating. One is that mathematics is essentially a language—a second language. Another is that mathematics and mathematical learning are, at heart, social activities.

Mathematics as a Language

Mathematics is more than a tool to aid thinking, more than a tool for discovering patterns, solving problems, or drawing conclusions. It is also an invaluable tool for communicating a variety of ideas clearly, precisely, and succinctly. In a very real sense, then, mathematics can be considered a language.* Indeed, it has been called the "language of science" (Dantzig, 1954) and serves as the language of engineering and commerce as well. Because people the world over can use it to communicate despite differences in their native tongues, it has even been called "the universal language" (Jacobs, 1982).

For children, mathematics is essentially a second or foreign language. When instruction focuses on memorizing terms rather than communicating ideas, many find mathematics impenetrable. Like Sally in Figure 2.11, they may make little sense of the technical terminology of mathematics. Children's difficulties in learning the new language of mathematics are compounded when it is introduced too quickly.

Mathematics Learning as a Social Activity

Like mathematics itself, mathematical learning is inherently a social activity (Schoenfeld, 1992). Unfortunately, a traditional approach overlooks the

---

* The language of mathematics is fundamentally different from natural languages, though, in that it describes ideal situations rather than ordinary situations (Layzer, 1989). For example, a circle is a geometric ideal; in a real circle-like figure, all the points of the circumference are only approximately the same distance from the center. Mathematical terms derive their meaning from axioms, *not* from ordinary experience.

social nature of mathematical learning, which may impede the mathematical development of children. Pupil-pupil interactions, as well as teacher-pupil communications, are important for nurturing children's mathematical potential.

Disadvantages of a Traditional Skills Approach. Traditionally, children have learned mathematics in isolation. By and large, they sat quietly as their teacher discussed and demonstrated the daily lessons. Afterward, with the exception of occasional teacher feedback, they attempted to make sense of assigned problems or worksheets alone. Largely unchecked, they misapplied their assumptions and misconceptions. When pupils encountered difficulties or puzzles, they dealt with them privately. In their solitude, children shamefully and surreptitiously used informal strategies, not realizing that many of their peers used similar strategies. Without the example and input of their peers, they sometimes persisted in using strategies that were inefficient or even inappropriate.

A highly individualistic approach can also work against problem-solving success; this is particularly true of children's early efforts. Often an individual child will lack the necessary background knowledge or the general problem-solving strategies needed to understand a problem or devise a solution strategy. If the teacher is unavailable to help, the child may simply have no idea of how to proceed. Sometimes individuals get off on a wrong track and, unless the teacher is available to check their progress, they remain blissfully ignorant of their errant approach.

In the individualistic and competitive situation of the traditional classroom, a few students shone brightly, most did not, and some failed miserably. The pupils' isolation often undermined confidence, many students concluding that they were not the chosen and gifted few. For some, isolation helped breed fear, anxiety, and avoidance.

Small-Group Work: Practical or Not? Small-group cooperative learning, or team study, has been suggested as a means for helping to minimize or to eliminate the difficulties created by the overly individualistic and competitive traditional approach (e.g., Davidson, 1990). However, is it really practical? *If given the opportunity to work together, will children really interact in productive ways?* For some different opinions, see Box 2.19.

Box 2.19: A Common Concern About Small-Group Work

Over lunch, Miss Brill commented, "When I was in college, we discussed small-group peer dialogue. Perhaps...."

"I wouldn't if I were you," interrupted Mrs. Battleaxe, rumored to have successfully fought off mandatory retirement for at least a dozen years. "You let them little whippersnappers talk, and you won't get anything done. You'll just have chaos. You want CHAOS, Missy?"

"But, but don't you think children have anything to offer each other?" gasped Miss Brill, surprised by Mrs. Battleaxe's outburst.

"Nothing worthwhile. You let them talk, they'll talk, but not about mathematics. They talk about their sports or fashions. Today they even talk about drugs and other unspeakable things. You want them to talk about anything worthwhile, *you* have to direct the talk." Then as abruptly as she had started, Mrs. Battleaxe was gone, perhaps to consult with her lawyer about her latest mandatory retirement suit.

Ms. Wise interjected, "A common concern among many teachers is that if children are allowed to talk to each other, they will tend to get 'off-task' and will accomplish little or nothing of educational value. I disagree with this pessimistic assessment of children. Undoubtedly, small-group work sometimes does lead to off-task behaviors. This is especially likely when a teacher has not planned the group work carefully. However, I feel that it is important that students have the opportunity to interact with other students, as well as the teacher. If a teacher is going to encourage students to take responsibility for their learning and foster autonomy, she must be willing to trust them. I use peer dialogue extensively and find that it is generally effective."

Do children, particularly young children, have the social skills necessary to benefit from group work? Piaget (1965) argued that because young children are egocentric (self-centered), they cannot put themselves in the "shoes" of their listener. As a result, they may not take into account what a listener does and does not know or make an effort to communicate in an organized and clear manner. Consider, for example, the exchange described in Box 2.20 between a boy, who is an avid videogames player, and his mother, who lives in a different world.*

Although research suggests that Piaget may have underestimated children's social and communication skills, there is general agreement with his conclusion that peer interaction is an important vehicle for furthering these skills. Piaget concluded that peer interaction is a key mechanism for overcoming self-centeredness. That is, playing and working together forces children to consider their peers' point of view. After all, alternatives include ending the activity, losing a friend (at least temporarily), or fighting (physical harm).

Benefits of Peer-Peer Communications. Pupil-pupil interactions can be important for constructing mathematical knowledge, developing problem-solving and reasoning competence, encouraging confidence, and acquiring social skills (e.g., Davidson, 1990; Lappan & Schram, 1989). These potential benefits of cooperative learning are explained in Table 2.3.

Box 2.20: A Case of Egocentric Speech

In the following exchange, note that the boy did not consider whether or not his mother shared the same frame of reference. Instead of prefacing his comments that he was discussing a videogame, the boy assumed his mother understood the context of his remark.

Boy: I can jump the Turtle now, mom.

Mother (conjuring up thoughts of a shelled, toothless, horny-beaked reptile and wondering where the creature could be): What turtles?

Boy: You know, the four Turtles.

Mother (hoping for the best): You found four turtles outside?

Boy: No, mom, downstairs [mother becomes faint] . . . you know, the Ninja Turtles in my Nintendo game [mother regains consciousness].

*As the example of the videogame player illustrates, children often appear self-centered. But then many adults frequently converse in a self-centered fashion also. Piaget argued that while older children and adults can take a listener's perspective if they try, young children are conceptually incapable of this. More recent research suggests that young children appear more conceptually able to take another's perspective than Piaget's research indicated. Children may appear more egocentric than most adults because they try less often to take a listener's perspective and because they have fewer communication skills.

Table 2.3: Advantages of Using Cooperative Learning

Cooperative learning can foster mathematical knowledge. Communications with peers can foster content learning, understanding, and strategy acquisition.

• To become mathematically literate, children must learn basic aspects of our culturally accumulated mathematical knowledge. Research suggests that cooperative-learning groups can promote higher mathematical achievement than can more individualistic approaches (Davidson, 1990; Johnson & Johnson, 1989; Slavin, 1983).

• To help children construct an understanding of mathematics, instruction must regularly challenge their thinking. Interaction with peers can greatly enhance the opportunities for this. Moreover, many children may feel less threatened when challenged by a peer than by an adult. Small-group work also gives children a chance to share questions and insights, which further promotes understanding (e.g., Cobb, 1985).

• Peer-peer interaction gives children a chance to share strategies. For example, a peer might point out a more efficient way of figuring out basic number combinations.

Table 2.3 continued

Cooperative learning can foster problem solving and reasoning. Communicating with peers can be an important ingredient in learning how to think like a mathematician and in solving genuine problems successfully.

• To become good mathematical problem solvers, children need to develop a mathematical point of view—a disposition, for instance, to notice patterns, to find similarities across situations, to see real-world situations in quantitative terms (e.g., analyzing music in terms of the number of beats per minute). Because this may be as important as acquiring "any particular set of skills, strategies, or knowledge...we may do well to conceive of mathematics education less as an instructional process (in the traditional sense of teaching specific, well-defined skills or items of knowledge), than as a socialization process" (Resnick, 1988, p. 58).

Key aspects of this socialization process include understanding the social nature of mathematics, building a mathematical community in the classroom, and serving a mathematical apprenticeship. Children need to understand that mathematicians usually do not solve problems in isolation, but typically build on the ideas of others and work as a member of a team. The best way to understand that mathematics is a community effort is to simulate such a community in the classroom. Developing both a mathematical point of view and problem-solving skill requires extensive practice. This apprenticeship can be made easier and more profitable with the support and help of peers in the following three ways (Noddings, 1985):

• Discussing problems in a small group of peers can help children analyze and solve problems thoughtfully (e.g., define the unknown, gauge what data are relevant, consider alternative solutions, and evaluate the reasonableness of a solution). It can also help them to examine and refine tentative ideas and solutions (Kilpatrick, 1985b). The challenges and disbelief of their peers force children to examine carefully their assumptions, strategies, and answers (Vygotsky, 1978). "Having to explain one's reasoning allows classmates . . . to check assumptions, clarify misconceptions, and correct errors in understanding" (Johnson & Johnson, 1989, p. 236). Small-group discussion of problems can help children understand that mathematics involves thinking (Cobb, 1985), and can provide a relatively secure haven for experimenting with mathematical thinking.

• A group of students is more likely to have the background knowledge necessary to understand a problem and to find a workable solution than is an individual. Two heads are better than one.

• Children may begin to internalize the general problem-solving strategies used by the group (Vygotsky, 1978).

Cooperative-learning can foster confidence (Johnson & Johnson, 1989). Research indicates that when children work in small groups, are required to reach consensus, and are encouraged to accept everyone's thinking and view errors as a mutual part of learning, they become more confident, autonomous, and persistent (Cobb, Wood, & Yackel, 1991; Cobb, Yackel, Wood, Wheatley, & Merkel, 1988). Small-group activities can actively involve more children than can whole-class activities, giving more children a chance to contribute. Small-group work puts a premium on children's thinking, not on a teacher's (or some other authority's) thinking. By sharing ideas and strategies, children may recognize that they are not alone in having a misconception or using a finger-counting strategy. Moreover, they can seek clarification or assistance either in the relative safety of their own group or by posing a question as a group.

Cooperative learning can foster social and communication skills (e.g., Noddings, 1985). Communication with peers is particularly important for the development of social skills and for honing communication skills. Children may learn, for example, that if someone does not understand what you are saying, you need to rephrase or simplify your comments. Children may learn how to check for signs of confusion and how to offer constructive criticism. They may even learn to assume the same position or orientation as a listener so that directions are not reversed.

BUILDING A MATHEMATICAL COMMUNITY

This subunit first addresses teaching mathematics as a language. Next, it focuses on how cooperative-learning groups can be used. It then discusses the role of justifications and group consensus in building a mathematical community.

Development of a Communal Language

For children to adopt mathematics as a communal language and use it effectively, this language needs to be introduced carefully. Like learning any second language, children need real, or at least realistic, opportunities to use mathematics. They need to move gradually from using their native tongue to this new language. Children also need to see how this new language corresponds to their native tongue and how it differs.

✍ **Use a Language-Experience Approach.** Like a whole-language approach for reading instruction, a language-experience approach provides a purposeful and meaningful way of teaching mathematics. "This personalized, reality-based approach encompasses activities such as listening, speaking, reading, and writing, where children are guided to express their reactions, ideas, and feelings regarding situations . . . in the classroom or on a field trip" (Curcio, 1990, p. 69) (see Box 2.21).

✍ **Formal definitions and notations should build on children's informal or existing knowledge.** Introduce mathematical and symbolic language gradually. Children can be encouraged to move through four stages of describing real mathematical situations:

(1) *Stage 1 or the Natural-Language Stage* entails using their own language;

(2) *Stage 2 or the Material-Language Stage* involves using the terminology of a concrete or a pictorial model;

(3) *Stage 3 or the Shorthand Stage* entails using a few words to summarize mathematical situations.

Box 2.21: A Purposeful Way of Introducing "Thirds"

✍ Note that Mr. Adams' "lesson" on fractions was introduced as a problem the class needed to solve so that they could play a game (which focused on another content area altogether). There are many opportunities during the school year to introduce basic mathematical skills and concepts in a purposeful manner as a means to achieving significant ends.

✍ Children are encouraged to speak and listen carefully about the genuine problem facing them. To further consolidate the learning experience, the teacher has the class write about fractions using a personally meaningful context.

Mr. Adams wanted his second-grade class to construct place-value mats so they could play a place-value game. He explained that the construction paper distributed to each child needed to be folded into three equal sections for a ones, tens, and hundreds portion. Mr. Adams asked the class how this could be done, and suggested using a regular piece of paper to experiment with. Several children tried folding the paper in the middle and found this did not work. Mr. Adams encouraged one of these students to explain what she had tried and why it didn't work. Barbara Ann noted, "The pieces aren't the same size if you do."

After some experimenting, Marcella found a way of doing it: "Fold one end halfway toward the other end and then fold the other end over it." The class listened and watched while Marcella explained and demonstrated. Afterward, Mr. Adams pointed out that the construction paper was folded into *thirds*. Later, he had the class write about whether they would rather share a yummy cake that was cut into two equal pieces ("halves"), three equal pieces ("thirds"), four equal pieces ("fourths"), or five equal pieces ("fifths").

(4) *Stage 4 or the Symbolic Language Stage* involves using mathematical terminology or symbols as an even more economical way to record mathematical situations (Irons & Irons, 1989).

An example of this four-stage process is illustrated in Box 2.22.

✐ **Relate mathematical terms to everyday expressions.** Help children connect formal terminology to their informal knowledge. For example, a discussion can help children connect the formal and unfamiliar term "plus" to their more intuitive and familiar term "add." The term subtrahend can be distinguished from minuend by pointing out that sub means "under," as in submarine (literally under the water).

✐ **It is important to compare and contrast mathematical language with everyday language.** Where the mathematical and everyday meaning of a term diverge, it is important to highlight the difference for children (see Box 2.23).

Box 2.22: Four Stages of Introducing Multiplication

1. **Natural Language:** *Ricardo's father gave him a block of stamps with Elvis' picture on it. The block had 4 stamps in each row and there were 3 rows. So Ricardo had 12 Elvis stamps altogether. I love stamps even without Elvis.*

2. **Material Language:** Three rows of 4 baby cubes makes 12 baby cubes altogether, which after trading is 1 long (ten) and 2 baby cubes (ones).

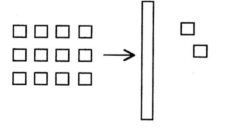

3. **Shorthand:** *3 rows of 4 → 12*

4. **Symbolic Language:** *3 × 4 = 12*

Box 2.23: What's Right About a Right Triangle?

A child correctly identified the form as a right triangle but not △. The child explained that a *right* triangle always faces right; the other triangle was a "left triangle" (Mason, 1989). Children need to understand that the right in right triangle refers to a triangle with a *right* angle, which is another name for a square (90°) angle, and has nothing to do with the everyday use of right to denote direction.

The Use of Cooperative Learning

Simply putting students together in small groups does not guarantee cooperation or success. Like any tool, using cooperative learning requires care.

Some Common Problems with Group Learning. Miss Brill had been using cooperative-learning groups for several weeks when she noticed that no one in LeMar's group, except LeMar, was working on the problem. "How about getting together to discuss this problem?" she suggested.

"Hey, I'm not going to say anything," responded Andy. "The last time I did, my answer was wrong and everyone blamed me."

"Well, it wasn't fair," snapped LeMar. "I had the right answer. We would have gotten it right if you had listened to me."

"Mr. Show Boat here thinks he's always right and always wants to do things his way," interjected Rodney. "What's the point of trying?"

"Well, I wouldn't have to do everything if you weren't such a veggie," retorted LeMar.

The incident above illustrates a number of common problems that teachers encounter with cooperative learning.

• When a group answers incorrectly, there is the human tendency to assign blame, to find a scapegoat. Students frequently turn on the perceived culprit, like Andy, with such invectives as, "You turkey; that was your idea. I knew you were wrong on that" (Noddings, 1985, p. 356). This happens with students of all ages, including college students.

• It is not uncommon for children to feel unfairly treated by their group. This can occur for many reasons. For example, a scapegoat may wonder why he or she was singled out. Proposing the correct solution only to have the group select an incorrect alternative (as LeMar had) is particularly hard for children to swallow.

• Some children may choose to remain passive (Good, Mulryan & McCaslin, 1992). Some students are willing to take a free ride—turn over responsibility and work to other students. This common problem is often tolerated by a group as long as their goals are not frustrated. However, freeloading can also lead to resentment and divisiveness.

• Low-achieving children are particularly likely to have difficulty adapting to and benefiting from small-group work (Good et al., 1992). Such children may be discouraged from active participation for a number of reasons. Their general sense of mathematical incompetence may carry over to the group setting. High-achieving students may become impatient with their questions or their slowness in completing a task. (Many children believe that completing a task quickly is an important measure of success.) In some cases, such as in Rodney's, students do so because of learned helplessness. (When their efforts repeatedly have no effect, many people simply stop trying.) This is particularly likely to happen when a bright student, such as LeMar, dominates a group.

• Group work does not guarantee that children will use or learn the social skills necessary for productive teamwork. For example, LeMar and Rodney did not realize that name-calling is not a profitable way of venting frustration and resolving conflicts.

Some Tips on Using Cooperative Learning. There are no simple solutions to the problems of small-group work. Clearly, though, a teacher must take an active role to ensure that cooperative learning is effective and productive. Some recommendations follow:

✐ **Start small.** To begin with, you may wish to use cooperative learning occasionally and then use it with increasing frequency. It may be easier to start by assigning pairs of students with relatively simple problems or tasks and work toward larger groups and more demanding problems.

✐ **Aim for a group size of about four.** Smaller groups may not generate sufficient input and discussion. Larger groups can be unwieldy and decrease the active involvement of the participants. Many children may find it more comfortable, safer, and easier to advance their ideas or explain their reasoning in a small group than in a large group.

✐ **Vary students' problem-solving experiences.** Research about the positive and negative effects of small-group problem-solving instruction is incomplete (Good et al., 1992; Lester, 1989; Noddings, 1985; Silver, 1985). It might be judicious, then, to provide opportunities for individual and whole-class problem-solving efforts as well as small-group activities.

✐ **Address problems directly.** Encourage students to discuss problems that arise in groups. This can provide an excellent opportunity to discuss social issues. Why do people need scapegoats? If a group makes a decision, does this free the individuals in the group from responsibility for the decision? If a majority agrees on a point, does it necessarily make it right? Is majority rule always fair?

✐ **Ensure individual accountability.** Students should know that group work is not an excuse to take a free ride. Randomly picking students to explain a group's strategy or answer, and questioning or testing individual students are two ways of ensuring accountability (Johnson & Johnson, 1989).

✐ **Foster mutual effort.** It is important to stress that a group is responsible for helping all of its members develop. A teacher may need to point out to more able students that simply giving other members of the group the answers is not really helping them in the long run. More able students should be encouraged to help their peers work problems out themselves. A teacher should underscore to everyone that several minds are frequently better than one, and that it is important to listen carefully to everyone. One device for encouraging cooperation is to require a consensus or unanimous agreement.

✐ **Foster social skills.** It is crucial that a teacher help children learn skills essential to cooperative enterprises. Consider William Golding's *The Lord of the Flies*. Children left to their own devices may not acquire the skills for a civilized society. A teacher should indirectly or directly discourage ineffective behaviors. For example, Miss Brill could have intervened in the dispute between Rodney and LeMar by asking, "Do you think name-calling is helpful?" She might have commented, perhaps emphatically, "Name-calling is hurtful, I will not permit it in my class." Moreover, a teacher needs to encourage students to consider how to vent frustrations, resolve conflicts, and otherwise work together cooperatively. For example, Miss Brill could have encouraged Rodney and LeMar to consider whether the other's complaint had any validity and, if so, what could be done about it.

✐ **Journals can help a teacher monitor and regulate cooperative-learning groups.** Journals can provide an invaluable means for individual students to identify problems in group work. The following journal entries made by college students in an elementary mathematics methods course illustrate two common difficulties:

1) Tammy wrote, *"How should we resolve a conflict when two or more people are adamant about their answers? [Would it not be better] to work together then submit our own answers?"*

2) Christine wrote, *"I feel...left out of my group. I think my group does not take me very seriously. It seems...that because of my lack of confidence (and ability sometimes)..., I'm the...object of ridicule...."*

Once aware of a problem, a teacher can help the group deal with it by, for example, discussing the issue with the group or the whole class. For Issue 1 raised by Tammy, it might help to discuss whether conflict is healthy. (It is not only inevitable but desirable. Consider what happens if everyone in a group readily agrees on an incorrect answer.) The class could then consider the advantages of Tammy's proposal (e.g., individually graded problems would better ensure individual responsibility) and its disadvantages (e.g., removing the need for a consensus may lessen the incentive to listen carefully to others' views or explain one's own cogently).

Besides helping students learn group-work skills, written and verbal comments on the journal entries have a number of other advantages. It concretely shows a concern for students' feelings and may help students take the initiative to change. In response to Christine's obvious anguish, her instructor wrote, "Have you voiced your concerns to the group? Is there anything I can do to help? We all start out with incomplete knowledge. Although some members of your group have had the advantage of good instruction, it is no reason to ridicule others...Your group has the opportunity to practice [with you the skills necessary for a good teacher, e.g., building confidence in someone less knowledgeable, rather than undermining it]." Christine resolved on her own to speak up more both in her group and in class. Although there is no guarantee that journal exchanges will always help, Christine's group did become cohesive and Christine became a regular contributor to class discussions, often insightfully so.

Fostering Mathematical Justifications

What role should explanations and proofs play in elementary instruction?

Explanations, Informal Proofs, and Mathematical Proofs. Mathematical justification can vary in sophistication. As children develop, they can be expected to use more sophisticated justifications. One way to view mathematical justification is to distinguish among explanations, informal proofs, and mathematical proofs (Balacheff, 1988).

• An *explanation* is an effort to convince others of the validity of your conjecture.

• An *informal proof* is an explanation (e.g., a description of a pattern, examples, or an informal deductive argument) accepted by a group.

• A *mathematical proof* refers to a formal proof using, for example, deductive logic.

The Role of Explanations and Proofs in Elementary Instruction. Fortunately, mathematical proofs are typically not introduced to elementary school children (Semadeni, 1983). Mathematical proofs are difficult enough for high school students to learn, and they are usually just memorized by rote and quickly forgotten anyway (Silver et al., 1990). Although elementary teachers need not concern themselves with teaching mathematical proofs, it is important for them to encourage explanations and informal proofs. A focus on explanations and informal proofs should help children appreciate that thinking (reasoning) and communicating are critical aspects of mathematics—even more important than memorizing and regurgitating information.

✍ **It is important to regularly ask children to** *justify* **their conjectures and answers.** A teacher should regularly follow up student responses with, "Why?" This will help children see that an explanation is at least as important as an answer. Moreover, posing probing questions and encouraging children to explain their thinking verbally or in writing can prompt reflection (NCTM, 1989). This can help children see connections, or discern gaps in their understanding.

✍ **It is important to involve the whole class in evaluating explanations.** Explanations are an important step to informal proofs. In the give-and-take of an open discussion, it should quickly become evident that not just any explanation will do. An explanation must be plausible—it must be convincing to others. All children need experience in fashioning arguments (explanations) that are convincing to others (Silver et al., 1990). An explanation that is convincing to the group achieves the status of informal proof.

✍ **As children increase in age and experience, they should be encouraged to use stricter standards for what is a convincing argument.** Whereas young children should be helped to see that one or two examples are not sufficient to prove a rule and should be encouraged to find additional examples, older children should be helped to see that even numerous examples do not constitute a proof and should be encouraged to adduce counterexamples. For instance, any number of whole number examples does not prove that multiplication *always* results in a product that is larger than the factors. Such a rule can be disproved by the counterexamples 0×8 or $\frac{1}{2} \times 8$. Children should also be helped to see that mathematical arguments begin with agreed-upon principles (premises) and must follow specific rules (rules of logic). Older students might even be encouraged to spell out an informal deductive argument with the challenge: "How can you prove that logically?" Fostering informal deductive reasoning can provide an invaluable basis for the formal deductive reasoning introduced in high school.

FOSTERING ALL ASPECTS OF COMMUNICATING

Instruction should help children to communicate mathematical ideas by representing, listening, reading, discussing, and writing. This subunit discusses the importance of each aspect and some teaching ideas for each, with particular emphasis on discussing and writing.

Representing

Representing involves re-presenting (translating) an idea or a problem in a new form (NCTM, 1989). It can entail, for example, translating a word problem into a concrete model with blocks, a picture, or a number sentence (written symbols). Representing ideas or problems can require a thoughtful analysis and, thus, actively involve children's thinking. It can also help children clarify key concepts. For example, constructing models of multidigit numbers (see, e.g., Figure 2.12) can help children understand that a numeral such as 23 denotes two tens and three ones. As noted earlier, representing a problem can help make its meaning clear and facilitate finding a solution strategy.

By experimenting with different representations and representing various situations, children can begin to understand the power of mathematics. By using and comparing various representations, they can discover some are easier to use than others. Such experiences can help children appreciate the economy and elegance of mathematical symbols (see, e.g., Figure 2.13 on page 2-108). Moreover, by using a

Figure 2.12: Representing the Place-Value Base-Ten Ideas Underlying Two-Digit Numerals

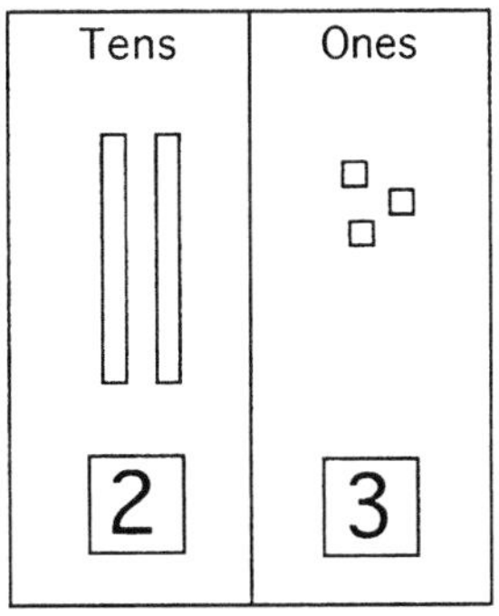

Figure 2.13: Various Ways of Recording the Points Collected During the Course of a Game

Relatively Direct Representation ——————————————→ Relatively Abstract Representation

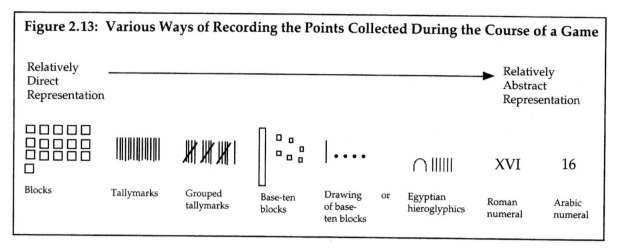

| Blocks | Tallymarks | Grouped tallymarks | Base-ten blocks | Drawing of base-ten blocks | or | Egyptian hieroglyphics | Roman numeral | Arabic numeral |

---

representation to illustrate a variety of situations, children can begin to appreciate the flexibility and usefulness of mathematics (NCTM, 1989). For example, the equation (number sentence) 5 + 3 = 8 can represent an infinite number of specific situations including the following:

Situation 1. Increasing an amount and finding a new total: Mortina started the period with 5 points. She scored another 3 points during the period. How many points does she have now?

Situation 2. Combining two parts to find a whole: Monica had five good volleys and three bad volleys. How many volleys did Monica take altogether?

Situation 3. Making an amount equal to an unknown amount: Ignacio was ahead on points. Joaquin, who had 5 points, got 3 more points to tie Ignacio. How many points did Ignacio have?

Situation 4. Comparing an amount with an unknown amount: Karem was ahead on points. Roderick, who had 5 points, was behind Karem by 3 points. How many points did Karem have?

Listening

Children must learn to listen carefully to the comments and questions of others. Adults and peers may offer ideas that help them see a new connection or clarify their reasoning. Others' questions may raise previously unconsidered issues for a child. Peers may have devised efficient strategies for completing a task. Listening carefully to others, then, can be helpful in constructing more complete mathematical knowledge or more effective strategies.

✎ **Teachers should also encourage students to think of questions to ask while they listen to others.** This underscores the importance of listening actively and critically.

✎ **Teachers should foster respect for others' views.** This essential element of listening carefully begins with good role models. Teachers (and parents) must take the time to listen to children's ideas. It is important to explicitly point out that we all—including teachers—have incomplete knowledge and can benefit from others.

Reading

The NCTM (1989) Standards recommend putting more emphasis on reading children's literature and gradually increasing the use of mathematical textbooks. Children's books on mathematics (e.g., the Young Math Book series originally published by Thomas Y. Crowell) and children's literature can introduce interesting mathematical ideas and applications as well as provide reading practice. Students should be encouraged to use their mathematics textbooks as a source of information and ideas, not merely a source of seatwork and homework assignments (Lappan & Schram, 1989).

Discussing

This section elaborates on the reasons for fostering class discussion, notes some suggestions for avoiding common problems with class discussions, and delineates some tips on helping children to practice oral-communication skills.

Rationale. We use language to think and learn as well as to communicate our thoughts—as a tool for reflection as well as a tool for expression (Britton, Burgess, Martin, McLeod, & Rosen, 1975). Whether alone or with others, we use oral language to think about and to make sense of what we are doing (Connolly, 1989). We talk to ourselves to plan, monitor, and evaluate our actions. We also use "private speech to puzzle through ideas—as a way of constructing new understandings. Through discussion, we make our inner thoughts or private speech public (Vygotsky, 1978). Such sharing can prompt children to reflect on, reconsider, reorganize, and clarify their ideas (Lappan & Schram, 1989). How many times have you thought you understood something until you tried to explain it to someone else? Talking about their ideas is an excellent way for children too to discover gaps, inconsistencies, or a lack of clarity in their thinking. (For similar reasons, teaching frequently results in the teacher understanding a topic more deeply.) A discussion can benefit listeners as well, perhaps giving them new insight.

Avoiding Class-Discussion Pitfalls. As Miss Brill discovered in Box 2.24 below, class discussions don't just happen. Verbalizing mathematical ideas can be difficult for students. Many feel insecure and threatened about speaking up, because they do not wish to appear ignorant or expose themselves to ridicule. Opportunities to practice verbalizing mathematical ideas in a nonthreatening atmosphere is essential. One method to accomplish this is by using **nonjudgmental recitations** (see Part I of Box 2.24). Students, particularly those accustomed to being spoon-fed, may be unresponsive. Many students have difficulty verbalizing mathematical ideas clearly and precisely. The lessons Miss Brill learned about fostering class discussions in Part II of Box 2.24 are summarized on page 2-111 immediately following Box 2.24.

Box 2.24: The Young and the Listless, or the Case of the Diffident Discussers

Part I: Recitation Revisited. Miss Brill was concerned about the lack of student participation in her class "discussions." "Why won't they talk? What should I do?" she asked the other fifth-grade teachers while waiting for a faculty meeting to begin.

"Recitation," announced Mrs. Battleaxe. "When I was a girl, my schoolmarm would call us before the class; we would have to put our solution to a problem on the chalkboard and we would have to defend our solution and answer. Great teaching method. Still use it in my class to this day. I can tell right away if they understand something or not. Sometimes it helps clarify a student's thinking real fast; with everyone's eyes on them, some kids think harder than they would otherwise and recognize their own mistakes and sometimes even correct themselves. It's good for other kids too. They can question and challenge the presenter, which really gets them whipped up at times. With any luck, a decent recitation will also help those out in left field understand the problem or lesson. Seems that if a student explains something, other students understand it better than if I try. Saves me a lot of wind." With that said, Mrs. Battleaxe left to talk with one of her cronies who had just arrived.

"Recitation?" Miss Brill asked.

Ms. Wise noted, "It was a technique used long before your time; it is seldom seen in the modern school. I find a modified version useful. As traditionally practiced, the instructor passed the ultimate judgment on the recitation, pointed out the correct procedure and answer, and then recorded a grade for the recitation performance in the grade book. Such a technique reinforced memorizing a prescribed view or procedure and listening to authoritative sources of information rather than thinking for yourself. It also produced an uncomfortable and even threatening situation where children were fearful to be wrong."

"Like in Mrs. Battleaxe's class," blurted out Miss Brill before she realized what she had said.

"It is essential to give children opportunities to discuss their thinking in an accepting atmosphere so that children do not fear being wrong," continued Ms. Wise, politely not agreeing with or contradicting Miss Brill's comment.

"But certainly not all answers are equally good," interjected Miss Brill.

"No, they certainly aren't," answered Ms. Wise. "But in an open atmosphere, children are more willing to examine their own ideas, admit they

Box 2.24 continued

erred, and correct themselves. If not, other children may disagree with a proposed solution or answer. And if this fails, a teacher can pose questions, note contradictions or inconsistencies, and otherwise help students re-evaluate their position.

"For such an approach to work—to help students risk being wrong—it is essential that a teacher help students understand that making errors is a natural process of learning. It is essential that a teacher help establish an atmosphere of mutual respect; we can disagree but we should do so without personal attacks. It is essential that a teacher help children to see that we should correct others in a spirit of helpfulness, not one-upmanship—in a way that we would like to be corrected."

Part II: Overcoming Discussion Difficulties. Miss Brill was still dissatisfied with the amount of student participation in her mathematics class. She tried a technique learned in an educational psychology course that involved inserting more questions into her lectures. Miss Brill hoped that more questions would keep the students alert, stimulate their thinking, and serve as a review of the key points. She was utterly astounded by the reaction of her class: silence. "They just sit there and don't say anything," complained Miss Brill in the teachers' room. "They don't even try to answer my questions," she said softly, almost in tears.
"What do you do when the class doesn't answer," asked Ms. Wise gently.

"Why I ... I tell them the answer," responded Ms. Brill. "After all, if no one knows the answer, it's important to tell them, isn't it?"

Instead of responding to her colleague's question, Ms. Wise asked another question, "How long do you wait before giving the class the answer?"

"Maybe 15 seconds," answered Ms. Brill.

"Why not wait longer?" probed Ms. Wise.

"If someone knows the answer, surely that will give them enough time to respond," answered Miss Brill. "Besides," she confessed, "the silence makes me nervous. If they don't answer right away I feel as though the question is not working—as though things are getting out of control."

"But consider what you're doing," explained Ms. Wise. "By always answering your own questions, you tell your students, 'Don't bother, she'll tell us in a moment.' In effect, they come to view all questions as rhetorical. Even if they know the answers, students may feel you are not really interested in hearing them. What you need to do is create the expectation that the students, not you, will answer your questions."

"How can I do that?" asked Miss Brill. "Just stand there and endure the silence?"

"Yes, this may be necessary, especially at first," confirmed Ms. Wise. "If you wait, it is clear that you really expect a student answer. After a long wait, you may want to give them a hint or some encouragement such as, 'What brave person will hazard an educated guess?' Though it may seem inefficient or even feel uncomfortable, it is important to wait for students to respond. Ultimately, it is in their best interest."

Steeled by Ms. Wise's advice, Miss Brill soon found that her class become more responsive to her questions. More specifically, as illustrated by the dialogue below, she found that her students had become comfortable answering questions that required responses of one or a few words.

Miss Brill:	In dividing this circle into two equal parts, the shaded area consists of how many parts?
Student:	Two.
Miss Brill:	The total area consists of how many parts?
Student:	Two
Miss Brill:	What fraction describes the area of this circle that is shaded?
Student:	One-half.
Miss Brill:	If I fold the circle in half the other way and draw in the line, the shaded area consists of how many parts?
Student:	Two.

Box 2.24 continued

Miss Brill:	The total area consists of how many parts?
Student:	Four.
Miss Brill:	What fraction describes the area of this circle that is shaded?
Student:	Two-fourths.
Miss Brill:	Has the area of the circle or the shaded amount changed?
Student:	No.
Miss Brill:	What can you conclude about the one-half and two-fourths?
Student:	They're the same?

Although pleased she had used precise questions to led the class to a logical conclusion, Miss Brill recognized that she still was doing most of the talking. Moreover, when she asked questions requiring responses of more than a couple of words, her students' replies were inadequate.

Miss Brill:	Describe a rectangle.
Student:	This piece of paper is a rectangle.
Student:	This square too.
Student:	Square angles.
Student:	Four-sided shape.

Although all of these responses described an aspect of the concept, none described a rectangle to Miss Brill's satisfaction. She sought a description that would distinguish a rectangle from other shapes—one that would sufficiently enlighten a person who had no previous knowledge of rectangles.

It was clear from this and other episodes that her students needed practice responding to questions that required them to articulate mathematical ideas more fully and carefully. To accomplish this and to increase the amount of student dialogue, she tried to phrase her questions so that the response required more than one or two words (e.g., "What would you do to find whether 156 is divisible by 3?" "How do you determine if 57 is a prime number?").

Miss Brill also found that her students frequently overused vague words such as "it," "them," "these," and "those." As a result, she and the other students often had difficulty understanding the explanation. Helpful-minded students would try to intervene to clarify the confusion but would often do no better. At first, Miss Brill would guess what the student meant. Usually she guessed correctly and the lesson proceeded. However, Miss Brill became concerned that her willingness to clarify the students' vague words was not promoting progress in the use of mathematical language or communication in general. She decided to insist on the use of proper terminology. Instead of "that number," for instance, she encouraged the use of "addend," "factor," "sum," "product," "numerator," "divisor," and so forth. Sometimes Miss Brill had her students write the answers to such questions first and then had them read to the class what they wrote. This motivated students to choose their words, and otherwise construct their arguments, more carefully.

✐ **Create the expectation that students should talk.** Give students the opportunity to respond and, if necessary, wait for them to respond.

✐ **Use questions that require a response of more than one word or a few words.** Questions requiring one- or two-word responses can be useful but do not provide sufficient experience for most students to become articulate in expressing mathematical ideas.

✐ **Encourage the use of proper terminology.** Model appropriate mathematical language and encourage students to substitute mathematically precise terms for vague everyday terms.

✐ **Occasionally have students write out their answers to questions and then read them to the class.** Writing a response can encourage students to concentrate on the use of words and the clarity of their ideas.

Practicing Oral-Communication Skills.
Children need to practice oral-communication skills regularly. Such practice can be done in an interesting fashion.

✍ **Use class presentations to practice communication skills.** To further improve communication skills, Miss Brill's students made mathematical presentations to the class. Sometimes students reported on a famous mathematician, a mathematics story from one of the mathematics magazines created for children, or a topic of personal interest.

✍ **Use small-group problem solving to practice communication skills.** On a regular basis, Miss Brill would have her students solve problems in small groups. Sometimes she would give each group a different problem. The students in a group discussed the problem and recorded their progress toward a solution. Next, the groups presented the problem to the entire class. Sometimes a group had not achieved a solution. Even so, attempts to reach a solution were described. Miss Brill encouraged the class to make any comments relevant to the problem in the form of clarifying questions, alternate solutions, insights, and so forth. Talking mathematics was a key goal of this activity.

✍ **Use games to practice communication skills.** Games can be an entertaining way of fostering the development of communication skills. Box 2.25 describes a game called **Talking Math**. This game can be enjoyed at any grade level. Early grades can have fun with words such as add, subtract, number, count, and equals. The list increases with each grade, eventually including possibilities such as dividend, equation, composite, Pythagorean triple, supplementary angle, rational number, and cosine. To facilitate their presentation to a class, words can be inscribed on 2" by 4" pieces of overhead projector transparencies.

🍎 Box 2.25: Talking Math

While driving home from school, Miss Brill was reflecting on her attempts to improve the use of precise mathematical language. Suddenly an idea popped into her mind. Once home, she took a stack of plain paper and wrote a single mathematical term on each piece. In class she would hold up a page and announce the term. Then Miss Brill would go around the room allowing each student to make a statement containing and/or describing the word. Each statement would have to be a complete sentence. One word or phrase would not be acceptable. When a word had been adequately described, Miss Brill would move on to a new word. To the word "triangle," class members made such responses as, "A triangle is a kind of shape"; "A triangle has three sides"; "Connect three points and you get a triangle"; and "A right triangle has a 90 degree angle."

Often the students' statements provided opportunities for further investigation and learning. "Try to draw three points that when connected will not result in a triangle," Miss Brill said as she wrote the challenge on the chalkboard. During spare moments that day, a number of students tackled the challenge, and some were successful. Before dismissal, students displayed their efforts and concluded that, indeed, three connected points sometimes did not result in a triangle. Miss Brill introduced a new word, "collinear," which was written on paper and added to the stack of math words.

One day an excited Lakesha asked, "Miss Brill, can we make our math words into a game show?"

"How could we do that?" a curious Miss Brill questioned.

"Well, we could have a host and teams of two," replied Lakesha. "The host would hold up a word that one team member and the class could see. The other team member would have her back to the host so that she could not see the word. The first team member would have to give clues so that the second team member could guess the word. If the 'guesser' got stuck, the 'clue-giver' could decide to 'pass' and proceed with the next word. The team would have one minute to try up to five words."

Miss Brill accepted the role of first host, shuffled the papers, and took the top five words for the first game. Lakesha served as the first clue-giver and her teammate Jessica served as the first guesser. Tom served as the timekeeper. Miss Brill held up the first word so that Lakesha and the class could see it, and Tom started a stopwatch.

Box 2.25 continued

Lakesha: A dot.

Jessica: A point.

Lakesha: A number with a dot in it.

Jessica: A decimal?

Miss Brill: Right. [displaying the second word]

Lakesha: What do you get when you divide?

Jessica: The answer.

Lakesha: The name for that answer .

Jessica: Oh, the remainder.

Lakesha: No, the name for the answer to eight divided by two?

Jessica: Four?

Lakesha: The answer to any division problem. [After it was clear Jessica was not going to respond, Lakesha decided to pass, and Miss Brill displayed the third word.] It's a round shape.

Jessica: A circle.

Miss Brill: Right. [holding up the fourth word]

Lakesha: Three, five, seven.

Jessica: Odd numbers.

Lakesha: No. Two, eleven, and thirteen.

Jessica: Primes.

Tom: Time's up.

Miss Brill: Primes is right. Lakesha and Jessica had three words correct.

The game was dubbed "Talking Math" and became a regular activity in Miss Brill's class. Whenever there were a few extra minutes, a student would suggest, "Let's play Talking Math!" When a pair of students were stuck on a word and ran out of time, their classmates were eager to suggest clues that could have been used. As new terms were introduced, Miss Brill wrote each on a piece of paper and placed it in the pile. The pages of words became worn quickly. Miss Brill transferred the words to sturdier cards. Multiple packs were made for students to use in smaller groups.

Some students invented a competitive variation of Talking Math that could be played by three children. In this variation, the host chose the words and gave the clues. The first of the two contestants to raise his or her hand could respond. Ties were handled by flipping a coin. If the first contestant was wrong, the second contestant was given an opportunity to respond. The contestant who identified the most words within a specified time or number of words won.

Activity 2.5 describes a communication game appropriate for any age level, including adults. Indeed, because this activity is a microcosm of didactic teaching, it can provide useful practice for anyone preparing for the teaching profession.

☞ Try Activity 2.5 (page 2-117) before going on.

Writing

How is writing relevant to learning mathematics? Writing across the curriculum is gaining popularity among elementary teachers. However, unlike other subjects such as science and social studies, where—if nothing else—children answer textbook questions, writing has never been viewed as a natural part of mathematics instruction (Wilde, 1991). The NCTM (1989) *Curriculum Standards* recommend putting more emphasis on expressing mathematical ideas in writing. To understand why, this section examines two instructional approaches to writing and then discusses the value of "writing to learn." It concludes with suggestions for how writing can be incorporated into mathematics instruction.

The Communicative Versus the Reflective Approach. Traditionally, writing instruction has focused on the process of communicating ideas. More recently, writing has been viewed as process of "thinking aloud on paper" (Rose, 1989). Table 2.4 compares the traditional "communicative approach" and the newer "reflective approach."*

Writing to Learn. Encouraged by proponents of the reflective approach, writing to learn has recently gained currency in the educational community. "The writing-to-learn movement is fundamentally about using words to acquire concepts" (Connolly, 1989, p. 5); it uses writing to *foster* reflection and understanding. Writing is a useful thinking tool, because it—more so than speaking—forces a child to slow down. "Its very slowness makes [writing] more deliberately self-conscious," which can enhance reflection (Connolly, 1989).

Writing to learn is fundamentally different from traditional instruction in several important ways (Connolly, 1989):

• Traditional uses of writing are based on the assumption that students should secure concepts first and then write about them. In fact, writing is an ideal way to help children discover gaps in their understanding, consider connections, and otherwise organize, reconsider, and clarify their ideas.

---

* In the educational literature, communicative writing is often called "transactional writing" and reflective writing is typically called "expressive writing."

• Talk in the traditional classroom is dominated by a few—largely by the teacher and more-able students; most students are passive. Writing provides a vehicle by which all students can be actively engaged.

• In the traditional classroom, knowledge is handed down ready-made to children by an authority. Writing to learn invests authority for learning in a child, enhancing the child's ownership of the learning, sense of power, and autonomy. It can help children see that knowledge is actively constructed, not passively absorbed—an important step in understanding the nature of their own learning. Through writing, children can experience mathematics as a creative activity (Rose, 1989).

Teaching Suggestions. Both communicative and reflective writing can play an important role in learning mathematics (Rose, 1989). Table 2.5 on the next page outlines ways each can be used in mathematics instruction. Note that in practice, the two types of writing are often blended. For example, a teacher may have students write about a concept to foster reflection about its meaning and then have them read their ideas to the class. While the emphasis may be on the students' ideas, the writing needs to be clear enough to communicate their meaning to others. Used in this way, writing serves to foster personal-reflection and public-communication goals. Activity File 2.8 on page 2-116 illustrates an easily implemented writing assignment. Some general guidelines about using writing in mathematics instruction are noted below:

Table 2.4: A Comparison of Two Approaches to Writing Instruction

Communicative Approach	Reflective Approach
• Public writing directed at an audience.	• Writing intended for personal use.
• Writing used to inform or persuade.	• Writing used to explore and reflect on ideas, plans, or feelings.
• Focuses on a polished finished product.	• Focuses on the messy process of exploration.
• Emphasizes style: clarity, organization, grammar, and spelling.	• Emphasizes content: meaningful reflection, not language skills.
• Uses a linear process: outline, draft, final product.	• Uses a recursive process: continual revisiting and revision of an idea.

Table 2.5: Some Uses of Writing[7]

Communicative Writing

• **Summaries:** To help students focus on the key points of a lesson, to evaluate their understanding, and to facilitate retention, have them summarize a lesson in their own words.

• **Questions:** To help students reflect and focus on what they don't understand, have them submit their questions (privately) in writing.

• **Explanations:** To foster reflection, understanding, and precise wording, have students explain their solution procedure, how to avoid an error, or the reasons for an answer or an error.

• **Definitions:** To help students think about the meanings of terms and clarify their understanding of terminology, have them write the definitions of terms in their own words.

• **Word problems:** To help students reflect on problems they don't understand, apply what they do understand, and develop a sense of power over word problems, have students rewrite word problems or write their own.

• **Reports:** To help students understand that writing is a key aspect of mathematics and to investigate mathematical topics, issues, or personalities, have students--as individuals or as groups--write a report.

• **Books:** To help students reflect on a mathematical topic, have them write and illustrate a book, which could be used to teach their peers or younger children about the topic.

Reflective Writing

• **Freewriting:** To help students think aloud on paper, have them record their thoughts and feelings. The assignment can be open-ended (unfocused) or channeled (focused). For focused writing, a teacher can, for example, pose a specific question such as: Was there anything I didn't really understand about yesterday's math lesson? What was the main idea of our discussion today? How did you feel about tackling today's problem? Focused writing is especially effective following hands-on activities (Wilde, 1991). Children can take a step toward communicative writing by sharing their freewriting with the teacher or class.

• **Letters:** To help students feel comfortable about expressing their thoughts and feelings, have them pretend to write a letter to a friend, a relative, a teacher, or a deity. The letter can describe what they have learned or what is causing them difficulty, what they would like to learn about, or how they feel about a particular topic or mathematics in general. Actually having children send the letters would combine reflective and communicative writing.

• **"Admit Slips":** To help students vent their worries, have them anonymously note their concerns, feelings and anxieties. If collected and read by the teacher, admit slips would become another step toward communicative writing.

• **Autobiographical Writing:** This can be done as communicative writing, reflective writing, or a combination of the two. To help students reflect on their personal experiences and become comfortable with writing, have them write a biographical narrative. This can be relatively open-ended (e.g., Mathematics makes me feel . . . or The best experience I have had in a math class is . . .), or more channeled (e.g., When I learned to multiply . . . or I use numbers to . . .).

• **Journals:** Like autobiographical writing, journals can be done as communicative writing, reflective writing, or a combination of the two. Thus, the audience, purpose, structure, and content of journals can vary. One type of journal is called the "Divided Page Exercise" (Tobias, 1989). On the lefthand side of the page, students think aloud, expressing whatever thoughts and feelings they wish. On the righthand side, they note their problem solutions, drawings, and calculations. The lefthand side gives students an opportunity to vent their feelings and anxieties. With experience, children may use this side of the page for metacognitive reflections. To prompt this, a teacher can have children respond to such questions as, "Do I really understand what I am doing? What might help me understand this problem? What confuses me about this problem? Why did I make the mistake I made?"

Activity File 2.8: Writing About Mathematics

◆ Examining beliefs about mathematics ◆ K-8
◆ Any number

To get a sense of how students view mathematics, a teacher can ask children to complete the expression, "To me, math is. . . ." Comparing children's responses at the beginning of the year to those at the end of the year can give you and them a sense of how their thinking about mathematics has evolved. Two samples from a third-grade class are shown below. Note that Matt views mathematics in a traditional vein—as doing written workbook pages—while Katie seems to view it in a more stimulating way—as something that involves solving problems and learning new concepts.

Matt

To me math is putting numbers in a book. Write math on papers.

To me math is fun because I like to figuour out things and learn new things.

Kane

✐ **Help children to understand the purposes of writing.** Some children may see writing as just an added burden. Explicitly point out that writing can serve as a tool for learning or a way of carrying out a dialogue with you (Marwine, 1989). It may also help to note that explaining how one got an answer is at least as important as getting the answer.

✐ **Begin with informal writing, which focuses on private reflection, and gradually work toward including formal writing, which focuses on public presentation.** To help children become comfortable with writing to think aloud, begin with purely reflective writing. Next, include tasks that blur the distinction between reflective and communicative writing. Lastly, introduce more purely communicative writing while continuing to practice more reflective writing.

✐ **Encourage children to write about their *reflections* of what they did, as well as what they did.** Younger children and those just introduced to writing about mathematics, in particular, will often simply write a narrative, a description of what hap-

pened. For example, a child might write: *"We used base-ten blocks to add."* An exposition entails commenting about the learning process or about what was learned (e.g., *"To add with base-ten blocks, you have to trade in 10 baby cubes for a long when you get too many baby cubes. I forget to trade sometimes but then I remember. Trading makes adding up scores easier"*). Although narrative writing may naturally lead into expository writing, some children will need to be encouraged to make this transition.

✐ **Help children overcome barriers that can make them reluctant to write.** Some children, particularly those accustomed to a communicative approach to writing, may be reluctant to write because of problems with style. For example, a child might be reluctant to write about his concept of multiplication because he cannot spell it. In this case, help the child to understand that expressing his or her ideas is what counts, not correct spelling.

✐ **As a step toward communicative writing, encourage children to share orally their reflective writing.** This can help children spot problems with their writing as well as their thinking. (You might wish to encourage children to read their writing to themselves before a public reading. Such a technique can be helpful in refining highly personal writing so that it can be understood by others.) Sharing also helps the other students in class by giving them exposure to content more than once and, possibly to new views of the content (Wilde, 1991).

✐ **Integrated language arts-mathematics assignments can provide another vehicle for writing about mathematics.** Writing a story that involves mathematics can be done, for instance, in conjunction with the classic assignment of writing a story that involves a week's vocabulary words. It could be done as a creative-writing assignment. Such activities provide an excellent opportunity to practice language-arts skills and to use one's imagination. They can help children connect mathematical knowledge to other subject areas and everyday life.

✐ **Encourage bilingual children to write in their first language first and then their second language.** This code switching may help bilingual children to better capture their thoughts and feelings as well as increase their fluency in their second language (Wilde, 1991).

⚫ Activity 2.5: Design Teaching

◆ Communication and social skills + geometry terminology ◆ K-adult ◆ Small groups

The aim of Design Teaching is for a "teacher" to communicate verbally a description of a design so that a "student" or small group of "students" can reproduce it. The design can be drawn (see Frames A, B, and C on the next page) or made of manipulative materials such as pattern blocks (see Frames D, E, and F) or geoboards and rubberbands (see Frames G, H, and I). The "teacher" can create his or her own design or a design can be provided. The complexity of the design can be tailored to the developmental level of the students.

The rules specify that the "teacher" may verbally describe the design but may not gesture or picture the design. To ensure that only verbal communication is used, the teacher could sit on one side of a barrier with the design and the "student(s)" could sit on the other side. The students may ask questions at any time. Indeed, a wise teacher encourages questions. The teacher should be given an opportunity to prepare a "lesson" on the design—to organize his or her thoughts about how to best communicate about the design. The activity can be played with a time limit, which can create pressure to communicate efficiently and add an element of excitement. The teacher's success can be gauged by whether or not the student reproduced the design. If there are a group of students, then success can be gauged by how many could accurately reproduce the design. With drawn designs, an accurate reproduction contains all the shapes in the original in the same proportions as the original, although the drawing need not be the same size as the original. Put in mathematical terms, a successful reproduction must be similar to the original design but it need not be congruent to the original. Try the activity with your group and then continue with the description of the activity below.

Several elements can facilitate communication and, thus, the effectiveness of one's teaching. One such factor is the use of precise language. For Item A, for example, it is most helpful to specify from the onset that the triangle has equal sides. This saves time trying to repair your description later. Moreover, without further explanation, it means that the squares that adjoin each side are the same size.

Communication is facilitated even further if the teacher and student both understand terms for a concept. For Item B, for example, if everyone understands the term equilateral octagon, the teacher can more easily communicate the central figure in the form. Compare this with trying to describe the form as an eight-sided figure in which all the sides are equal. Some people might even have difficulty imagining such a shape. Helping children acquire mathematical terms and their related concepts is important for fostering shared meanings, which can facilitate communication.

Incidentally, this exercise illustrates well the importance of relating information to a person's existing knowledge. A useful technique for achieving this end both in this exercise and in teaching, in general, is the analogy. In Item E, for instance, a powerful analogy for the central figure in the form is a stop sign, for which many people have a mental image. For Item C, the analogy of an arrow or a one-way street sign could greatly facilitate communication.

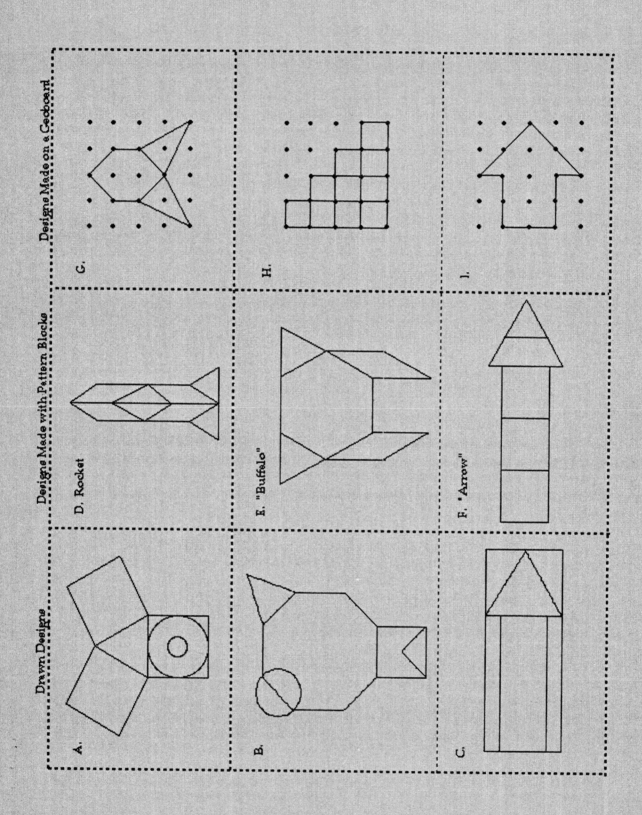

Drawn Designs

A.

B.

C.

Designs Made with Pattern Blocks

D. Rocket

E. "Buffalo"

F. "Arrow"

Designs Made on a Geoboard

G.

H.

I.

Reader's Notes

FOR FURTHER EXPLORATION

SOME INSTRUCTIONAL RESOURCES

☞ **About Teaching Mathematics: A K-8 Resource** by Marilyn Burns, © 1992 by Math Solutions Publications, 150 Gate 5, Suite 101, Sausalito, CA 94965. Distributed by the Cuisenaire Company of America, Inc., 10 Bank Street, White Plains, NY 10606-1951 (800-237-3142).

This invaluable reference evolved from the coursebook for the widely acclaimed *Math Solutions* inservice workshops. The book has three main parts. Part I, Raising the Issues, examines the role of arithmetic in the mathematics curriculum, common arithmetic errors, using word problems to develop arithmetic understanding, going beyond word problems to foster problem solving (including problem-solving heuristics and arguments against and for problem solving), how children learn mathematics, and managing the classroom for problem solving.

Part II, Problem-Solving Activities in the Strands, illustrates how problem solving can be integrated with content instruction on number (developing a number sense), measurement, patterns and functions, geometry, probability and statistics, and logic. For example, "Palindromes," an activity from the number strand, involves looking for number patterns as well as practicing multidigit arithmetic. A palindrome is a number that has the same value whether read forward or backward. For example 77, 707, 757, and 7557 are all palindromes; 72, 700, 756, and 7547 are not. A nonpalindrome can be converted into a palindrome by adding its reverse (e.g., 72 + 27 = 99). Sometimes this process must be repeated once (e.g., [1] 75 + 57 = 132; [2] 132 + 231 = 363); sometimes more often (e.g., [1] 78 + 87 = 165; [2] 165 + 561 = 726; [3] 726 + 627 = 1353; [4] 1353 + 3531 = 4884). With this background, pose the following problem:

■ **Palindromes 0 to 99.** What are all the palindromes between 0 and 99? What numbers can be converted into a palindrome in one step, two steps, three steps, and so forth? You may wish to warn students that 89 and 98 require persistence. (Each requires 24 steps.) Are there any patterns that emerge? (Recording the data on a 0 to 99 chart can be helpful.)

Part III, Teaching Arithmetic, examines why arithmetic should be taught in a meaningful manner and how this can be done. It includes an assortment of independent activities (menus) for beginning number concepts, place value, addition and subtraction, multiplication, division, fractions, decimals, and percents. Cross-Out Singles, for example, is a useful game for practicing addition.

🍎 **Cross-Out Singles** can be played with two or more players. Using a 0 to 9 spinner, a number is chosen. A player records the number anywhere they wish to on a 3x3 grid. This process is repeated until all 9 grids are filled in. Each player then sums the rows, a diagonal, and the columns and records the result of each in the appropriate circle. Any sums that appear only once are crossed out. The sum of the remaining circles is a player's score.

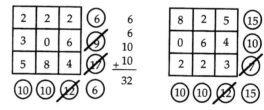

☞ **Activities with Attributes: Experiences in Logical Problem Solving** by Maria Marolda, © 1993 by Dale Seymour Publications, P.O. Box 10888, Palo Alto, CA 94303 (800-USA-1100).

This resource contains numerous games and activities to challenge children's thinking. In **What Is Missing in the Square?**, children must fill in blank squares with attribute blocks with two sizes, four shapes, and four colors. The catch is that blocks in squares sharing a side must differ by three qualities. Try solving the example below. Are there other possible solutions? How many can you find?

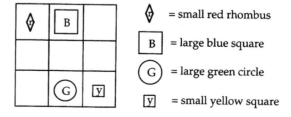

This resource illustrates how problems can be solved with the aid of Venn diagrams and provides numerous problems for practice. Consider the problem below:

■ A math teacher conducted a survey of her classes. 42 students chewed gum in class; 55 talked incessantly; and 25 fell asleep during class. Four people both talked and fell asleep but didn't chew gum. Six students fell asleep and chewed gum but at least didn't talk. Forty students only talked. Ten students talked and chewed gum but didn't fall asleep. How many students were there in all? How many students talked and chewed gum and fell asleep (UGH)?

☞ **The Elementary Mathematician** published by COMAP, 57 Bedford St., Suite 210, Lexington, MA 02173 (617-862-7878; FAX 617-863-1202).

Subscriptions to this newsletter are *free* to all elementary educators. (COMAP is a nonprofit organization originally supported by the National Science Foundation.) The newsletter, supported by the Exxon Education Corporation, consists of articles and information (e.g., instructional materials development projects) that teachers will find useful. It also includes challenging problems such as Activity 1 (The Chain Letter) described below. Note that this problem can involve a discussion of number names up to a billion (place-value content), making a table (problem-solving heuristics), and the use of calculators.

■ **The Chain Letter.** Suppose you start a chain letter by sending a letter to five of your friends, asking them to send a copy of the letter to five of their friends, and so on. Suppose, further, that it takes only one day for each of these notes to arrive, so if you send your notes on day 1, then your friends receive it on day 2, their friends receive it on day 3, etc. Assuming there are 6 billion people in the world and no one receives more than one letter, how long would it take for everyone in the world to receive a letter?

For extension, have students consider what would happen if each recipient sent only 2 new letters or if they sent 10 new letters? Try solving the Chain Letter and its extensions yourself.

☞ **Learning by Logic**, © Invicta Plastics Ltd. and published by Ebenezer Baylis & Son Ltd. of Leicester and London, England.

This resource illustrates various games and activities with attribute blocks. In **Gate Game I**, for instance, a gatekeeper checks each player's ticket (an attribute block) and allows those with a valid ticket (the chosen characteristic) to enter. For example, if the gatekeeper has chosen red, a player with a small, thin, red triangle or a large, thick, red square would be allowed to enter. A player who choses a small, thin, yellow triangle or a large, thick, blue square would be denied entry. The first player to identify the rule becomes the new gatekeeper. Such a game would be appropriate for children as young as kindergarten.

This game underscores the usefulness of incorrect answers. Consider the following scenario. On her first turn, Kerry chose a large, thin, blue square but was not allowed to enter by the gatekeeper. Ebenezer then chose a small, thick, red circle and was not allowed to enter. Micah then chose a large, thin, yellow triangle. He was allowed to enter but incorrectly concluded that the rule was yellow. What should Kerry do on her turn? What kind of reasoning was required to determine what Kerry should do?

☞ **Make it Simpler** by Carol Meyer and Tom Sallee, © 1983 by Addison-Wesley, Route 128, Reading, MA 01867 (800-447-2226).

This book has numerous problems elementary school children may find challenging. If the problems are solved in order, children encounter a relatively simple version of a problem first and then a more elaborate version later. A teacher can use the book, then, to underscore the heuristic of *relating a new problem to a familiar problem*. Consider the example below from page 224:

■ **Planting the Orchard.** My neighbor has a peculiar orchard. He has five apple trees, five peach trees, five pear trees, five apricot trees, and five plum trees. The trees are planted in a square of five rows of five trees each. Each row (in each direction) has exactly one tree [of] each variety and so do the center diagonals. How are the trees planted?

What is the solution? For primary children especially, the chances of successfully solving this problem can be increased by introducing a simpler version of the problem first. This can be done by reducing the number of rows and columns and/or eliminating the constraint that the diagonals must contain different items. For example, the simpler version of Planting the Orchard, which appears earlier in *Make It Simpler*, involves arranging four rows of four coins each so that each horizontal and vertical row has exactly one penny, one nickel, one dime, and one quarter.

☞ **The Pattern Factory: Elementary Problem Solving Through Patterning** by Ann Roper and Linda Harvey, © 1980 by Creative Publications, 5040 W. 111 Street, Oak Lawn, IL 60453 (800-624-0822).

This resource contains numerous problems that entail undercovering a pattern. The cow-fence problem was discussed in Box 2.6. Below is another example from page 60:

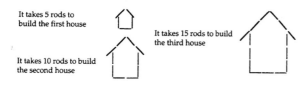

How many rods will it take to build the sixth house?

House	1st	2nd	3rd
Number of rods	5	10	15

Set theory is introduced concretely with aid of Venn and Carroll Diagrams. An example of the latter is shown below.

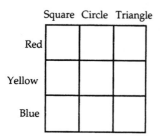

Consider how you would modify the diagram to illustrate the attribute of size (large versus small) as well as shape and color.

☞ **The Problem Solver 3: Activities for Learning Problem Solving Strategies** by Shirley Hoogeboom and Judy Goodnow, © 1987 by Creative Publications, 788 Palomar Avenue, Sunnyvale, CA 94086.

This valuable resource is representative of recent efforts to introduce children to problem solving strategies. Paralleling Polya's four-phase systematic approach to problem solving, it introduces a four-step method: FIND OUT, CHOOSE A STRATEGY, SOLVE IT, and LOOK BACK. It introduces 10 heuristics: (1) ACT OUT or USE OBJECTS, (2) MAKE A PICTURE OR DIAGRAM, (3) USE OR MAKE A TABLE, (4) MAKE AN ORGANIZED LIST, (5) GUESS AND CHECK, (6) USE OR LOOK FOR A PATTERN, (7) WORK BACKWARDS, (8) USE LOGICAL REASONING, (9) MAKE IT SIMPLER, and (10) BRAINSTORM.

The third-grade volume described here is part of a set that spans the elementary years. Each volume has a preface that describes the problem-solver program and general teaching suggestions. The preface also includes a table listing each problem in the volume, the applicable heuristic, and similar problems in the previous and successive volumes. The set, then, can aid teachers in finding problems that are developmentally appropriate for their grade level and that encourage the *relate-a-new-problem-to-familiar-problems* heuristic, which is briefly mentioned in the reference.

The first section, **Teaching the Strategies**, describes the four-step method and heuristics and presents teaching problems for illustrating them. The second section consists of practice problems similar to the teaching problems but presented in a haphazard order. Unlike the teaching problems, the students must decide for themselves which heuristic is appropriate.

Illustrated on the next page is a student workbook page from the first section. What is the solution to Problem 45 shown below? The teaching plan (not shown) includes: **EXTEND IT:** • How many sides would get painted if Ron put 10 blocks in each row? What is the solution to this extension problem? What would be the solution to the problem if 100 blocks were pushed together?

2-123

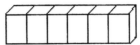 **MAKE IT SIMPLER**   Name

45 Ron and Rebecca Robot work in a factory. Ron pushes 6 blocks together in a row on a table, and Rebecca sprays paint on the blocks. Every block has 6 sides. The sides that touch the table or sides of other blocks don't get painted. How many sides of the blocks in a row get painted?

FIND OUT
- What is the question you have to answer?
- How many blocks are in each row? Are the blocks touching or not touching?
- How many sides does each block have?
- What sides of the blocks don't get painted?

CHOOSE A STRATEGY
- Circle to show what you choose.

SOLVE IT
- What are you going to keep track of in the organized list started on your paper?
- Begin with 1 block. How many sides touch the table? How many sides touch sides of other blocks? How many of the block's sides get painted?
- Now try 2 blocks. How many sides touch the table? How many sides touch the sides of other blocks? How many sides of 2 blocks get painted?
- Now try 3 blocks. How many sides touch the table? How many sides touch the sides of other blocks? How many sides of 3 blocks get painted?
- How many sides of 4 blocks get painted?
- Do you see a pattern in the number of sides getting painted?
- How many sides of 6 blocks get painted?

Number of blocks in the row	Number of sides that get painted
1	5
2	8
3	
4	
5	
6	

LOOK BACK
- Look back to see if your answer fits with what the problem tells you and asks you to find. Read the problem again. Look back over your work. Does your answer fit?

The Problem Solver 3   T•89   © 1987 Creative Publications

The facsimile of page T•89 is represented with the permission of the publisher.

☞ **Problem-Solving Experiences in Mathematics: Grade 7** by Randall I. Charles, Robert P. Mason, Joan M. Nofsinger, and Catherine A. White, © 1985 by Addison-Wesley Publishing Company, Menlo Park, CA.

This book is part of a series of books that outlines a problem-solving program for grades 1 to 8. The problems at a given grade level have been extensively field tested for interest and appropriate difficulty. This resource, then, provides another valuable source of grade-appropriate problems for the classroom teacher.

The Overview includes a chart indicating what heuristics might be helpful in solving specific problems, tips on creating a classroom climate conducive to problem solving, and suggestions for evaluating students' problem-solving efforts.

A SAMPLE OF CHILDREN'S LITERATURE

☜ **The I Hate Mathe-matics! Book** by Marilyn Burns, © 1975 by Little, Brown and Company, Boston.

Although written for intermediate-level students, this book can be an entertaining source of problems and teaching ideas for teachers. It begins by reassuring readers that "some of the nicest people hate mathematics," especially those who equate it with arithmetic (p. 7). After listing examples of disparaging comments made by children about mathematics (e.g., "Mathematicians have little pig eyes"), readers are encouraged to vent their own feelings about mathematics. The book suddenly changes tack, noting it will use fun and games to change mathematical weaklings into mathematical heavyweights. The secret, it announces, is that "YOU ARE A MATHEMATICAL GENIUS IN DIS-GUISE!" and that all it takes is to reorganize what is already in the reader's head (p. 9). In other words, it advances the beliefs that anyone can develop mathematical aptitude by learning to exploit their existing knowledge more effectively. The book goes on to note that "the password of mathematics is patterns" (p. 9). The book includes problems on combinations and permutations, ratios, large numbers, primes, and probability. One problem involves cutting sidewalks:

■ **Cutting Sidewalks.** Consider a square or a rectangular section of a sidewalk. What is the greatest number of pieces it could be cut into with one straight line? Two? Three? Four? Complete the table below. Then consider the relatively difficult cases of using five and six straight lines.

Number of straight lines	1	2	3	4	5	6
Greatest number of pieces						

☜ **Mathematical Games for One or Two** by Mannis Charosh, © 1972 by Thomas Y. Crowell Company of New York.

This resource describes a number of games that can be played by one or two children as young as primary age. One example, **Nim** games, involves two rows of objects, drawn circles, etc. On their turn, players eliminate as many items as they wish from *one* of the rows. The player who eliminates the last item wins. In "Equal Nim," the rows begin with an equal number of items. There can be any number in each row. Example A below shows four items in each row. In "Unequal Nim," the rows begin with an unequal number of items as in Example B below.

```
O O O O        O O O O O
O O O O        O O O O
```
A. Equal Nim   B. Unequal Nim

Devise a winning strategy for Equal Nim. Some children may want to play these games with beaucoup items in the rows. Is this a good idea when you are trying to find a winning strategy? (Put differently, what heuristic is applicable?) Does it matter whether there are an odd or an even number of items in each row? Next, try finding a winning strategy for Unequal Nim. Consider how what you know about Equal Nim may help. Then try "Odd Equal Nim": an odd number of rows with the same number of items or circles in each row. This game using three rows is illustrated below:

```
O O O O
O O O O
O O O O
```

What is the winning strategy for this game? Consider what you already know about Nim games. Does "Even Equal Nim" have the same winning strategy?

☜ **Venn Diagrams** by Robert Froman, © 1972 by Thomas Y. Crowell Company, New York.

This book introduces Venn diagrams as a tool for sorting things out. Particularly interesting is the section on using Venn diagrams to solve problems. It presents what appears to be an unsolvable problem and illustrates how a Venn diagram can be used to determine the answer. The problem below is similar in structure to that presented in the book. Try using a Venn diagram to solve it.

■ Professor Cloud would never be accused of being a fashion plate. During the course of a week, he wore a white sock seven times, a brown sock four times, and a rust sock three times. If he wore matched white socks twice and a white and brown mismatch three times, how many times during the course of the week did Professor Cloud wear a pair of socks with matching colors?

TIPS ON USING TECHNOLOGY

Calculators

⌨ **Cooperative Problem Solving with Calculators** by Ann Roper, Shirley Hoogeboom, and Judy Goodnow, © 1991, and **The Problem Solver with Calculators** by Terrence G. Coburn, Shirley Hoogeboom, and Judy Goodnow, © 1989, both published by Creative Publications, 788 Palomar Avenue, Sunnyvale, CA 94086.

The first resource is a collection of 72 problems suitable for children in grades 4 to 6. "The problems are designed to be solved by groups of four students, using calculators" (p. iii). A four-step strategy is suggested for solving problems: (1) FIND OUT; (2) CHOOSE A STRATEGY; (3) ESTIMATE, CALCULATE, AND SOLVE; and (4) LOOK BACK. The resource also provides hints about what heuristic (Make a Table, Look for a Pattern, Make a Picture or Diagram, Make an Organized List, Guess and Check, Make It Simpler, Use Logical Reasoning, and Work Backwards) might be helpful—hints that a teacher can provide as needed. A sample problem from page 26 is:

■ Moko and Indmy live in a solar system 10 billion light years from Earth. Moko is 1006 years old. Indmy is 3026 years old. In how many years will Indmy be exactly three times as old as Moko?

The hint that can be provided is: "**Make a Table**. Write down the two ages now, add one year, and see how many times older Indmy will be than Moko then." (Consider what operation students need to use to determine this.) By extending the table students should be able to solve the problem.

The second resource includes 60 problems suitable for students in grades 4 to 6 and 60 problems suitable for students in grades 7 to 8. It also provides a convenient table to indicate which heuristic can be used with each problem. The following problem is from page 3:

■ There are long weeks, but no months, on the Willyturf calendar. On the planet Willyturf, the year is 365 days long, and the year is divided into weeks. The first day of the week is named A-day, the second day of the week is named B-day, and so on to the last day, which is named

Z-day. The Willyturfs love H-days! Every H-day is a holiday and all the Willyturfs celebrate. Day 1 of the year 2005 falls on H-day. How many holidays will the Willyturfs have in the year 2005?

Beside the problem, the handout for the students includes suggestions for choosing a strategy and solving the problem: "Use [a] pattern to identify the H-days after the first day of the year. Record the H-days in a table.... Use the constant. Begin with these keystrokes: Multiples of 26 (+1): [C] 1 [+] 26 [+] [=] [=] [=]. Continue filling in the table.

H-day	1	2	3	4	5	...
Day of year	1	27				

A teacher might choose to give students the problems only and have them try to come up with their own solution strategies first, reserving the worksheet with its suggested solution strategy for those groups that need help.

⌨ **Problem Solving Using the Calculator** by Joan Duea, George Immerzeek, Earl Ockenga, and John Tarr. Chapter 12 (pp. 117-126) in *Problem Solving in School Mathematics*: 1980 Yearbook, edited by Stephen Krulik and Robert E. Reys and published by the NCTM, Reston, VA.

This chapter describes how calculators can be used to foster problem solving and provides numerous example problems. Consider the following:

■ The product of...two facing pages [pages 40 and 41] is...1640. Where would you open the book so the product of the two facing pages' numbers is 12,656? (p. 118).

⌨ **Using the Math Explorer™ Calculator** by Gary G. Bitter and Jerald L. Mikesill, © 1990 by Addison-Wesley, Menlo Park, CA.

This resource includes chapters on Learning to Use the Math Explorer Calculator, the Calculator and the Curriculum, Using the Calculator as a Teaching Tool, Curriculum Considerations for the Use of the Calculator, Interdisciplinary Calculator Projects, Career Applications and Career Project Ideas, Estimating with an Emphasis on Place Value, and Exponents and Scientific Notation. It also has three chapters on Using a Calculator to Develop Higher Order Thinking Skills for grades K to 3, grades 4 to 6, and 7 to 9. The problem described below is from Activity 2 of the grade 4 to 6 section (pages 132-134).

■ **Super Product**. Arrange the digits 1 to 5 in the boxes below, arrange them so that the resulting product is the largest possible value. You may use each of the five digits once.

Students are encouraged to make educated guesses and check their guesses on the calculator. The extension suggested is: Arrange the five digits to make the smallest possible product.

Computers

Learning how to program a computer is a challenging task that requires logical reasoning and the precise use of (a computer) language. If a student fails to reason logically or use a computer language carefully, the computer is uncompromising. It will refuse to work or will produce something other than what was desired. The book described below introduces children to programming using a flow chart.

🖳 **Computers** by Jane Jonas Srvastava, © 1972 by the Thomas Y. Crowell, New York.

This book gives an overview of how computers work. One observation that children might find interesting: computers are counting machines; they do arithmetic by counting. The book also introduces some computer terminology such as "program" (a set of instructions that tell a computer what to do) and "flow chart" (a road-map like plan for writing a program). For example, it illustrates a flow chart for counting from 0 to 10 and then challenges readers to create a flow chart for counting 20 to 30. Readers are encouraged to give their flow charts to friends who serve as computers to see if they work. Because the friends can only do what they are instructed, whether or not they successfully count from 20 to 30 depends on the precision of the flow charts. Thus, children can be introduced to the exacting demands of programming, even without the availability of a computer.

1. Shown below is a flow chart. Follow its instructions and determine its purpose.

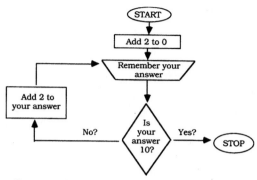

Note: An oval indicates where the flow chart (logic) starts and ends. The rectangle is a process symbol. (In the programming language BASIC, these would be LET statements.) The trapezoid represents other instructions. The diamond is a decision symbol. (In BASIC, IF statements.)

2. Construct a flow chart for (a) counting by ones from 1 to 10; (b) counting by ones from 20 to 30; (c) counting by fives from 5 to 45.

🖳 **Computers in Elementary Education** by Douglas H. Clements, © 1989 by Prentice-Hall, Englewood Cliffs, NJ 07632.

This invaluable resource has chapters on computer programming (including a discussion of LOGO), problem solving, and logical foundations and number. It lists commercially available software and provides helpful comments on numerous instructional programs.

🖳 **The Adventures of Jasper Woodbury videodisk problem-solving series** created by the Cognition and Technology Group, Peabody College of Vanderbilt University, © 1993 and published by the Optical Data Corporation, 30 Technology Drive, Warren, NJ 07059 (800-524-2481; FAX 908-668-1322).

This series uses a humorous story format to present challenging and realistic (applied) problems that require (Grades 5-8) students to use a variety of mathematical concepts, skills, and strategies. The series is squarely predicated on a problem-solving approach: presenting a single complex problem before children have been introduced to subject-matter content. In one episode, for example, children are confronted with the problem of calculating the rate at which an airplane travels. Research on the materials indicates that intermediate-level students working in groups can intuitively discover that distance traveled is a function of the rate of travel multiplied by the time. (It is probably a good idea for teachers to help students summarize such intuitive discoveries as a formula: in this case, that $D = R \times T$).

Calculating rates leads students into the area of partial units, creating a need to explore decimals. The episode also gets into other subject matter domains such as science, specifically aerodynamics. The videodisk allows students to go back to any part of the story and access information needed to solve the problem. The problems are open-ended in the sense that there is no one correct solution. Extension of the original problem is provided by asking students "what if?" questions (e.g., What if the plane only carried 5 gallons of gas?) Research indicates that students generally respond enthusiastically to the rich problems (Pellegrino et al., 1991).

The King's Rules by Thomas C. O'Brien, © 1984 by Sunburst Communications, Inc., Pleasantville, NY 10570.

Appropriate for intermediate students, this program involves inductive reasoning and can be used with Apple, Commodore 64, or TRS-80 Model III-4 computers. The aim is to advance into the heart of a castle and confront a king. To advance beyond the first level (the Castle Gate), a student must solve three relatively transparent number riddles: number patterns involving small upward or downward jumps. A riddle is posed as three numbers, which are related by a "secret" rule. Consider the example: 29 24 19. Players can then check their hunch (hypothesis) about the secret rule by posing their own set of numbers. For our example, posing 30 25 20 or 38 33 28 would elicit the response from the computer: It fits the rule. When the player feels ready, the computer poses a five-question quiz. After successfully completing this diagnostic test, the players go on to the next riddle.

After completing the first level, the players face increasingly difficult number patterns. The patterns of the second level (The Guard's Room) entail multiplying or dividing by a number from 1 to 5 (e.g., 2 10 50 or 48 12 3). Level 3 entails 10 new rules such as ends in 9. From the clue, guesses (hypotheses), and feedback shown below, can you decipher the rules for Riddles A and B?

	Clue	Guess 1	Feedback	Guess 2	Feedback
A.	27, 87, 93	25, 36, 72 (a<b<c)	Does not fit the rule	3, 5, 7 (odd numbers)	Does not fit the rule
B.	12, 48, 92	4, 12, 16 (divisible by 4)	Fits the rule	5, 10, 15 (divisible by 5)	Fits the rule

A key to hypothesis testing is to collect disconfirming evidence as well as confirming evidence. The former allows you to discount plausible alternative explanations while the latter confirms your explanation (hypothesis).

In Problem B above, the first hypothesis is confirmed. It might be tempting to conclude from the clue and test that the rule is: divisible by 4. The players, though, wisely sought to disconfirm other hypotheses before taking the Quiz. They tried 5 10 15 fully expecting the feedback to indicate this set of numbers did not fit the rule. To their surprise, it did. Clearly, their initial hypothesis (divisible by 4) was not general enough. What rule would fit all three sets of numbers shown for Riddle B?

Level 4 (The Magician's Study) involves riddles in which the third number is the result of an operation on the other numbers shown and, in some cases, a constant. Can you decipher Riddles C and D from the evidence given?

	Clue	Guess 1	Feedback	Guess 2	Feedback
C.	5, 3, 4	6, 3, 9	Fits the rule	7, 3, 16	Fits the rule
D.	5, 3, 80	3, 1, 40	Fits the rule	6, 3, 90	Fits the rule

Level 5 (The Royal Suite) includes patterns that are apparently obvious but which are not. Consider Riddle E below. It appears from the clue that the rule is add 100. At this level, though, it is especially important to consider plausible alternative hypotheses and to seek evidence to disconfirm them. This is what the players have done with Checks 1 and 2. What other plausible alternative rules can you think of?

	Clue	Guess 1	Feedback	Guess 2	Feedback
E.	100, 200, 300	2, 4, 6 (divisible by 2)	Does not fit the rule	1, 2, 3 (numbers in ascending order)	Does not fit the rule

In the sixth and last level (confrontation with the King), the riddles are very difficult because the rule may apply to only one or two of the numbers in an example. For instance, the numbers given may be 64, 66, and 68, and the rule is the middle number is even.

Teacher's Resource Book for Addison-Wesley Computer Literacy and Addison-Wesley Programming in BASIC for the Apple II Series, Commodore 64, TRS-80, and IBM-PC by Gary G. Bitter, © 1986 and published by Addison-Wesley.

The first part of this resource (Toward Computer Literacy) includes a list of computer-literacy objectives, safety do's and don'ts, and resources (Computer Books for Teachers, Computer Magazines and Newsletters, and Computer Books for Students). The second part describes an activity-based approach to teaching children about computers and how to use them. This part includes chapters on Word Processing: Writing Made Easier, Data Bases: Finding Information Fast, Spreadsheets: Tools for Decision Making, and Programming: Taking Steps to Solve Problems.

QUESTIONS TO CONSIDER

1. In the Peg Game, a player must interchange the light and dark pegs (e.g. white and blue golf tees) on a board like that shown below in the fewest moves possible. The rules specify that the light pegs may move only toward the right by sliding into the next empty hole or by jumping over a single peg into an empty hole. The same holds for dark pegs, except that they can only move toward the left.

With two pegs on a side, as shown above, the minimum number of moves to switch the position of the light and dark pegs is 8. With 3 pegs, it takes 15 moves, and with 4 pegs, 24. Determine for yourself how many moves it would take to interchange one light and one dark peg. Note that the light peg must end up in the position originally occupied by the dark peg and vice versa. Now consider how many moves it would take to interchange 5 pegs on each side.

(a) What heuristic(s) would be useful in solving the problem above? Briefly justify. (b) What is the answer? (c) Does solving this problem involve inductive reasoning, deductive reasoning, or both? Briefly justify your answer. (d) How might this task be simplified so that it is appropriate for primary children?

2. Problem 9 in Probe 2.3 on page 2-28 (Golf Balls) may be very difficult for children. It might help them to solve a simpler version before trying this problem. (a) Write a simpler version of the Golf-Ball problem. (b) Try rewriting the problem so that it involves repeated subtraction. (c) Rewrite the problem so that it involves repeated addition.

3. In mathematics, the meaning of some terms such as "or" are restricted to just one of their everyday meanings. In everyday language, "or" can mean one thing or another but not both (the exclusive meaning), *or* it can mean at least one of two things and perhaps both (the inclusive meaning). An example of the exclusive meaning—and more common everyday usage—is an insecure beau presenting an ultimatum to his girlfriend, "What's it going to be, him or me?"

Implied is a choice; having both beaus is not acceptable. An example of the inclusive meaning is a woman looking forward to having children who says, "I'd like boys or girls." In this case, the woman does not have a preference and would be satisfied with either boys, girls, or both. For each of the following, decide whether an exclusive or an inclusive meaning of or applies. (a) The italicized or in the second sentence above; (b) I want to be a beach bum or a medical doctor when I grow up; (c) I don't care whether you take a train, plane, or car, just get here by tomorrow; (d) I'd like a tie, a pen set, or a new Mercedes for my birthday; (e) The union of two sets: mathematically, a set of items possessing the property of one set or another (e.g., 8, 16, 24... are both even numbers and multiples of 8).

4. (a) Evaluate the following argument. Is it valid or invalid? (b) Draw a Venn diagram to illustrate your answer.

> People who do not have enough money to pay their bills are not happy. All rich people have enough money to pay their bills. Therefore, all rich people are happy.

5. A sports column had the following passage: "In the second half, the home team led by an ever-increasing margin of 21 to 7, 28 to 7, 35 to 7, 35 to 10, 42 to 10, and 45 to 10." Evaluate the accuracy of this written communication.

SUGGESTED ACTIVITIES

1. Examine a mathematics textbook at the grade level you plan to teach. Find two routine problems and transform them into nonroutine problems. Share your examples of routine problems and new-and-improved nonroutine problems with your group or class. Explore how your new-and-improved nonroutine problems could be improved further.

2. Examine a mathematics textbook at the grade level you plan to teach. Find two goal-specific problems and transform them into nongoal-specific problems. Share your examples of goal-specific and new-and-improved nongoal-specific problems with your group or class. Explore how your nongoal-specific problems could be improved.

3. Start collecting a file of problems appropriate for

the grade level you plan to teach. Particularly helpful are references like *The Joy of Mathematics: Discovering Mathematics All Around You* by T. Pappas (1989). You may wish to keep your file on 3x5-inch cards or in a computer. You may wish to cross-reference your index so that you have the title and topic.

4. As you read the newspaper or a weekly news magazine, be alert for real-world problems you could use in the classroom.

5. Collect examples of faulty reasoning. The Letters-to-the-Editor section of your newspaper and ads can be rich sources of examples.

6. Find an example of how inductive reasoning appears (or could be used) in the instruction of other content areas such as reading, spelling, science, or social studies at the grade level you plan to teach. Do the same for deductive reasoning.

7. Devise a magic square for the mathematics instruction appropriate to your chosen grade level.

8. The text notes that attribute blocks are a useful manipulative for activities involving sorting, classifying, and reasoning. Make up your own set of attribute materials. For example, draw pictures of Zorks or other space aliens on a 3 x 5 card. Choose about four characteristics to vary (e.g., hairy versus hairless; one-, two-, or three-eyed; round, oval, or pear-shaped; red, orange, green, or purple eyes).

9. Stories can provide an opportunity for introducing, discussing, or practicing mathematical content.

   • *Write your own stories to address the mathematical content (and other content) you wish to focus on.* The fabricated story about Dudley the Dawdler in Box 2.26 would be suitable for upper elementary and middle-school students. Note that the story involves a rate problem and fraction arithmetic. It could also serve to introduce vocabulary such as dawdle, tardiness, vexed, steely, and sarcastic. (You could tailor your stories to include the vocabulary specified by your English curriculum.)

■ **Box 2.26: Dudley the Dawdler**

Dudley was late for school again, arriving just in time for lunch.

"Dudley," Miss Fern inquired impatiently, "Were you dawdling again?"

Dudley suspected he knew what Miss Fern was talking about, but to buy some time and to put Miss Fern off the track, he inquired in a most earnest manner: What does dawdle mean, Miss Fern? It sounds like a most interesting word, and I surely would like to add it to my vocabulary."

"To move slowly," said Miss Fern softly just a bit surprised by Dudley's sudden interest in the language arts. "Did you walk to school slowly or is there some other reason for your tardiness?"

"Slowly, Miss Fern? Could you be more precise?" replied Dudley.

Even more vexed now, Miss Fern asked in a steely tone, "Dudley, how far is it from your house to the school?"

"One quarter of a mile," answered Dudley cheerfully, not recognizing the trap that Miss Fern was setting.

"And how long did it take you to walk to school?" she pressed.

"Oh, a half an hour," replied a still unsuspecting Dudley.

"Tell me, Dudley," inquired Miss Fern in a sweet, sarcastic tone, "how fast were you walking then?"

And finally, Dudley recognized that he had a formidable adversary in Miss Fern. He was going to like this school year with her, he thought to himself.

What arithmetic operation should Dudley use to figure out his rate? What was his rate? If *casually* walking a mile required 30 minutes, how much faster or slower would this pace be than Dudley's *rate*?

- *Start compiling a list of children's literature books that contain mathematical content at the grade level you plan to teach.* Use a computer file or index cards. You may wish to cross-reference entries by title, author and mathematical content. Plan how you could use these opportunities to introduce, discuss, or practice mathematics skills in concepts.

- *Examine the basal reader or set of stories used in the reading program at the grade level you plan to teach.* Note what mathematical content is mentioned and how you might use the references to explore mathematics.

QUESTIONS TO CHECK UNDERSTANDING

1. This chapter distinguishes among an exercise, a problem, and an enigma. How would the moderate novelty principle (discussed in Chapter 1) predict how children might respond to each of these? Briefly justify your answers.

2. Mrs. Perkie gave her first graders the following word problem: Ruffus the dog muddied nine rugs in the morning and six rugs in the afternoon. How many rugs did he muddy altogether? Ginger did not know the answer, but she knew how to get it. She tried using her fingers but did not have enough. Ginger then tried another familiar strategy; she put out 9 blocks and 6 blocks and counted all the blocks. For Ginger, was this word problem an exercise, a problem, or an enigma? Why?

3. Without explaining what a magic square was, Mr. Adams put the magic square shown below on the chalkboard and asked his second-grade class what the missing number might be.

1	6	5
8	4	0
3	2	

Much to his surprise, a number of children quickly raised their hands. Marisal indicated she thought the missing number would be seven. Mr. Adams asked if anyone else had a different answer. Gerald thought the missing number

was nine. Mr. Adams recorded a 7 and a 9 on the board. After asking again for answers, a number of students indicated they agreed with Marisal and some indicated they agreed with Gerald. Mr. Adams then asked Gerald to explain his answer. The boy noted that "the numbers were like counting," so after eight comes nine. Mr. Adams then asked Marisal to justify her answer. Marisal pointed out that she counted (0, 1, 2...) and found that seven was missing: "See, there's a six and an eight but no seven."

a. Evaluate how Mr. Adams handled the lesson described above? More specifically, what things did he do to foster or dampen a spirit of inquiry?

b. Mr. Adams was surprised by how his children determined the missing number. He had expected them to add and to discover that the rows and/or columns all had the same sum. Even with encouragement to look for patterns, the students persisted with counting patterns and overlooked addition patterns. Mr. Adams concluded that his first example of a magic square was a mistake. What example or examples should he present his class now to help them discover the rules underlying a magic square?

c. After analyzing several more examples of magic squares and discussing them, the class arrived at a definition of magic squares. Mr. Adams then gave the class several more magic squares. Raymond came to Mr. Adams with a completed magic square and asked, "Is this right?" How should Mr. Adams respond to Raymond?

4. In an effort to put more emphasis on problem solving, Miss Brill created the following word problems. Because she wanted to encourage a thoughtful analysis of problems, she included various types of nonroutine problems, including nongoal-specific problems. For each problem below indicate whether the word problem is routine (write R), nonroutine but goal specific (write NR), or nonroutine and nongoal specific (write NGS). Justify your choice.

a. Mrs. Smith bought a 9 lb. bag of dry cat food for $2.00 for their cat Haphazard. Ruffus the dog found the bag in the pantry, chewed a hole in it, and ate 2/3 of the dry cat food before he was discovered and forced to stop. How many pounds of dry cat food did Ruffus eat?

b. The next week Mrs. Smith again had to buy a 9 lb. bag of dry cat food. Ruffus found this bag also and ate 3/5 of it before he was driven off by the furious Haphazard. Over the two weeks, how many pounds of Haphazard's dry cat food had Ruffus consumed?

c. If Ruffus ate 2/3 of a bag of dry cat food and 3/5 of another, what fraction of a bag did Ruffus eat?

d. The next time Mrs. Smith went shopping, she bought ten 9 lb. bags of dry cat food. Because she bought in bulk, the store manager marked down the regular $2.00 price 20%. Mrs. Smith also had a coupon for $2.00 off. Write and solve as many word problems as you can.

e. Given the information in question d, how many weeks would the ten 9 lb. bags of dry cat food last if Ruffus were kept from eating any of it? How long would it last if Ruffus found this supply?

f. Rosi is 7 years old. Isauro is 5. How old was Rosi when Isauro was 2 years old?

g. Juan had five baggies, and Soncee had four baggies. Juan put two pebbles in each of his baggies; Soncee put three pebbles in each of her baggies. Note questions you could make from the information and write out their answers.

5. a. Transform the goal-specific question below into a nongoal-specific question.

> Mrs. Dingle baked a cherry pie and a banana-cream pie for supper. Each pie was cut into 8 pieces. Ruffus the dog licked 3 pieces of the cherry pie and 3 pieces of the banana-cream pie. What fraction of the 16 pieces of pie had Ruffus ruined for human consumption?

b. Kazan's effort to transform the goal-specific question above into a nongoal-specific question is shown below:

> Mrs. Dingle baked a cherry pie and a banana-cream pie for supper. Each pie was cut into 8 pieces. Ruffus the dog licked 8 pieces. Draw a picture to show *all* the ways Ruffus could have licked the pies.

Evaluate Kazan's effort. Is her transformed question a nongoal-specific question? How many different ways could Ruffus have licked 8 pieces of pie?

6. Examine the problem titled, "The Importance of Paper Conservation," on page 2-136 of the Problems section. What type of nonroutine problem is it? (a) That is, would it qualify as a complex translation problem, a process problem, an applied problem, or a puzzle problem? (b) Would it qualify as a goal-specific or a nongoal-specific problem?

7. Using a deck of 40 cards with a number from 0 to 9 on each card, a moderator played Guess Who I Am with Alexi and Alison (both aged 8). After the moderator drew a card, the players could, in turn, ask questions with yes - no answers or try guessing the number drawn. Alison asked if the number was more than five. The answer was no. Alexi asked if the number was even. The answer was no. Alison then guessed one, which was incorrect. Alexi brightened and said, "I know what the answer has to be. It's got to be three." He was stunned to learn that the number was not three.

(a) What kind of reasoning did Alexi engage in to determine his answer of three? (b) What went wrong with his reasoning? (c) What would a teacher need to clarify for Alexi?

8. Folding a form is one way of determining whether or not a form such as a rectangle is divided in half. If the two parts cover one another, then the parts are indeed halves.

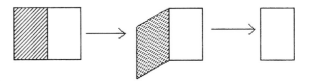

A form could not be folded in two so that the pieces covered one another. Therefore, the parts of this form cannot be one-half of the form. (a) What kind of reasoning was involved in drawing this conclusion? (b) Is the argument valid? Why or why not?

9.[8] Judi was excited about what she had discovered over the weekend while helping her father tile the floor of their family room. "Miss Brill," she explained, "did you know that as the perimeter of a rectangle increases, its area increases. I can *prove* it, see." Judi drew the following diagram on the chalkboard, illustrating the two areas of the family room she helped tile:

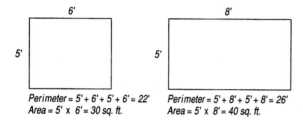

Perimeter = 5' + 6' + 5' + 6' = 22'
Area = 5' x 6' = 30 sq. ft.

Perimeter = 5' + 8' + 5' + 8' = 26'
Area = 5' x 8' = 40 sq. ft.

Miss Brill had never considered the relationship between perimeter and area, but it seemed obvious now that Judi had pointed it out. "Good for you—that makes a great deal of sense," the teacher noted. "Class, Judi has made a very interesting discovery that I'd like her to share with you."

a. Judi used what type of reasoning to arrive at her conclusion about the relationship between the perimeter and area of a rectangle? Her justification to Miss Brill was (i) an explanation, (ii) an informal proof, or (iii) a mathematical proof?

b. What type of reasoning did Miss Brill use to conclude that Judi was correct? Evaluate the soundness of Miss Brill's conclusion.

c. Evaluate the way Miss Brill handled Judi's discovery: What things did this new teacher do that were commendable? What might she have done to make this incident more profitable for Judi and the class?

d. Evaluate Judi's conclusion about the relationship between the perimeter and area of a rectangle. Was it a conjecture or not?

Briefly justify. Did her explanation *prove* her conclusion was true? Is Judi, in fact, correct about the relationship she described? Briefly explain why or why not.

10. Julie was asked to identify the type of reasoning involved in three examples. The instructions indicated that she should write A if the example illustrated intuitive reasoning; B, if it illustrated inductive reasoning; and C, if it illustrated deductive reasoning. Julie confidently answered C for the first example and B for the second example but was unsure about the third example. Julie reasoned, "It makes sense that all the letters should be used. I've used letters B and C already. So, the answer to the third example must be A." Julie was later surprised that her answer to the third example was marked incorrect. (a) What kind of reasoning did Julie use to reach the conclusion that the answer to the third example must be A? (b) Why was her conclusion not true?

11. In Figure 2.9, Charlie Brown reasons, *"If someone is reading a book about something, [then] I guess you have to trust her."* Charlie Brown appears to be using if-then (deductive) reasoning. Unfortunately, his conclusion was not true. Is the italicized argument above really deductive reasoning or is it intuitive reasoning? Briefly justify your answer.

12. The NCTM (1989) *Curriculum Standards* include the following example of a pattern: 121   12321   1234321. Is this a repeating or a growing pattern? What is the pattern?

13. Mr. Adams played Guess My Shape with his second grade. He created a shape on a geoboard. The first group to create a congruent shape (same-sized shape) on their geoboard won. On their turn, a group could pose a question that could be answered yes or no. The first group made a triangle on their geoboard and asked Mr. Adams "Is this the shape you made?" When Mr. Adams answered, "No," the second group made a square and asked the same question. When Mr. Adams again responded, "No," the third group switched tactics and asked if his shape had 5 nails in the middle (5 nails not touched by rubber bands). What is the problem with these students' questions? What should Mr. Adams encourage his students to do?

14. a. Miss Brill asked her class to make a Venn diagram showing the relationship of all boys, all girls, and all people with freckles. Evaluate Andy's solution shown below. Is it satisfactory? Why or why not?

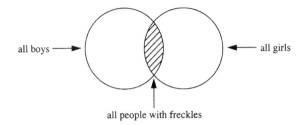

all boys ⟶   ⟵ all girls

all people with freckles

   b. Miss Brill instructed her class to make a Venn diagram illustrating who had visited Springfield, who had visited Chicago, who had visited both Springfield and Chicago, and who had visited neither. Rodney noted that four loops would be needed. Andy commented, "No, knothead, you need three." Evaluate these answers.

15. Activity 2.4 discussed how Euler diagrams can be used to check the validity of arguments. Show how such diagrams could be used to illustrate the validity or invalidity of the following arguments:

   a. No women have been president of the ALLMEN Society. Alexis Harbough was a president of ALLMEN. Alexis Harbough was not a woman.

   b. All goos are moos. All boos are toos. All toos are doos. All moos are boos. Therefore, all doos are goos.

   c. All triangles inscribed in semicircles are right triangles. Some of the triangles Miss Brill showed her class were inscribed in a semicircle. At least some of the triangles Miss Brill showed her class were right triangles.[9]

16. (a) Evaluate each of the following arguments. Give at least one counterexample for questionable (invalid) arguments. (b) Show how an Euler diagram could be used to spot the invalid arguments.

   i. If Anita comes to visit, then Delbert is happy. Delbert is happy. Anita must have come for a visit.

   ii. If Jamellah is studying for a test, then she smokes. She is not smoking. So Jamellah must not be studying for a test.

   iii. If Mr. Tomlin eats pizza, then he gets heartburn. Mr. Tomlin has heartburn. He must have eaten pizza.

   iv. If Haider studies hard, then he gets good grades. Haider did not study hard for his Social Studies test. Thus, he will not get a good grade.

17. Consider the following premise: If all Bs are As and all nonBs are nonCs. Use an Euler diagram to determine which of the following conclusions are valid:

   i.   All As are Cs
   ii.   All Bs are Cs
   iii. All Cs are As
   iv.   All Cs are Bs

18. A question that sometimes comes up when cooperative learning is used is, "If we study together as a group, why can't we take the test together as a group?" How can a teacher address this question?

19. Successively larger triangles can be made from pattern blocks:

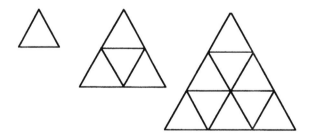

Note that it takes nine blocks to make the third triangle.

(a) What kind of pattern do successively larger triangles represent: a repeating pattern or a growing pattern? (b) How could a teacher encourage students to create a table and to use patterns or relationships rather than laboriously use manipulatives or pictures to determine the answer? (c) Complete the table below. (d) How might intermediate-grade students figure out the last five entries in the table below differently from younger students? Why?

Triangle Number	1	2	3	4	5	6	7	8	9	10
Number of blocks needed	1	4	9							

20. Miss Brill was exasperated with her students' efforts to solve a problem. "Stop guessing," she instructed. As the mathematics coordinator, how would you evaluate Miss Brill's directive?

21. A preservice teacher recorded the following in her journal: "Very quickly...I realized that I am the slowest 'solver' in my group. It takes me longer to think through a problem than it does for the other members of my group....I am not sure how I would solve this problem if it occurred in my own classroom." What advice would you give to this prospective teacher?

PROBLEMS

Some of the problems below will not be problems to you because you can readily determine a solution procedure and the answer. Where you feel the need (for genuine problems), try Polya's four-step approach to problem solving and heuristics (see Figure 2.7 on page 2-18). Record your solution procedures as well as your answer.

■ Even Man Out

Any number of people can play Even Man Out. Put out a row of chairs equal to the number of people playing. Contestants line up 10 yards away from the row of chairs. At "Go," contestants rush to take a chair. The judge begins with the first chair in a row and counts, "Odd." The next chair is counted, "Even," and the contestant in that chair is out of the game. The third chair is counted, "Odd." The fourth chair is counted, "Even," and the contestant in the chair is out of the game. The same pattern is used to count the remaining chairs. After the row has been counted, the process is repeated by continuing the odd-even count until there is only one chair left. The person sitting in the chair is the winner. The counting process is illustrated below for seven contestants. Note that o = an odd count, e = an even count, and x = eliminated on a previous count.

row of chairs:	1	2	3	4	5	6	7
first count	o	e	o	e	o	e	o
second count:	e	x	o	x	e	x	o
third count:	x	x	e	x	x	x	o
final result	x	x	x	x	x	x	o

The winner is the contestant in Chair 7.

(a) Who will win if there are 37 contestants?
(b) How can you predict the winner given any of the contestants?

■ Devising a Formula for an Arithmetic Series

(a) After reading about and/or discussing the solution to Problem 6 in Probe 2.3 on page 2-28 (Sum of An Arithmetic Series), devise a formula for computing the sum of an arithmetic series. Organizing the data from various examples in a table may be helpful. (b) Will the formula you devised work for an arithmetic series with an odd number of numbers (e.g., 1 + 2 + 3 + 4 + 5)? (c) Will the formula you devised work for an arithmetic series that begins with a number other than one and increases by increments of one (e.g., 2 + 3 + 4 + 5 + 6 + 7)? (d) Will the formula work for an arithmetic series that increases by increments of a number greater than one (e.g., 2 + 4 + 6 + 8 + 10 + 12 or 1 + 4 + 7 + 10 + 13 + 16)? (e) Devise a formula that will work for all the situations above.

■ How Many Games Did You Say We Have to Play?

The rage at Chaos Middle School was a new "mind" game called Easy Money in which players take the role of S&L Bank officials trying to outwit bank regulators and treasury agents so as to amass fortunes for themselves. Herbert, president of the Easy Money Club, proposed a tournament. Vinnie, a compulsive Easy Money player, recommended that all 160 members of the club play each other. The player who amassed the greatest number of wins would be crowned the champion.

Taking into account that a game of Easy Money took on average 6 hours to complete, Herbert asked how many games such a tournament would require.

How many games would the 160 members of the Easy Money Club have to play if each member played all the other members once?

Mystic Rose

The book *Problems with Patterns and Numbers* (Shell Center for Mathematical Education, 1984) presents an interesting problem. Mystic Rose is a diagram made by connecting all 18 points on a circle to each other point with straight lines. If every point is connected to every other point, how many straight lines are there altogether? This seems like an overwhelming problem. Consider, then, some simpler cases. How many straight lines can be drawn between two points on a circle? Three points? Four points? Five points? Six points? Is there anything you notice?

Two-Colored Helmets

Three alert soldiers—Joe, Kevin, and Luke—stood in a row at attention as their Captain read them their orders. The Captain indicated that he needed three men to work in the pits of the rifle range changing targets—a dusty and, if you were not careful, a dangerous job. He also needed two safety officers who would sit in a tall tower behind the shooters and who would watch for unsafe practices. As the three soldiers had marched to the Captain's office, they had seen three white helmets (for pit crew members) and two red helmets (for safety officers) sitting out on a table. The Captain, being a man of few words, went to the table behind the soldiers, chose three helmets, and put them on the three soldiers from behind. Because the Captain was a timid man and did not like to confront complaining, he did not tell the men what color helmet (assignment) he had given them. He simply ordered them to march to the rifle range where they would discover their assignment well out of his earshot.

As they marched, Luke, the last soldier in line, teased, "I have no idea what color helmet I'm wearing, but I know *the color* you two guys have."

Much to Luke's surprise, Joe, the first soldier in line, replied, "Well, I know what color helmet I'm wearing."

What color helmet was Joe wearing? How did he know when Luke did not? What kind of reasoning did Joe employ? Hint: Pay special attention to Luke's comment.

Two-Colored Helmets Problem Revisited

Given the same situation described in the Two-Colored Helmets Problem above, assume that the conversation among the soldiers proceeded as follows:

As they marched, Luke, the last soldier in line, teased, "I have no idea what color helmet I'm wearing, but I know what color each of you is wearing."

"Well," said Kevin, the second soldier in line, "I don't know what color helmet I'm wearing, but I know Joe's color."

Joe, the first soldier in line who could not see the color of any of the helmets said, "Well, thanks for telling me my assignment, guys."

The last two soldiers in line were astounded and asked if Joe had somehow seen the helmet put on his head. "No," said Joe, "You gave me all the information I need."

Does the change in what Luke says change the problem? Justify your answer. Is it possible for Joe to know what color helmet he is wearing or is he just teasing Luke? If the problem is solvable, what color is Joe's helmet and how do you know? If the problem is not solvable, explain.

Clock Chimes

A clock chimes once at 1 A.M. and 1 P.M., twice at 2 A.M. and 2 P.M., three times at 3 A.M. and 3 P.M., and so forth. During the course of one day, how many times does a clock chime? Assume that a day begins at 12:01 A.M. and ends at 12 P.M. midnight.

Guesses Needed for the Number-Guess Game

In the Number-Guess Game (page 2-70) described in Probe 2.12, if the range of numbers is 1 to 5, an efficient strategy can invariably determine the chosen number in three (or fewer) guesses. Assuming an efficient strategy, how many guesses are required to determine the chosen number if the range is 1 to 10? 1 to 20? 1 to 50?

Increasing Numbers

The numbers 1234 and 1357 can be called "increasing numbers," because any of their digits are bigger than the digits to the left. How many increasing numbers are there between 2000 and 7000?

Don't Want to Go Last

Two people play this game. Set blocks, chips, pennies, or other objects out in the following configuration:

```
          o   o   o
        o   o   o   o
      o   o   o   o   o   o
```

The rules of Don't Want to Go Last are: (1) on your turn, you may take objects from any *one* row; and (2) you may take any number of objects from that row. The aim of the game is to force your opponent to remove the last object(s). What is a winning strategy? Hint: The player who goes first can always win by taking one item from any of the rows and thereafter making the right moves.

A Number Riddle

Which pair of numbers summing to 24 has the largest product?

How Far the House Revisited

(a) Larry and Marv live on the same straight road 3 miles apart. Marv and Philippe live on the same straight road 4 miles apart. How far apart do Larry and Philippe live? (b) In this revised problem and the original problem (Problem 4 of Probe 2.5 on page 2-30), the roads are described as straight. What if these problems did not specify this? Would it make any difference to the answer?

Confusing Flower Arrangements

Kip was in charge of ordering flowers for the class dance. The Dance Committee decided on a red rose for the Queen and her attendants, a white rose for the King and the escorts of the Queen's attendants, a yellow carnation for adult chaperones, a white carnation for any boy escorting an adult chaperone, and a pink carnation for any girl escorting an adult chaperone. At the florist, Kip read through her notes. Though she had noted there was a total of six boys, she could not remember how many were supposed to wear white carnations (chaperones' escorts) and how many were supposed to wear white roses (the King and boy court members). Moreover, although she had noted there were five girls, she could not remember how many were supposed to wear pink carnations (chaperones' escorts) and how many were supposed to wear red roses (the Queen and girl court members). If there were three adult chaperones to escort, what should Kip buy?

Brother, Can You Spare a Tire?

A four-wheel car is equipped with tires that will last exactly 20,000 miles. What is the least number of spare tires that must be carried so that a marathon race of exactly 30,000 miles can just be completed? Describe how the tires would be used.

Archery Practice

Robin shot six arrows at a target with rings worth 1, 3, 5, 7, and 9 points. All his arrows hit the target. Which of the following could be Robin's total score: 5, 19, 25, 36, 47, or 56? Hint: Examine the values of the target rings and consider which total scores are possible and which are impossible.

A Strange Social Studies Assignment

Tracy was given an unusual assignment by her social-studies teacher. She was to read 1/3 of the pages on Monday, 1/4 of the remaining pages on Tuesday, 2/5 of the then-remaining pages on Wednesday, and 1/8 of the then-remaining pages on Thursday. On Friday she read the final 63 pages. How many pages did Tracy read altogether?

The Importance of Paper Conservation

How much paper does your College (School or Department) of Education use in a semester? How many average-sized trees are needed to supply this amount? What conservation measures could be implemented? How much paper would this save a semester?

ANSWERS TO SELECTED QUESTIONS

Problem 2.2 (page 2-10)

On the second trip, the farmer can take the cabbage. However, he must then undo Step 1: take the goat back. On the third trip, he can take the wolf and, on the last trip, the goat again. Is there another way you can solve the problem?

Probe 2.2 (page 2-16)

Whether the problem is an enigma, a genuine problem, or an exercise cannot be judged from the problem itself. It could be any of the three depending upon the readiness of a child. Problems 1 and 2 are routine problems used to reinforce addition and subtraction skills. The reminder instructs children to look for the key words *in all* or *left*. The instruction could be improved by reminding children to *think carefully about the words in the word problems and how they are used.* This heuristic encourages children to consider other words or phrases that mean the same as "in all," and whether it implies adding in *this* context. (Note that this gets us into the area of language arts.)

Problem 2.13 (page 2-20)

Slim was dividing the amount paid in by 3 and subtracting 1 from that (or subtracting 3 from the amount paid in and dividing the remainder by 3). Poor Jeb was getting less than 1/3 of what he sold. For $10 paid in, he would get only $2.33.

Problem 2.19 (page 2-24)

(a) A table of the given data shows that for side 2, all the possibilities but 5 have been eliminated. Thus, we can conclude (deduce) that 5 must be opposite 2. (b) If so, 3 must be opposite 4. Because 4 and 5 are already eliminated, 6 must be opposite 1. Note that all the pairs sum to 7. (c) The reasoning involved eliminating possibilities, a form of deductive reasoning.

Adjacent Numbers

Side	1	2	3	4	5	6
1	X	yes	yes			
2	yes	X	yes	yes		yes
3	yes	yes	X			yes
4		yes		X		yes
5					X	
6		yes	yes	yes		X

Problem 2.21 (page 2-24)

Hint: If the smallest disk is first put on Peg B, then the medium-sized disk will have to be put on Peg C. This results in a dead end in that one can now never move the largest disk. The key is to move the smallest disk to Peg C first.

Problem 2.22 (page 2-25)

Although 8 five-packs (40) and 4 three-packs (12) make 52, this is not the most inexpensive way to purchase the batteries. Completing a table should help uncover the most economical way to purchase the 52 batteries.

Problem 2.23 (page 2-25)

There are two ways Ebb could have scored 24: 2 nines, 1 five, and 1 one; or 1 nine, 3 fives, and 0 ones. There are no ways to make 26 from 9, 5, and 1.

Probe 2.3 (pages 2-27 and 2-28)

Problem 1. One straightforward way to solve this problem is to draw a number line to represent the drips per minute. Mark off a segment to represent 1 minute and divide the segment into thirds. Underneath this representation draw another number line. Again mark off a segment to represent 1 minute, but this time, divide the segment into five equal pieces.

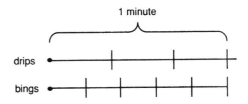

1 minute

drips
bings

Inspection of the diagram indicates that the leaks would produce the following pattern: bing, drip, bing, bing, drip, bing, drip-bing.

Problem 2. A drawing can help a problem solver either conceptualize this problem and choose a strategy to begin with or check the solution. By examining the sketch below carefully, the carpenter should have noticed that dividing 128" by 8" gives him the *number of 8-inch segments in 128 inches: 16.* However, the second floor serves as the step for the top-most 8-inch segment (the sixteenth step). Thus, he needed

15 steps, not 16. (Note that the problem illustrates how mathematical skills such as division and problem-solving heuristics can be applied to everyday situations.)

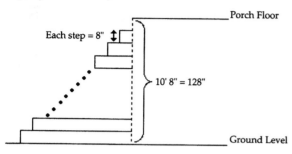

Problem 3. A drawing can help clarify that Ralphie can run 50 yards in the same amount of time that it takes Quickie Karl to run 45 yards. If Ralphie starts 5 yards behind the starting line, then the two rabbits will be neck and neck 45 yards from the starting line—5 yards short of the finish line. Because Ralphie is speedier, he will complete the last 5 yards before Quickie and win. Ralphie is no dumb bunny.

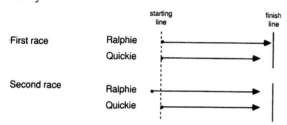

Have students consider other scenarios. For example, how would the race end if Ralphie gave Quickie a 5-yard head start? A 4-yard head start?

Problem 4. Making a chart of the data reveals an interesting pattern. Below, the couple's days off are charted for a 6-week period (A = Abby's days off; B = Bartheleme's days off). What does the chart make clear about the unfortunate couple?

	Sun	Mon	Tue	Wed	Thu	Fri	Sat
1	A	B		A			A
2	B		A			A	B
3		A			A	B	
4	A			A	B		A
5			A	B		A	
6		A	B		A		

Problem 5. Making a table of the possibilities and cross-checking them can lead to the answer. Delineated below are all the possible amounts up to $1.00 that would leave a remainder of 2 if grouped by fives.

counts by 5, r 2:	7	12	17	22	27	32	37	42	47	52	57	62	67	72	77	82	87	92	97
counts by 2, r 1:			X		X		X		X		X		X		X		X		X
counts by 3, 1 r:				X		X				X		X				X		X	
counts by 4, 1 r:	X												X						

Note that because the count by twos left a remainder, the amount has to be odd. In the chart all even amounts have been crossed. By following a similar procedure for the count by threes and fours, you can narrow Nyugen's penny count to two possibilities: 37 and 97.

Problem 6. One way to solve this problem is to consider a simpler problem and look for a pattern. Consider the relatively simple arithmetic series 1+2+3+4. Adding left to right indicates that the sum is 10. Another way to sum the digits is add the first and the last, second and the next to the last:

$$\overset{5}{\overbrace{1 + 2 + 3 + 4}}$$
$$\underbrace{}_{5}$$

The sum of each pair is 5 and there are two pairs, so the sum is 10.

Consider the somewhat larger arithmetic series involving the numbers 1 to 10. Use a calculator to determine the left-to-right sum. If the numbers are paired up as shown below and added, the sum is the same.

$$1 + 2 + 3 + 4 + 5 + 6 + 7 + 8 + 9 + 10$$

The sum of each pair is 11 and there are five pairs, so the sum is 55.

Now consider the arithmetic series 1 to 100.

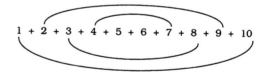

The sum of each pair is 101 and there are 50 pairs. The sum of this arithmetic series is then . . . ?

Problem 7. Mathematics is useful, in part, because it attempts to detect and explain the underlying commonality among various problems or situations that on the surface appear very different. Problem 7 is essentially the same as Problem 6 above.

Many students, though, may not see the connection between the two situations. Indeed Civil (1990) found that her preservice teachers could not solve the staircase problem soon after they had solved the arithmetic-series problem. It is important, then, to encourage children to look for commonalities among problems, even those that do not appear similar (to use the relate-a-problem-to-a-familiar-problem heuristic).

Problem 8. Let x = the page number of the first page. So x + 1 and x + 2 must be the page numbers of the second and third consecutive pages, respectively. Therefore, x + (x + 1) + (x + 2) = 534. The page number of the first consecutive page can be determined by solving for x.

Problem 9. Working backwards can make solving this problem much easier. Before encountering the third member of the Fleadirt gang, the boy must have twice two plus two or six golf balls. The answer can be determined by repeating this process for the second and lastly the first gang member encountered.

Probe 2.4 (page 2-29)

Problem 1. Once students recognize that they can extend lines beyond the area encompassed by the dots, a solution is possible. One solution to problem 1 is shown below.

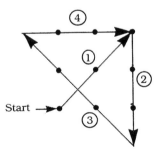

Problem 2. Many people assume that the term *squares* in the question implies only the small dark or light squares on the checkerboard used to play checkers. (There are 8 rows of 8 or 64 of these small squares.) One key to solving this problem, though, is realizing that the small squares can be combined to make larger squares. For example, four small squares

can be combined to make a 2 x 2 square, and nine small squares can be combined to make a 3 x 3 square. What other size squares can be made by combining the small squares? What is the largest square that can be made from small squares? A second key to solving this problem is realizing that larger squares can *overlap*. Thus, for instance, the checkerboard can be partitioned into more than 16 2 × 2 larger squares. When you take into account overlapping larger squares, you should see a pattern emerge for the number of 1 × 1, 2 × 2, 3 × 3 . . . squares. If you have not already solved the problem, try to now.

Problem 3. This problem is solvable if one of the utility lines crosses a line representing a house. Although not mentioned by the constraint, many people assume the direction applies to the lines of the house as well as the utility lines. (Of course, in the real world of 3-dimensional space, one utility line could pass above or below another utility line or below a house.) Two possible solutions are shown below:

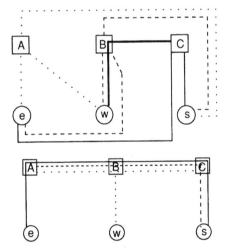

Probe 2.5 (page 2-30)

Problem 1. Some students see the phrase "cutting consumption" and decide to divide 5/8 by 3/4, arriving at an answer of 5/6 (5/8 ÷ 3/4 = 5/8 x 4/3 = 5/6). However, this answer makes no sense, because the amount he ate before the diet (5/8 pound) is just over half a pound while the amount after the diet (5/6 pounds) is nearly a whole pound. Multiplying 5/8 by 3/4 puts you on the right track but the answer 15/32 is not reasonable if you stop and think about it. After all, 15/32 is just under half a pound. If Hammond was eating just over half a pound and cut out 3/4 of this, you would expect the answer to be less than a quarter pound, not just less than half a pound. The answer 15/32 indicates how many pounds of hamburger Hammond cut out of his daily diet. The amount in his new diet is 5/8 − 15/32 = 25/32 − 15/32 = 5/32. (Note that it is important to decide whether your solution answers the question.)

Problem 3. An answer of 30 minutes answers the question "How long before the 72 people in front of her board a bus and leave for campus?" Rosalie will have to wait for the *fourth* bus to come, which will be 40 more minutes.

Problem 4. By drawing out a picture, a student may recognize there are two possible solutions.

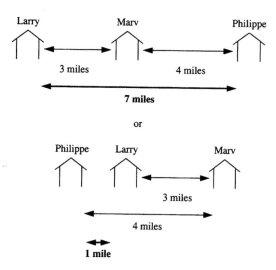

Probe 2.6 (pages 2-48 and 2-49)

Is This What Polya Had in Mind? (1) Workbook page 89 is an attempt to teach problem-solving strategies via problem solving. They represent an effort to teach children specific heuristics and Polya's 4-step problem-solving process directly and to use word problems to teach this content. Although it is an effort to teach *about* problem solving *via* problem solving, it does not involve teaching *for* problem solving. You might say it is an integrated approach that is missing a key ingredient and, thus, is not done well.

(2) It is commendable that the workbook makes an effort to foster the use of heuristics (analyzing the wording of problems and drawing a picture). It is also useful for children to relate pictorial or informal representations of problems (Step 1) and their formal representation (Step 2).

(3) Rather than encourage children to think about which strategies might be helpful, the worksheet prescribes how each step should be implemented. Step 1 tells children to draw a picture—whether or not they need to do so to understand the problem. By requiring a child to use a heuristic, instruction encourages the thoughtless use of heuristics and robs children of the opportunity to make decisions and to develop self-reliance (autonomous critical thinking). Step 2 tells the children *the* plan. This implies that devising a plan merely entails knowing the one acceptable solution procedure.

(4) Why not allow the children to devise their own method for each step and then discuss them. If needed, a teacher might, for Step 1, prompt, "Would it help you to understand the problem if you drew a picture?"

A Case of Unhelpful Heuristic Instruction: Question 1. Civil (1990), who posed Problem 1 to preservice teachers, found that using a diagram to find an answer was foreign to many of them. Several of her students appeared to draw their diagrams to match the answer they had already determined, rather than using the diagrams to find the answer.

The heuristic of drawing a diagram could be used to facilitate an informal solution:

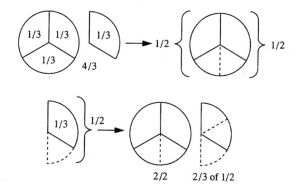

Three-thirds is equivalent to 2 halves (2/2). The remaining third, however, does not make up an entire 1/2. By partitioning this last half into equal segments, it is clear that 1/3 is 2/3 of 1/2. So the answer is 1 2/3 *halves*.

The problem can be solved in a variety of other ways. Some other solution methods are noted below:

• The problem could also be solved by considering equivalent fractions: 4/3 = 8/6 and 1/2 = 3/6. Because 3/6 can fit into 8/6 twice with 2/6 left over (3/6 + 3/6 = 6/6; 8/6 − 6/6 = 2/6), there must be 2 2/6 halves in 4/3.

• Formally, the problem could be solved by dividing 4/3 by 1/2: 4/3 ÷ 1/2 = 4/3 × 2/1 = 8/3 = 2 2/3.

• The problem could also be solved algebraically using a proportion: Let n = the unknown (the number of halves). So, how many halves fits into (equals) four-thirds translates into the expression n/2 = 4/3. You can solve for n by cross multiplying: 3n = 8. You can then isolate the n by dividing each side by 3:

$$\frac{3n/3}{} = 8/3; \ n = 8/3$$

Do you have yet another solution procedure?

Probe 2.7 (pages 2-50 to 2-52)

Problem 6. Hint: Actually manipulating concrete objects (pennies themselves or a substitute) is immeasurably useful in solving this problem. Inverting a triangle of 10 pennies can be done in three turns:

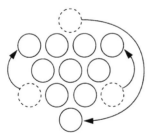

Hint: 21 pennies can be done in less than 8 moves.

Probe 2.8 (page 2-53)

Riddle 1. Six women players scored.

Riddle 2. A nickel and a quarter. One is a nickel and one is not.

Riddle 3. The two did not play each other.

Riddle 4. Three.

Riddle 5. Seven.

Riddle 6. You don't bury survivors.

Riddle 7. None; a hole consists of air.

Riddle 8. One hour. The alarm would go off at 9 P.M.

Riddle 9. White.

Riddle 10. 12.

Riddle 11. One hour.

Riddle 12. Yes, and a fifth and a sixth of July too.

Riddle 13. All 12 months have 28 days.

Riddle 14. The match.

Probe 2.9 (pages 2-54 and 2-55)

Problem 1. The transformed problem is a good nonroutine problem because, it entails multiple answers. It is not really an open-ended question, because a student is asked to find all (10) the ways the eggs can be painted.

Problem 2. Open-ended, roughly equivalent in difficulty.

Problem 3. This is a two-step nonroutine problem.

Problem 4. This nonroutine problem has insufficient information and cannot be answered. It is not really an open-ended problem then.

Problem 5. The routine workbook exercise has been translated into a nongoal-specific problem. The new problem provides practice constructing a table as opposed to simply filling one in. Even so, it is a reasonable substitute for the original routine exercise.

Problem 6. The transformed problem is open-ended but requires more sophisticated mathematical knowledge than the original problem. The latter required children to add two two-digit numbers without renaming (carrying) to get a two-digit sum. One of the simplest problems that can be constructed from the open-ended question is the cost of two oranges, four apples, and three pears—the addition of three two-digit numbers with renaming and a three-digit sum. This may or may not be problematic. Other problems (e.g., How many oranges can Doreen buy for $2.00?), though, might outstrip the student's mathematical knowledge.

Probe 2.11 (page 2-64)

1. The missing numbers are 1 (lower right-hand cell) and 7.

2. a. Concluding that it was possible to determine the missing numbers involves intuitive reasoning because it was based on an assumption. There was no guarantee that you would be able to determine the missing numbers.

   b. By examining different rows, columns, and diagonals (examples), it is possible to induce the following general rule: all the rows, columns, and diagonals add up to a particular number. Discovering a rule by examining specific cases is inductive reasoning.

   c. Once the rule has been induced, you can use it to figure out what number fits into each missing cell. Because the complete rows, columns, and diagonals sum to 34, the rightmost column (or bottom row) should also sum to 34: $13 + 8 + 12 + X = 34$ ($4 + 15 + 14 + X = 34$). Thus, you can conclude that the missing value in the lower right-hand corner should be 1. Reasoning from a general premise (the induced rule) to draw a conclusion about a specific unknown case is deductive reasoning.

Activity 2.1 (pages 2-65 to 2-67)

1. In a magic square the rows, columns, and diagonals all have the same sum.

2. As Example 1e shows, the numbers comprising a magic square do not have to form an arithmetic sequence. A trial-and-error approach quickly shows that using the same three numbers will not work.

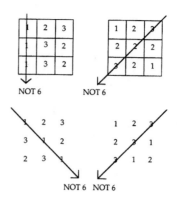

The left-hand column, for example, must have some combination of numbers other than 1, 2, and 3. The choices are limited because the combination must sum to six. The combination of 1, 5, and 0 can be eliminated, which leaves only the combination 1, 4, 1 for the left-hand column. Thus, the center column has to be 2, 2, 2 and the right-hand column has to be 3, 0, 3.

4. Magic square A_1 was formed by adding 4 to each number of A_0; A_2, by adding 10. A_3 was created by subtracting 4 from each number of A_0. A_4 was manufactured by multiplying each number in A_0 by 4; A_5, by multiplying by .01. A_6 was formed by multiplying each number in A_0 by 10 and adding 100. A_7 was generated by multiplying each number in A_0 by .1 and adding .2.

5. The set of numbers in the first magic square form the arithmetic sequence 1, 2, 3...9; in the second, 2, 3, 4...10; in the third, 3, 4, 5...11; and in the fourth, 4, 5, 6...12. In each magic square the second, fourth, sixth, and eighth number in the sequence form the corners, and the middle number is in the center cell. The remaining numbers are then placed so that the rows and columns have the same sum as the diagonals. The first example is illustrated below:

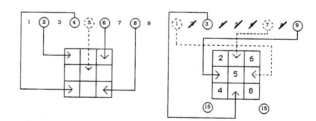

Probe 2.12 (page 2-70)

Mastermind. From Arianne's third try (B,B,B,Y) it is clear that the answer contains neither blue (B) nor yellow (Y). *If* these colors can be excluded and if the second try (B,Bk,B,W) contains two correct colors, *then* the solution must contain a black (Bk) and a white (W) in the positions shown. Moreover, *if* black is included in the answer, *then* try 1 (Bk,Y,R,G) means that the solution does not contain yellow, red, green. This means we have eliminated all but white and black from consideration. From this it follows that if black cannot occupy the first space (step 1), *then* white must occupy it. Therefore, we can conclude that the pattern is W, Bk, W or Bk, W. In brief, Arianne had a 50-50 chance of getting the correct answer on the next play. Because it involves if-then reasoning to eliminate possibilities, Mastermind involves a form of deductive reasoning.

Probe 2.13 (page 2-72)

4.　I.a.　If George makes his sister cry (A), then he is sent to his room (B). Not A, so Not B: invalid Type 4 (inverse) reasoning. There are other reasons why George might be sent to his room (e.g., he talked back to his mother, or he intentionally broke a dish).

　　b.　A, so B: valid Type 1 (detachment) reasoning.

　　c.　B, so A: invalid Type 3 (converse) reasoning. As noted for a above, there are many other reasons George might have been sent to his room.

　　d.　Not B, so not A: valid Type 2 (contrapositive) reasoning. We have found that some third graders have difficulty with this type of question because they do not accept the premise as a given. They argue—logically from their point of view—that George could have made his sister cry but escaped punishment because his parents did not find out. Although this can be the case in the real world, reasoning deductively in this case requires us to assume that the premise is true: making sister cry automatically leads to punishment.

　　II.a.　Argument Type 3 (converse): invalid. Figure A could be an equilateral pentagon, equilateral hexagon, and so forth.

　　b.　Argument Type 2 (contrapositive): valid.

　　c.　Argument Type 1 (detachment): valid.

　　d.　Argument Type 4 (inverse): invalid. Figure D could be some other equilateral shape.

Probe 2.14 (page 2-78)

Drawing a diagram makes clear how the various clues fit together.

G > S > B > J > M > L > A

1.　If Geraldo liked Bonita more than Junice and Junice more than Mercedes, it follows that he liked Bonita more than Mercedes.

2.　Using transition reasoning, if B > J, J > M and M > L, then B > L.

3.　If S > B and G > S, then it follows that Gabrielle was at the top of Geraldo's hit parade.

4.　Bonita was a third fiddle.

5.　Azure was last in Geraldo's affections.

Box 2.16 (page 2-80)

1.　No.

2.　It is important to examine many examples when attempting to induce an underlying rule or pattern. Examining only a few examples can be misleading because the rule or pattern common to these examples may not hold for other examples. Making and checking predictions is an important way to evaluate the generality of an induced rule.

3.　The pattern discovered by Tara's group and shown in the table below is *not* entirely correct.

Number of items	1	2	3	4	5	6	7	8	9	10
Player who wins	2	1	1	2	1	1	2	1	1	2

Can you discover the error? Drawing a picture can help. Consider the case of 4 items. If the first player crosses out 1 item (/), then the second player can cross out (x) two, leaving the first player with last (poisoned) item.

If the first player crosses out 2 items (/), then the second player can cross out one, leaving the first player again to be poisoned.

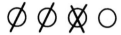

4. From the analysis above, it should be clear that you never want to be placed in a position where there are only 4 items left. You want your opponent to be in the unfortunate position. If you are playing with 8 items, how can you maneuver your opponent into this position? How many items should you take on your turn? Use a drawing and logical reasoning to check out what you should do to win with up to 16 items. Do you see a pattern that can help you predict what to do if a game has 20 items?

Problem 2.38 (page 2-86)

B = 6, C = 12, P = 6.

Problem 2.39 (page 2-86)

Six did not vote: 1 + 6 + 2 + 10 + 2 + 12 + 3 = 36; 42 − 36 = 6.

Probe 2.15 (page 2-95)

Problem 1. The first step in solving a problem is understanding the problem. This problem can help underscore the importance of reading problems carefully. Note that the wording of the problem does *not* imply that 40% are taking French *only* and that 25% are taking Spanish *only*. If the wording indicated this, the solution would be relatively straightforward: 40% + 25% + 10% = 75% taking French, Spanish, or both; 100% − 75% = 25% taking none.

A second erroneous answer is 35%, which is derived from adding 40% and 25% and subtracting the sum from 100%.

Drawing a picture can be most helpful in avoiding these errors and solving the problem. A Venn diagram is a particularly useful way to represent this problem and an invaluable aid in reasoning out the answer.

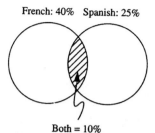

French: 40%   Spanish: 25%

Both = 10%

Such a representation can help make clear that the 10% taking both languages is *part* of the 40% taking French and the 25% taking Spanish. Thus 30% are taking French only, 15% are taking Spanish only, and 10% are taking both: 30% + 15% + 10% = 55%; 100% − 55% = 45% not taking a foreign language.

Problem 2. A Venn diagram can help in reasoning through this problem:

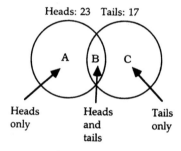

Heads: 23   Tails: 17

A   B   C

Heads only   Heads and tails   Tails only

If both coins come up tails three times, then C must be equal to 6. Now, consider what numbers must go in each part of the Venn diagram so that B + 6 = 17 and A + B = 23.

Problem 3. We know that A + B = 9, B + C = 10, and A + C = 13. Use trial and error to check out the possibilities. If A = 5, then B must = 4, and C must = 8. In this case, A + B does = 9 and A + C does = 13, but B + C = 12, not 10. Clearly, then, A cannot be 5.

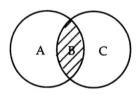

A = Conscious first half
B = Conscious both halves
C = Conscious second half

Activity 2.4 (pages 2-96 to 2-98)

Example 2. Point q goes outside Circle A, which also places it outside Circle B. The conclusion then is true—the product cannot be a multiple of 4.

Example 3. Point r must be placed inside Circle A. However, it may or may not go inside Circle B. Because it is unclear whether Point r goes inside or outside Circle B, the conclusion that the product is a multiple of 4 is questionable.

Example 4. Clearly, Point s must be placed outside Circle B. However, it may or may not go inside Circle A. Because it is unclear whether Point s goes inside or outside Circle A, the conclusion that the product cannot have 4, 8, 2, 6, or 0 in the ones place is questionable.

3. (a) Correct; (b) Incorrect; (c) Incorrect; (d) Correct

4. Jennifer's conjecture is always correct for situations in which the *if* portion of a premise is a sufficient condition for the *then* portion of a premise. Recall that a sufficient condition is but one of many possible conditions that could cause the result (the then portion).

5. A. (a) Invalid: the dot showing Samir's age may be inside or outside the outer circle.
   (b) Samir may be ineligible for a driver's license for many reasons. For instance, he may be legally blind, he may not know English and be able to read road signs, or he may currently be in jail.

   B. (a) Invalid (see diagram A below).
   (b) Failing a health inspection is only one of many reasons why a restaurant might be closed (e.g., bankruptcy, criminal activity by the owner, condemnation to make way for a highway).

   C. (a) Invalid (see diagram B below).
   (b) Rain is only one of many reasons why Lorraine might take the bus (e.g., she had a broken leg, felt lazy, was in a hurry, didn't like walking in an ice storm).

   D. (a) Valid: because the dot showing not getting a dollar is outside the outer circle and, hence, the inner circle.
   (b) There are various reasons why Hank might not get a dollar (e.g., he did not do his chores, he owed his parents money).

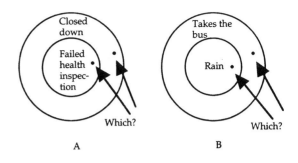

A   B

6. a.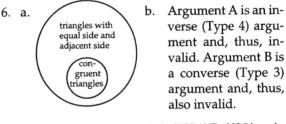

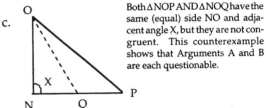

b. Argument A is an inverse (Type 4) argument and, thus, invalid. Argument B is a converse (Type 3) argument and, thus, also invalid.

Both △NOP AND △NOQ have the same (equal) side NO and adjacent angle X, but they are not congruent. This counterexample shows that Arguments A and B are each questionable.

Some Instructional Resources (page 121)

Make it Simpler. Using a model can be an invaluable aid in solving the Orchard Problem. Students might want to use five different-colored squares. One way of solving the problem is to start by putting four different colors in each corner and in the middle. This is a logical implication of the constraints placed on the solution. One could then determine what had to go into the remaining two positions of each diagonal. Finally, consider what could go in each row in turn.

In the diagram below, R = red, O = orange, G = green, P = purple, and W = white. Note if the top row is O, R, P, G, W, then the bottom row has to be G, W, O, R, P. If the top row is O, P, G, R, W, then the bottom row must be G, R, W, O, P.

O (R/P)	P/G	G/R	W
R	G	W	P	O
W	P	R	O	G
P	O	G	W	R
G (W/R)	O/W	R/O	P

A Sample of Children's Literature (page 2-124)

Venn Diagrams. Pairs of three possible colors can be represented with three intersecting circles.

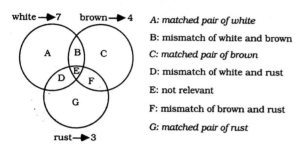

A: *matched pair of white*
B: mismatch of white and brown
C: *matched pair of brown*
D: mismatch of white and rust
E: not relevant
F: mismatch of brown and rust
G: *matched pair of rust*

If A is 4 (2 pairs of matched white socks) and B is 3 (3 pairs of mismatched white and brown), then C would have to be 0 (4 − 3 = 1 and 1 brown sock is not enough for a matched pair of brown socks). If C = 0, then F must be 1. If F = 1, then G must be 2. Thus, Professor Cloud wore a matched pair of socks a total of three times: matched white socks twice and matched rust socks once.

Questions to Consider (page 2-128)

1.   (a) Examining some examples to detect a pattern is a particularly useful heuristic for solving the Peg-Game problem. It might also help to organize the data in a table to make looking for the pattern easier.

Number of pegs on a side	1	2	3	4	5
number of moves to interchange pegs	?	8	15	24	?

(b) 1➔3; 5➔35.

(c) Examining specific instances or examples to induce a rule is inductive reasoning. Testing the rule with other examples entails if-then (deductive) reasoning. For example, the rule *multiply by four* would explain the second entry (2 → 8). *If* this rule is correct, *then* 3 pegs on a side should require 4 x 3 or 12 moves, which is not the case. Clearly, the rule needs to be modified or abandoned. Summarize the function governing the Peg-Game data.

(d) The problem could be simplified for primary children by using a halving, adding, or subtracting rule.

2.   (a) A simpler version of the Golf Ball problem would have each gang member taking one-half of the golf balls, instead of one-half plus two. An understanding of halving and doubling develop relatively early, so such a problem would not be inappropriate for many primary children. What would the answer be for the revised problem?

(b) To create a repeated-subtraction problem, each gang member could take, say, three golf balls. If the boy was left with two, how many would he have begun with? What kind of nonroutine problem is such a problem?

(c) To create a repeated-addition problem, the boy could have begun with an unknown number of golf balls, and on three occasions found, for instance, four balls and ended up with a total of 15. Consider what skills would be practiced solving this version of the problem.

3.   (a) Exclusive. (b) Probably exclusive. Realistically, the choice of one life style excludes the other. (c) Inclusive. (d) Inclusive. Any or all of the gifts would be welcomed. (e) Inclusive. An element in the union of two sets can come from either one of the sets or the other.

4.   (a) The argument is invalid. Rich people may be unhappy for any number of reasons other than an inability to pay bills (e.g., loss of a loved one). (b) Note that in a Venn diagram, the area for rich people (C) does not overlap with not able to pay bills (A) but could overlap with not happy (B).

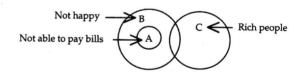

5.   It would be inaccurate to say the home team built an *ever*-increasing margin. With the score 35 to 7, the opponents scored 3 points to make the score 35 to 10 and *reduced* the margin to 25 points. The sports writer needs lessons on how to communicate mathematical ideas accurately.

NOTES

Chapter 2

[1]Our thanks to Dr. Steve Tozer of the University of Illinois for contributing this case.

[2]The Case of Sherry was originally reported in A. J. Baroody and H. P. Ginsburg's chapter, Children's Mathematical Learning: A Cognitive View, published in *Constructivist Views on the Teaching and Learning of Mathematics* (pp. 51-64), edited by R. B. Davis, C. A. Mahr, and N. Noddings and published by the National Council of Teachers in Mathematics in 1990 (*Journal for Research in Mathematics Education* Monograph Number 4). The case is used with the permission of the publisher.

[3]We are grateful to Jason Millman of Cornell University for the rain analogy.

[4]This is based on an activity developed by Patti Stoffel, a third- and fourth-grade teacher at the Prairie School, Urbana, IL.

[5]Our thanks to Linda Moore, a second-grade teacher at the Sangamon Elementary School (Mahomet, IL), and Dianne Dutton, a third-grade teacher at the Lincoln Trails Elementary School (Mahomet, IL) for allowing me (AB) to teach this and other lessons in their classroom.

[6]Our thanks to Sam's teacher Jo Lynn Baldwin, Lincoln Trails Elementary School (Mahomet, IL), for inviting me (AB) to work with the class. Brandi's teacher was Dianne Dutton.

[7]Based on Rose (1989).

[8]This question is based on a problem (Responding to Students' Novel Ideas: Perimeter/ Area, Proof) in Kennedy, Ball, McDiarmid, & Schmidt (1991).

[9]Item adapted from Ennis (1969).

REFERENCES

Balacheff, N. (1988, April). *A study of students' proving processes at the junior high school level.* Paper presented at the annual meeting of the National Council of Teachers of Mathematics, Chicago, IL.

Baratta-Lorton, M. (1976). *Mathematics their way.* Menlo Park, CA: Addison-Wesley.

Baroody, A. J. (1987). *Children's mathematical thinking: A developmental framework for preschool, primary, and special education teachers.* New York: Teacher's College Press.

Britton, J. B., Burgess, T., Martin, N., McLeod, A., & Rosen, H. (1975). *The development of writing abilities (11-18).* London: Macmillan Education Ltd.

Bryant, P. E., & Trabasso, T. (1971). Transitive inferences and memory in young children. *Nature, 232,* 456-458.

Campione, J. C., Brown, A. L., & Connell, M. L. (1989). Metacognition: On the importance of understanding what you are doing. In R. I. Charles & E. A. Silver (Eds.), *The teaching and assessing of mathematical problem solving* (pp. 93-114). Reston, VA: The National Council of Teachers of Mathematics.

Carpenter, T. P. (1986). Conceptual knowledge as a foundation for procedural knowledge: Implications from research on the initial learning of arithmetic. In J. Hiebert (Ed.), *Conceptual procedural knowledge: The case of mathematics* (pp. 113-132). Hillsdale, NJ: Lawrence Erlbaum.

Carpenter, T. P., Corbitt, M. K., Kepner, H. S., Lindquist, M. M., & Reys, R. E. (1980). Solving verbal problems: Results and implications from National Assessment. *Arithmetic Teacher, 28*(1), 8-12.

Carpenter, T. P., Matthews, W., Lindquist, M. M., & Silver, E. A. (1984). Achievement in mathematics: Results from the National Assessment. *Elementary School Journal, 84,* 485-495.

Charles, R. I., & Lester, F. K. (1982). *Teaching problem solving: What, why and how.* Palo Alto, CA: Dale Seymour Publications.

Civil, M. (1990). *Doing and talking about mathematics: A study of preservice elementary teachers.* Doctoral dissertation, University of Illinois, Urbana.

Cobb, P. (1985). A reaction to three early number papers. *Journal for Research in Mathematics Education, 16,* 141-145.

Cobb, P., Wood, T., & Yackel, E. (1991). A constructivist approach to second grade mathematics. In E. von Glasersfeld (Ed.), *Constructivism in mathematics education* (pp. 157-176). Dordrecht, Holland: Kluwer.

Cobb, P., Yackel, E., Wood, T., Wheatley, G., & Merkel, G. (1988). Creating a problem-solving atmosphere. *Arithmetic Teacher, 36* (1), 46-47.

Connolly, P. (1989). Writing and the ecology of learning. In P. Connolly & T. Vilardi (Eds.), *Writing to learn mathematics and science* (pp. 1-14). New York: Teachers College Press.

Curcio, F. R. (1990). Mathematics as communication: Using a language-experience approach the elementary grades. In T. J. Cooney & C. R. Hirsch (Eds.), *Teaching and learning mathematics in the 1990s: 1990 yearbook* (pp. 69-75). Reston, VA: National Council of Teachers of Mathematics.

Dantzig, T. (1930/1954). *Number: The language of science.* New York: The Free Press.

Davidson, N. (1990). Small-group cooperative learning in mathematics. In T. J. Cooney & C. R. Hirsch (Eds.), *Teaching and learning mathematics in the 1990s: 1990 yearbook* (pp. 52-61). Reston, VA: National Council of Teachers of Mathematics.

Davis, R. B. (1992). Reflections on where mathematics education now stands and on where it may be going. In D. Grouws (Ed.), *Handbook of research on mathematics teaching and learning* (pp. 724-734). New York: Macmillan.

DeGuire, L. J. (1987). Geometry: An avenue for teaching problem solving in grades K-9. In M. M. Lindquist & A. P. Shulte (Eds.), *Learning and teaching geometry, K-12: 1987 yearbook* (pp. 59-68). Reston, VA: National Council of Teachers of Mathematics.

Donaldson, M. (1978). *Children's minds.* New York: W. W. Norton & Co.

Ennis, R. H. (1969). *Ordinary logic.* Englewood Cliffs, NJ: Prentice-Hall.

Ennis, R. H. (1975). Children's ability to handle Piaget's propositional logic: A conceptual critique. *Review of Educational Research, 45,* 1-41.

Evans, J. St. B. T. (1982). *The psychology of deductive reasoning.* Boston: Routledge & Kegan Paul.

Feinberg, M. M. (1988). *Solving word problems in the primary grades: Addition and subtraction.* Reston, VA: National Council of Teachers of Mathematics.

Garofalo, J. (1987). Metacognition and school mathematics. *Arithmetic Teacher, 34* (9), 22-23.

Gelman, R. (1982). Basic numerical abilities. In R. J. Sternberg (Ed.), *Advances in the psychology of intelligence* (Vol. 1, pp. 181-205). Hillsdale, NJ: Erlbaum Associates.

Good, T. L., Mulryan, C., & McCaslin, M. (1992). Grouping for instruction in mathematics: A call for programmatic research on small-group processes. In D. Grouws (Ed.), *Handbook of research on mathematics teaching and learning* (pp. 165-196). New York: Macmillan.

Holt, J. (1964). *How children fail.* New York: Delta.

Inhelder, B., & Piaget, J. (1964). *The growth of logical thinking.* New York: Norton.

Irons, R. R., & Irons, C. J. (1989). Language experiences: A base for problem solving. In P. R. Trafton & A. P. Shulte (Eds.), *New directions for elementary school mathematics: 1989 yearbook* (pp. 85-98). Reston, VA: National Council of Teachers of Mathematics.

Jacobs, H. R. (1982). *Mathematics: A human endeavor* (2d ed.). San Francisco: W. H. Freeman.

Jacobson, M. H., Lester, F. K., & Stengel, A. (1980). Making problem solving come alive in the intermediate grades. In S. Krulik & R. E. Reys (Eds.), *Problem solving in school mathematics: 1980 yearbook* (pp. 127-135). Reston, VA: National Council of Teachers of Mathematics.

Jamski, W. D. (1989). Dürer's magic squares. *Arithmetic Teacher, 37*(4), 2.

Johnson, D. W., & Johnson, R. T. (1989). Cooperative learning in mathematics. In P. R. Trafton & A. P. Schulte (Eds.), *New directions for elementary school mathematics: 1989 yearbook* (pp. 234-245). Reston, VA: National Council of Teachers of Mathematics.

Kamin, L. J. (1974). *The science and politics of I.Q.* Potomac, MD: Erlbaum Associates.

Kennedy, M. M., Ball, D. L., McDiarmid, G. W., & Schmidt, W. (1991). A study package for examining and tracking changes in teachers' knowledge (Technical Series 91-1). East Lansing, MI: The National Center for Research on Teacher Education at Michigan State University.

Kilpatrick, J. (1985a). Doing mathematics without understanding it: A commentary on Higbee and Kunihira. *Educational Psychologist, 20,* 65-68.

Kilpatrick, J. (1985b). A retrospective account of the past twenty-five years of research on teaching mathematical problem solving. In E. A. Silver (Ed.), *Teaching and learning mathematical problem solving* (pp. 1-15). Hillsdale, NJ: Erlbaum Associates.

Kouba, V. L., Carpenter, T. P., & Swafford, J. O. (1989). Numbers and operations. In M. M. Lindquist (Ed.), *Results from the Fourth Mathematics Assessment of the National Assessment of Educational Progress* (pp. 64-93). Reston, VA: National Council of Teachers of Mathematics.

Lappan, G., & Schram, P. W. (1989). Communication and reasoning: Critical dimensions of sense making in mathematics. In P. R. Trafton & A. P. Shulte (Eds.), *New directions for elementary school mathematics: 1989 yearbook* (pp. 14-30). Reston, VA: National Council of Teachers of Mathematics.

Layzer, D. (1989). The synergy between writing and mathematics. In P. Connolly & T. Vilardi (Eds.), *Writing to learn mathematics and science* (pp. 121-133). New York: Teachers College Press.

LeBlanc, J. F., Proudfit, L., & Putt, I. J. (1980). Teaching problem solving in the elementary school. In S. Krulik & R. E. Reys (Eds.), *Problem solving in school mathematics: 1980 yearbook* (pp. 104-116). Reston, VA: National Council of Teachers of Mathematics.

Lester, F. K., Jr. (1980). Research on mathematical problem solving. In R. J. Shumway (Ed.), *Research in mathematics education*. Reston, VA: National Council of Teachers of Mathematics.

Lester, Jr., F. K. (1989). Reflections about mathematical problem-solving research. In R. I. Charles & E. A. Silver (Eds.), *The teaching and assessing of mathematical problem solving* (pp. 115-124). Reston, VA: The National Council of Teachers of Mathematics.

Lindquist, M. M. (1989). It's time for change. In P. R. Trafton & A. P. Shulte (Eds.), *New directions for elementary school mathematics: 1989 yearbook* (pp. 1-13). Reston, VA: National Council of Teachers of Mathematics.

Maher, C. A., & Alston, A. (1989). Is meaning connected to symbols? An interview with Ling Chen. *Journal of Mathematical Behavior, 8,* 241-248.

Marwine, A. (1989). Reflections on the uses of informal writing. In P. Connolly & T. Vilardi (Eds.), *Writing to learn mathematics and science* (pp. 56-69). New York: Teachers College Press.

Mason, M. M. (1989, April). *Geometric understanding and misconceptions among gifted fourth graders.* Paper presented at the annual meeting of the American Educational Research Association, San Francisco.

McLeod, D. B. (1992). Research on affect in mathematics education: A reconceptualization. In D. A. Grouws (Ed.), *Handbook of research on mathematics teaching and learning* (pp. 575-596). New York: Macmillan.

Musser, G. L., & Shaughnessy, J. M. (1980). Problem-solving strategies in school mathematics. In S. Krulik & R. E. Reys (Eds.), *Problem solving in school mathematics: 1980 yearbook.* (pp. 136-145). Reston, VA: National Council of Teachers of Mathematics.

National Council of Teachers of Mathematics. (1989). *Curriculum and evaluation standards for school mathematics.* Reston, VA: Author.

National Research Council. (1989). *Everybody counts: A report to the nation on the future of mathematics education.* Washington, DC: National Academy Press.

National Research Council. (1990). *Reshaping school mathematics: A philosophy and framework for curriculum.* Washington, D.C.: National Academy Press.

Noddings, N. (1985). Small groups as a setting for research on mathematical problem solving. In E. A. Silver (Ed.), *Teaching and learning mathematical problem solving: Multiple research perspectives* (pp. 345-359). Hillsdale, NJ: Erlbaum Associates.

Palincsar, A. (1986). Metacognitive strategy instruction. *Exceptional Children, 53,* 118-124.

Pappas, T. (1989). *The joy of mathematics.* San Carlos, CA: Wide World Publishing/Tetra.

Pellegrino, J. W., Hickey, D., Heath, A., Rewey, K., Vye, N. J., & the Cognition and Technology Group at Vanderbilt (1991). Assessing the outcomes of an innovative instructional program: The 1990-1991 implementation of the "Adventures of Jasper Woodbury" (Tech. Rep. No. 91-1). Nashville, TN: Vanderbilt University Learning Technology Center.

Piaget, J. (1965). *The child's conception of number.* New York: Norton.

Polya, G. (1973). *How to solve it* (39th ed.). Princeton, NJ: Princeton University Press.

Polya, G. (1981). *Mathematical discovery: On understanding, learning, and teaching problem solving.* New York: John Wiley & Sons.

Reeve, R. A., & Brown, A. L. (1985). Metacognition reconsidered. Implications for intervention research. *Abnormal Child Psychology, 13,* 343-356.

Resnick, L. B. (1988). Treating mathematics as an ill-structured discipline. In R. Charles & E. Silver (Eds.), *The teaching and assessing of mathematical problem solving* (pp. 32-60). Reston, VA: National Council of Teachers of Mathematics.

Riley, M. S., Greeno, J. G., & Heller, J. I. (1983). Development of children's problem-solving ability in arithmetic. In H. P. Ginsburg (Ed.), *The development of mathematical thinking* (pp. 153-200). New York: Academic Press.

Rose, B. (1989). Writing and mathematics: Theory and practice. In P. Connolly & T. Vilardi (Eds.), *Writing to learn mathematics and science* (pp. 15-30). New York: Teachers College Press.

Schoenfeld, A. H. (1982). Some thoughts on problem-solving research and mathematics education. In F. K. Lester, Jr., & J. Garofalo (Eds.), *Mathematical problem solving: Issues in research* (pp. 27-37). Philadelphia: Franklin Institute Press.

Schoenfeld, A. H. (1985). *Mathematical problem solving*. New York: Academic Press.

Schoenfeld, A. H. (1992). Learning to think mathematically: Problem solving, metacognition, and sense making in mathematics. In D. Grouws (Ed.), *Handbook of research on mathematics teaching and learning* (pp. 334-370). New York: Macmillan.

Schroeder, T. L., & Lester, Jr., F. K. (1989). Developing understanding in mathematics via problem solving. In P. R. Trafton & A. P. Shulte (Eds.), *New directions for elementary school mathematics: 1989 yearbook* (pp. 31-42). Reston, VA: National Council of Teachers of Mathematics.

Semadeni, Z. (1983). Integration of content and pedagogy in preservice training of mathematics teachers. In M. Zwen, T. Green, J. Kilpatrick, H. Pollock, & M. Suydam (Eds.), *Proceedings of the Fourth International Congress on Mathematics Education* (pp. 96-98). Boston: Birkhäuser.

Shapiro, B. J., & O'Brien, T. C. (1970). Logical thinking in children ages six through thirteen. *Child Development, 41*, 823-829.

Shell Center for Mathematical Education. (1984). *Problems with patterns and numbers*. Manchester, England: Joint Matriculation Board (Printed by Richard Bates Limited).

Sherrill, J. M. (1987). Magic squares and magic triangles. *Arithmetic Teacher, 35*(2), 44-47.

Silver, E. A. (1982). Knowledge organization and mathematical problem solving. In F. K. Lester & J. Garofalo (Eds.), *Mathematical problem solving: Issues in research* (pp. 14-24). Philadelphia: The Franklin Institute Press.

Silver, E. A. (1985). Underrepresented themes and needed directions. In E. A. Silver (Ed.), *Teaching and learning mathematical problem solving: Multiple research perspectives* (pp. 247-266). Hillsdale, NJ: Erlbaum Associates.

Silver, E. A. (1990). Contributions of research to practice: Applying findings, methods, and perspectives. In T. J. Cooney (Ed.), *Teaching and learning mathematics in the 1990s* (pp. 1-11). Reston, VA: National Council of Teachers of Mathematics.

Silver, E. A., & Carpenter, T. P. (1989). Mathematical methods. In M. M. Lindquist (Ed.), *Results from the Fourth Mathematics Assessment of the National Assessment of Educational Progress* (pp. 10-18). Reston, VA: National Council of Teachers of Mathematics.

Silver, E. A., Kilpatrick, J., & Schlesinger, B. (1990). *Thinking through mathematics: Fostering inquiry and communication in mathematics classrooms*. New York: College Entrance Examination Board.

Silver, E. A., & Thompson, A. G. (1984). Research perspective on problem solving in elementary school mathematics. *Elementary School Journal, 84*, 529-545.

Slavin, R. (1983). *Cooperative learning*. New York, NY: Longman.

Sovchik, R. (1989). *Teaching mathematics to children*. New York: Harper & Row.

Stanic, G. M. A., & Kilpatrick, J. (1989). Historical perspectives on problem solving in mathematics curriculum. In R. I. Charles & E. A. Silver (Eds.), *The teaching and assessing of mathematical problem solving* (pp. 1-22). Reston, VA: The National Council of Teachers of Mathematics.

Steen, L. A. (Ed.). (1990a). *On the shoulders of giants: New approaches to numeracy*. Washington, D.C.: National Academy Press.

Steen, L. A. (1990b). Pattern. In L. A. Steen (Ed.), *On the shoulders of giants: New approaches to numeracy* (pp. 1-10). Washington, D.C.: National Academy Press.

Sutton, R. E., & Ennis, R. H. (1985). Logical operations in the classroom. In T. Husen & T. N. Postlethwaite (Eds.), *International encyclopedia of education: Research and studies* (pp. 3129-3139). Oxford: Pergamon Press.

Tobias, S. (1989). Writing to learn science and mathematics. In P. Connolly & T. Vilardi (Eds.), *Writing to learn mathematics and science* (pp. 48-55). New York: Teachers College Press.

Vygotsky, L. (1978). *Mind in society*. Cambridge, MA: Harvard University Press.

Wertheimer, M. (1945/1959). *Productive thinking*. New York: Harper & Row.

Wilde, S. (1991). Learning to write about mathematics. *Arithmetic Teacher, 39* (6), 38-43.

Wood, E. F. (1989). More magic with magic squares. *Arithmetic Teacher, 37*(4), 42-46.

WE VALUE YOUR OPINION--PLEASE SHARE IT WITH US

Macmillan Publishing and our authors are most interested in your reactions to this textbook so that we can improve upon it in future editions. We'd be interested in knowing how well the text helped you learn how to teach problem solving to children and how the unique format affected your learning. How might we make it a more useful educational tool in future editions? Your comments will be seriously considered by the authors and their editors. Since you are the ultimate consumer of the text, we value your opinions and thank you for any additional comments you might like to supply.

Problem Solving, Reasoning, and Communicating, Grades K-8: Helping Children Think Mathematically
Arthur J. Baroody

Your Name (Optional) _____

University/College _____

Course Title and Number _____

Instructor's Name _____ Your Major _____

Your Class Rank (freshman, sophomore, junior, senior, graduate, etc.) _____

Were you required to take this course? _____ Yes _____ No   Course Length _____ Qtr. _____ Sem.

Were you required to buy this text? _____ Yes _____ No   Was it new or used? _____ New _____ Used

Was this book used in your course as the main text or a supplement? _____ Main _____ Supplement

Do you feel this book is worth keeping for your professional use as a teacher? _____ Yes _____ No
Why or why not? _____

_____

****

1) Overall, how does this text compare to other texts you've used?

_____ Superior _____ Better Than Most _____ Average _____ Worse Than Most

2) Please grade the text in the areas listed below by circling your response, using the following scale:
A = superior, B = above average, C = average, D = below average, E = poor

User-friendly Writing Style	A	B	C	D	E
Readability and Clarity of Ideas	A	B	C	D	E
Ease of Use	A	B	C	D	E
Relevance to Pre-service Teachers	A	B	C	D	E
Organization	A	B	C	D	E
Accuracy	A	B	C	D	E
Layout and Design	A	B	C	D	E
Illustrations/Cartoons	A	B	C	D	E
Use of Examples	A	B	C	D	E
Problems/Exercises	A	B	C	D	E
Topic Coverage	A	B	C	D	E
Up-to-date Coverage	A	B	C	D	E
Explanation of Difficult Concepts	A	B	C	D	E
Applications to Real Life	A	B	C	D	E

3) What did you like most about this text? _____

_____

4) What did you like least about this text? _____

_____

5) What was the most useful part of the book? _____

_____

6) How did your instructor have you use the Probes and Activities? _____

_____

7) How easy was it for you to locate the Probes and Activities? _____

_____

8) Would you prefer to have the Probes and Activities located elsewhere in the book? Please explain. _____

_____

9) Did your instructor cover the entire book? _____ Yes _____ No If not, what areas did you skip?

_____

10) Please comment on the length of the book. _____

_____

11) If you are planning to be an elementary teacher, will you use any part of this book with your students? If

so, what will you use? _____

_____

12) What would be one suggestion for improvement that you would give to the authors as they write the next

edition of this text? _____

_____

Other Comments:

May we quote you in our advertising? _____ Yes _____ No

Please Mail to: Linda Scharp, Editor
                        College Division Research/Merrill Education
                        Macmillan Publishing Company
                        445 Hutchinson Avenue
                        Columbus, OH 43235